Dialogue at the Margins

Dialogue at the Margins
Whorf, Bakhtin, and Linguistic Relativity

Emily A. Schultz

The University of Wisconsin Press

The University of Wisconsin Press
114 North Murray Street
Madison, Wisconsin 53715

3 Henrietta Street
London WC2E 8LU, England

Printed in the United States of America

The figures on pages 101, 102, 103, 104, and 113, are reproduced courtesy of the M.I.T. Press from *Language, Thought, and Reality: Selected Writings of Benjamin Lee Whorf,* edited with an introduction by John B. Carroll, published in 1956. Copyright © 1956 by The Massachusetts Institute of Technology.

Library of Congress Cataloging-in-Publication Data

Schultz, Emily A. (Emily Ann), 1949–
    Dialogue at the margins: Whorf, Bakhtin, and linguistic
relativity / Emily A. Schultz.
        192 pp.   cm. — (New directions in anthropological writing)
    Includes bibliographical references.
        1. Whorf, Benjamin Lee, 1897–1941. 2. Bakhtin, M. M. (Mikhail
Mikhailovich), 1895–1975. 3. Sapir-Whorf hypothesis. I. Title.
II. Series.
P85.W48S38   1990
306.4'4—dc20   90-50097
ISBN 0-299-12700-1   CIP
ISBN 0-299-12704-4 (pbk.)

For Rob

It is customary to speak about the authorial mask. But in which utterances (speech acts) is there a *face* and not a mask, that is, no authorship?

Bakhtin
Speech Genres and Other Late Essays

Contents

Preface

From the time I first encountered them, the essays of Benjamin Lee Whorf impressed me as exciting, puzzling, and ultimately frustrating. I studied them, accepted conventional explanations about what was wrong with them, and went on to other things. In 1985, however, while preparing the chapter on language for a cultural anthropology textbook, I had an opportunity to read Whorf again, at length and closely. This led me to question the traditional interpretations of Whorf's work, even as it renewed my original frustration with it. At the same time, I was growing increasingly annoyed by a series of attacks on "relativism" that were appearing in the writings of some philosophers and literary critics. I resolved that I would study Whorf's texts intensively until I was able to find a more satisfactory way to explain why his words, which seem so straightforward on first reading, become so elusive on closer analysis. At the same time, such a study offered the opportunity to respond to the critics of "relativism," since they were often also critics of Whorf.

Some months into the project, I had produced a 78-page manuscript— too long for a journal article, too short for a book. Ivan Karp read the manuscript, and suggested that I write a paper comparing Whorf with Mikhail Bakhtin. The more Bakhtin I read, the more I came to perceive a striking affinity between Bakhtin and the Whorf I had come to know as a result of my own research. It seemed increasingly clear to me that the most important of Bakhtin's works, in terms of his affinity with Whorf, was *Problems of Dostoevsky's Poetics.* Indeed, I originally intended to call my own book *Problems of Whorfian Poetics,* though cooler heads eventually prevailed. The question of what to do with the original 78-page manuscript was solved, as it was reworked from a Bakhtinian perspective to produce (with few subsequent changes) the present volume.

Seeing any scholarly project through, from embryonic conception to finished product, always depends on the circle of support provided by friends and colleagues. Carol Levin, of the Owen D. Young Library, St. Lawrence University, was extremely helpful in the early days, when I was poring over citation indexes and making heavy use of interlibrary loan. Colleagues in St. Cloud helped sharpen my understanding of the theoretical issues I was addressing, as well as serving as a sounding board for some of the conclusions I was reaching. Especially generous were Carolyn North, Judy Parham, Sid Parham, Bela Petheo, and Joanne Saltz. At crucial stages in the project, Michael Silverstein, Richard Bauman, and especially Michael Herzfeld, provided positive critical feedback. Gordon Lester-Massman, Barbara Hanrahan, Raphael Kadushin, and Susan Tarcov made it a pleasure to work with the University of Wisconsin Press.

For good or ill, however, this book would not be what it is without the crucial influence of four people. Jacques Périvier first taught me the significance of the word with a loophole, a lesson I have never forgotten. Wilfred Cantwell Smith, whose work has inspired me for many years, read the first draft of this manuscript and sent favorable comments at a time when they were particularly welcome. Ivan Karp has provided encouragement and sound advice at every stage in this project; he is the very model of an exemplary colleague. Finally, Robert Lavenda has long been both my most fervent supporter and my most incisive critic. He is the ideal dialogic partner, in every dimension and in all senses. It is to him that I dedicate this book.

Dialogue at the Margins

Introduction

As the shadow of poststructuralist criticism has cast itself more and more fully over the study of language in recent years, the confidence which linguists once expressed in finally, once and for all, explaining the nature of their subject has eroded. In particular, the confidence of some formal linguists has been shaken, to the extent that certain of their early pronouncements today sound ironic indeed. Nowhere is this clearer than when one examines the stand taken on linguistic relativity. Following that period in the first part of the century when relativism was first proclaimed, and evidence to support it eagerly sought, there came a period in which relativism was criticized and devalued, to be replaced by a search for universals in culture and language. The transformational linguistics of Chomsky represented the forefront of this search. In the flush of early success, an enthusiast could proclaim that the "battle may have been won by the linguistic relativists, but the war was lost to the Rationalists. For a priori Rationalism died in mid-twentieth century scepticism of our ability to know, in 'scepticism of the word,' but Rationalism was revived and innate ideas (now called linguistic universals) are now posited on empirical evidence" (Penn 1972:56).

Penn also observed that "it may not be a coincidence that Rationalism has become more popular at the same time that linguistic relativity has fallen into disrepute" (1972:11). In the late twentieth century, however, "Rationalism" has, in the eyes of many, fallen into disrepute. This fall has coincided, as some have pointed out, with the failure of the revolutionary hopes of the 1960s to issue in the anticipated concrete social changes which could save the West (or particular Western nations) from decline. Others, of course, believe that the radicalism of the 1960s, far from promising salvation, was responsible for accelerating decline. The fall of rationalism is made more poignant by the defensive efforts of those who fear that, if rationalism goes, nihilism follows (as indeed it does for those who believe that unless some universal a priori rationalism can unite human beings, nothing can do so, since we begin as self-enclosed individuals with no natural ties to one another). And the fall becomes deeply sinister if we can point to no overriding standard to resolve our uniquely individual (and therefore endlessly varied) points of view. On what grounds can we condemn the Nazis, or the defenders of apartheid, and sympathize with their victims? The loss of universal rationalism seems to entail the loss of all ability to distinguish good from evil, which can only lead to the tyranny of the many, to anarchy, to the end of civilization as we know it.

It is therefore hardly surprising that the single most acrimonious debate among practitioners of the human sciences revolves precisely about the nature of human rationality and the extent to which it can be identified and described apart from the cultural, historical, and biographical contexts in which we encounter it. In anthropology and related disciplines, this debate centers on the meaning, and value, of the concept known as "cultural relativism." The defenders of rationalism take as their single most pressing mission the need to discredit the concept of relativism. The word has become a battleground between different scholarly traditions, and the battle is over the control of discourse. The issue, simply put, concerns who will define the "true meaning" of "relativism." That the battle is so fierce and engages both sides so deeply suggests that the defenders of relativism are worthy dialogic partners for the defenders of rationalism. Particularly within American anthropology, it seems to me that a careful reconsideration of the tradition of cultural relativism in the light of modern scholarship can reveal why this is indeed so. It can also help to move the debate to a plane, beyond subjective individualism and objective determinism, which may even reassure rationalist opponents that commitment to a relativistic perspective is the opposite of nihilism and far from debilitating.

In the context of such a debate between "rationality" and "relativism," a reexamination of the writings of Benjamin Lee Whorf is therefore most appropriate. Despite the fact that Whorf's ideas about the nature of language were shared to a greater or lesser degree by other students of language (Humboldt, Boas, and Sapir, for example), it remains true today that the concept of linguistic relativity is most closely associated with Whorf, and is even called by many the "Whorfian hypothesis." Indeed, in recent years a number of scholars in different disciplines have begun to reconsider Whorf's ideas—or, in many cases, the ideas attributed to him by others. For only rarely has this return to Whorf been accompanied by a return to Whorf's texts.

This book is based on such a return. I argue that Whorf is eminently worth rereading and pondering in these poststructuralist times. If many view "deconstruction" as the reanimation of relativism in the late twentieth century, early relativists like Whorf might be seen as precocious "deconstructors." Handler, for example, has argued that "nowhere is the fundamentally comparative dimension of destructive analysis more apparent that in Whorf's . . . masterly analysis of the implicit ontology built into Hopi and "Standard Average European" (SAE) languages" (1985:176). Whorf's goal, in Handler's view, was primarily to undermine the ontology of SAE and celebrate the alternative ontologies of the Native American languages he studied: "the rhetorical force of Whorf's essay is brought primarily to bear on Western thought. . . . Hopi functions as 'a mirror held up to' SAE, which becomes, for the moment, a familiar object subjected to destructive analysis" (1985:177).

All this is true, as far as it goes. But what I wish to urge in this study is that Whorf's own writings be scrutinized, since, as I hope to show, the "implicit ontology" they contain is anything but straightforward. Whorf's writings beg to be "deconstructed," precisely because some have tried to assimilate his work into the main line of linguistic anthropology, while others have viewed it, and continue to view it, as scandalous. One cannot read Whorf and avoid (with a clear conscience) being drawn into the dialogical struggle. And to be drawn in means to encounter as perplexing, as elusive, as sly, as perverse, and possibly even as tragic a figure as any of the postmoderns. It is because of this, I believe, that his writing continues to generate as much exasperation as it generates interest.

In this study I propose to do the following things:

1. Examine the nature of the Whorfian "canon," and demonstrate how attempts to delimit this canon illustrate one (largely unsuccessful) means of attempting to reduce Whorf to consistency and manageability by finding a single voice for him.

2. Attempt to separate out the different voices in Whorf's texts. This undertaking was prompted by the effort of Christopher Norris (1985) to deconstruct Wittgenstein, by the effort of Ranjit Chatterjee (1985) to compare Wittgenstein with Whorf, and by Michael Holquist's suggestions (e.g., 1986: ix, 171n) of linkages between Whorf and Mikhail Bakhtin. It will involve locating the "undecidable paradoxes" in Whorf's texts where the struggle between voices is most intense. It will also involve a focus upon works usually taken as "marginal" to the Whorfian

canon, in order to assess what they suggest about the views Whorf is ordinarily said to have propounded.

3. After proceeding in this way, however, I hope to show the superior analytic power that can be achieved when the bare bones of deconstruction are fleshed out by a dialogic perspective. Bakhtin will serve as "a mirror held up to Whorf." But while this permits Whorf to be deconstructed, it also allows him to be put back together again in a far more intriguing shape. I believe that a dialogue between Bakhtin and Whorf makes exceptionally clear the fact that Whorf's "message" to his readers cannot be reduced to one or more explicit position statements, but lies rather in his compositional strategy, including both verbal and nonverbal means. This helps explain why readers can disagree, sometimes violently, about what Whorf "actually said." For example, it may be true, as Michael Silverstein has observed, that Whorf's claims about linguistic relativity can be usefully (and noncontroversially) understood as a way of pointing out how "the user's native ideology of reference . . . is systematically related to, and at least in part systematically derives from, the grammatical structure of the language" (1979:193–94). Yet if this were all Whorf had to say (or, indeed, all that he *did* say) it is unlikely that he would have become so controversial.

Indeed, it is precisely the question of *how* he said what he said, the question of stylistics (or poetics), that must be addressed if one wishes to make progress with Whorf. Whorf, I claim, was a writer of "artistic prose" which, in the view of Mikhail Bakhtin, is closely bound up with novelistic prose. Whorf is a master of double-voiced discourse and the intentional dialogized hybrid construction. This is why explicit position statements can never be taken at face value in his articles. Whorf always makes such statements serve, at the same time, a constructive role in his larger compositional strategy, and this second role alters the way they may be understood.

But there is more. In his most successful artistic prose constructions (which are also his most controversial texts), Whorf fleshes out the dialogized voices, turning them into speakers of Amerindian and Standard Average European languages. The scope of the dialogue is restricted primarily to issues of grammar and reference, of course; this restriction is significant and will be explored later. Yet even in such a restricted context, Whorf is able to make the part revealed hint at the richness of the unseen whole, is able to convince readers who believe that primitives really exist, that perhaps they ought to reconsider. Put another way, Whorf's texts are polyphonic in the same way (according to Bakhtin) that Dostoevsky's novels are polyphonic. The images of the

Hopi or the Shawnee or the Nootka which he constructs for his readers are, like Dostoevsky's characters, "capable of standing *alongside* their creator, capable of not agreeing with him and even of rebelling against him" (Bakhtin 1984[1929]:6). How to create ethnographic images of other peoples that achieve this goal is currently the focus of some of the most important theorizing in cultural anthropology today (e.g., Marcus and Fischer [1986], Marcus and Clifford [1986], Fernandez [1986,1982]). Yet it is precisely this, Whorf's greatest accomplishment, that is, at the same time, the source of the greatest tension in his work. It is also the source of the many accusations of self-contradiction and inconsistency leveled at Whorf over the years.

In my view, we can improve our understanding of Whorf's texts by applying to them some of the same critical categories and operations which Bakhtin applies to Dostoevsky's texts. Such an analysis further suggests (as did Bakhtin's analysis of Dostoevsky criticism in his day) that much traditional criticism of Whorf ends up blaming or praising only one voice in the polyphonic chorus, rather than blaming or praising Whorf himself. As Bakhtin observes (1984[1929]:43), "It seems that each person who enters the labyrinth of the polyphonic novel somehow loses his way in it and fails to hear the whole behind the individual voices. . . . Everyone interprets in his own way Dostoevsky's ultimate word, but all equally interpret it as a *single* word, a *single* voice, a *single* accent, and therein lies their fundamental mistake."

The Whorfian Canon

Who was Benjamin Lee Whorf? What did he actually say? The facts of his biography, outlined in John Carroll (1956) and supplemented by Peter Rollins (1980), seem inadequate by themselves as answers for these questions. Whorf was born in 1897 and died at the age of forty-four, in 1941. He studied chemical engineering at the Massachusetts Institute of Technology and spent his professional career working as a fire prevention engineer for the Hartford Insurance Company. Whorf's personal struggle to resolve the competing claims of science and religion led him to focus on the study of language as a likely source of insight. Although he began linguistic studies on his own, in the early 1930s he studied formally with Edward Sapir at Yale. Up until his death, alongside his regular duties as an insurance executive he continued to produce scholarly analyses of a high calibre on a number of Amerindian languages.

Whorf is notoriously difficult to pigeonhole or pin down. Rollins, who makes the most sustained attempt at psychohistory, concludes that "whether he should be described as a philosopher, linguist, or mystic does not matter; he should be recognized as a daring and independent thinker" (1980:17). Richard Bernstein's remarks about Peter Winch and Thomas Kuhn, two other celebrated "relativists," could just as easily have been made about Whorf: "Winch is ambiguous and, at times, ambivalent. His style, like Kuhn's, is frequently provocative and all too easily lends itself to conflicting interpretations" (1982:97). Yet, again as with Winch and Kuhn, Whorf's ambiguity, ambivalence, and provocative style have not led scholars to ignore him. As George Miller notes, "if the Whorfian hypothesis is gone, it is not forgotten, for there is something right about it" (1978:95). Still, as Stephen Murray observes, "Despite a widespread feeling that 'There's something there,' no one has established quite what it is" (1982a:158). Well aware of this perplexing state of affairs, Miller refers to the "Whorfian hypothesis" as an "intellectual inkblot": "Anthropologists, psychologists, and linguists have projected different interpretations onto it, and what they have projected says at least as much about them as about Whorf" (1978:95).

Interpreters of Whorf have all, in their own ways, followed the time-honored critical procedure of seeking after consistency in his writings, of searching for the single, authentic authorial voice. Consistency, of course, has ordinarily been defined relative to the reader's own disciplinary interests. This search for consistency has involved two procedures, each of which is parasitic on the other. One procedure has been to delimit a canon of "serious" Whorfian writings, within which one may then seek the consistent principles underlying his thought. The other procedure has been to follow up one or another theme of interest in all (or most) of Whorf's works, deciding which items belong in the canon by discovering which items most fully contribute to the development of the theme in question.

Both procedures are part of those discourse practices that define a scholarly discipline both for its practitioners and in distinction to other disciplines. Terry Eagleton's remarks about the origin of the "literary canon" illuminate the ways in which anthropologists, linguists, philosophers, and others have set about delimiting the Whorfian canon: "Literary theorists, critics and teachers, then, are not so much purveyors of doctrine as custodians of a discourse. . . . Certain pieces of writing are selected as being more amenable to this discourse than others, and these are what is known as literature or the 'literary canon' " (1983:201).

This view is similar to that expressed by Bakhtin in his discussion of canonization of linguistic forms by literary language. For him, canonization takes place in a context of heteroglossia. Heteroglossia (or "many-voicedness") refers to the situation of coexistence of many different language varieties (e.g., dialects, jargons) with a *single* "national language"—that is, a language as linguistics defines it, such as English or Russian. Heteroglossia, for Bakhtin, is the normal state of affairs in language, sometimes further complicated by polyglossia ("many-languagedness"). A speech community characterized by polyglossia draws its language varieties from more than one national language, and is usually described as bi- or multilingual. Literary language is thus only one of many simultaneously coexisting language varieties available to the author as a socially, culturally, and historically situated being. To be the custodian of a discourse is to police the boundaries of *one* of these langauge varieties, and to admit into one's speech and writing only those forms which "have lost their flavor of 'belonging to another language' " (Bakhtin 1981c[1940]:418). The debate over "what Whorf really said" is related to the struggle between the "languages" of anthropology, linguistics, psychology, and other scholarly disciplines for the right to decide which of his writings were worthy of serious scholarly attention. This is simultaneously a struggle to decide whether all, or part, of what he wrote can be made amenable to their (or anyone else's) discourse.

Attempts to isolate those of Whorf's writings deserving of serious scholarly attention began in 1949 with the publication by the Foreign Service Institute, Department of State, of *Four Articles on Metalinguistics* (reprinted in 1952). The four articles included were "Science and Linguistics" (1940), "Linguistics as an Exact Science" (1940), "Languages and Logic" (1941), and "The Relation of Habitual Thought and Behavior to Language" (1939). The first three of these articles were written for the *Technology Review* at MIT, Whorf's alma mater, and, as Carroll reminds us, "were addressed to lay audiences" (1956:18). The fourth article, however, was prepared for the festschrift in honor of Edward Sapir, edited by Leslie Spier, and can thus be presumed to be addressed to an audience of linguistic experts.

All four articles have not been accorded equal importance. Harry Hoijer, one of Whorf's early supporters, identifies the festschrift article, "The Relation of Habitual Thought and Behavior to Language," as the most important of Whorf's papers (1953:560). Similarly, in an early review of the *Four Articles on Metalinguistics,* Robert Longacre, though highly critical of Whorf, also singles out the festschrift article for particular consideration, observing that it "is marked by a caution and breadth not characteristic of the other articles" (1956:307).

The Whorfian canon was augmented in 1956 with the publication of John Carroll's edited collection, *Language, Thought, and Reality.* This volume contains the original four articles on metalinguistics, plus an additional fourteen pieces, some of which were previously published and some of which were not. This book has not gone out of print, so far as I know, since its first appearance. Indeed, it has become for most scholars, in practical terms, the Whorfian Bible.

Carroll's bibliography contains, in addition to a list of Whorf's publications, and a list of publications about Whorf, a third list of "selected" unpublished manuscripts by Whorf (1956:275–76). Since Carroll chose to include some unpublished materials in his collection, yet excluded others, questions naturally arise concerning his criteria for inclusion and exclusion. And here again, the politics of discourse enter the scene. Carroll apparently found himself having to select pieces in which Whorf's voice harmonized with the discourses of psychology, anthropology, and linguistics as they were constituted in the mid-1950s. This meant excluding works in which Whorf seemed to question or contradict the behavioristic and positivistic discourse practices dominant in these disciplines at that time.

Most embarrassing was the frankly religious or mystical cast of some of the material which Carroll nevertheless felt obliged to include in his volume. He anticipated possible objections by remarking that "it may come as a surprise to some that Whorf's interest in linguistics stemmed from one in religion" (1956:7). He then attempted to make such a distasteful discovery more palatable by relating Whorf's achievements to those of other scholars who, though working on religious texts for religious motives, nevertheless made great contributions to our understanding of language. And he tried to still any remaining doubt in skeptical readers by reassuring them that Whorf "was not interested in any translation of the Bible, at least not in any ordinary sense; he seriously believed that fundamental human and philosophical problems could be solved by taking a new sounding of the semantics of the Bible" (1956:7).

Responses by scholars to this widened canon have differed. Max Black, for example, held to the same opinion first articulated by Hoijer and Longacre, calling the paper for the Sapir festschrift Whorf's "best essay" (1962[1959]:245). This position has been echoed by Stephen Murray, who argues that the festschrift piece "should be viewed as the definitive presentation since it was the one in which Whorf presented his views to professional linguists" (1982a:153). All these commentators thereby marginalize and devalue articles addressed to lay audiences. Black and Murray, moreover, are as suspicious of the religiously tinged materials as Longacre. Black detects "a vaporous mysticism" which "blurs perspectives already sufficiently elusive" (1962[1959]:245); Murray declares:

"[In 'The Relation of Habitual Thought and Behavior to Language'] Whorf set forth a nuanced and serious set of ideas proposing a relationship between language and thought, not a mystic or messianic message claiming to explain all of cognition or to introduce the millennium for linguistics" (1982a:155).

Suspicion of the religiously tinged materials widens into outright criticism in the work of Rollins, who expands the Whorfian canon in his own work to include the most scientifically embarrassing of Whorf's unpublished works. Indeed, he goes beyond the unpublished materials listed in Carroll's select bibliography to examine works described by Carroll in his introduction (1956:7) but not listed, including the "130,000-word manuscript" on the conflict between science and religion, which was completed in 1925 and rejected by several publishers (see bibliography in Rollins 1980 for a complete list of the materials he examined). Rollins' thesis (though sometimes undercut by his own more nuanced observations about Whorf) is that Whorf was a "WASP drowning in change" whose work in linguistics was all bent toward reaffirming the truths of his ethnic and religious heritage and reconciling them with the truths of Einsteinian physics. From this perspective, Whorf's achievements in linguistics are an epiphenomenon, and his supposed relativism is a mirage: "Whorf was in search of metaphysical truths. In this respect, he was embarrassingly like his bete noir [sic], Herbert Spencer. Both the American believer and the British agnostic pursued a single, correct way of looking at the universe: both were certain that ultimate truths could be unveiled" (Rollins 1980:23).

Paul Friedrich, by contrast, values much in Whorf that others find problematic. Although he criticizes Whorf (as he criticizes Bloomfield, Chomsky, and Wittgenstein) for rooting his theories of language in a "personal credo" with venerable "theological wellsprings," and urges students of language to "turn from these theologically tinged linguistic mechanisms—or rather, these irrational faiths in the total ordering of language and culture" (1986:138–39), he also praises Whorf for sharpening the issues surrounding relativism "with an almost hallucinatory theoretical clarity; in his writings there is a beautiful integration of reason and intuition" (1986:6). Indeed, he regards highly the most "mystical" of all the articles in Carroll's reader, "Language, Mind, and Reality," first published in the *Theosophist* in Madras, India, in 1941, observing that in this "remarkable, posthumously published article [Whorf] moved very far toward a more pragmatic, action- and event-based position (consonant with shifting to semantically complex examples from American English)"(1986:6). Moreover, Friedrich *objects* to those elements in

Whorf which, in the 1950s, made his work amenable to the discourses of anthropology, linguistics, and philosophy: his "scientism, the occasional misuse of theory from the natural sciences, an overemphasis on morphology and structure in Amerind (as against acts of discourse), and his almost total neglect of the unique individual" (1986:6).

That Murray and Friedrich, in the 1980s, could disagree so completely on what is of value in Whorf's work suggests that the discourse practiced in the human sciences today has changed significantly since Carroll's reader first appeared. Views such as Friedrich's can get a serious hearing today, even if people like Murray are still likely to dismiss his views (which are tinged with their own brand of metaphysics) for the same reasons they are likely to dismiss the "mystical" and "messianic" elements in Whorf. Their opposed positions, indeed, reflect the contemporary struggle between competing modes of discourse within the human sciences. George Miller has described more explicitly than any other contemporary interpreter of Whorf the positions from which different scholarly traditions claim to have revealed the true importance of Whorf's insights. He contrasts the positions of social anthropologists (who, he says, fault Whorf for being too eager to derive meaning from grammar rather than context), theoretical linguists (who "regard language as the only term in Whorf's synthesis that can be seriously analyzed" and for whom "mapping culture onto habits of thought has all the clarity of mapping mish onto mash"), and cognitive psychologists (whose "professional bias leads them to neglect cultural differences and concentrate on the relation of language to thought. They seem to assume that, if Whorf was right, the fact that your native language is English should cripple you in some discoverable way") (1978:95–96).

Surprisingly, many scholars outside anthropology, linguistics, and pyschology who refer to Whorf rarely demonstrate awareness of the multiple interpretations the linguistic relativity principle has received. Thus, Rudolf Arnheim protests the conclusions of those analysts of visual art who insist on making visual apprehension dependent on linguistic processing. In a classic article, Arnheim lays the blame for the notion that "the world is invisible without words" on the importation into art criticism of the "extraordinary perversion" of "the so-called linguistic determinists," among whom he includes Herder, Humboldt, Cassirer, Sapir, and Whorf (1972).[1] Fifteen years later, Douglas Arrell makes the same charges in an article attacking Nelson Goodman's thesis that pictorial representation is based on arbitrary denotation rather than resemblance: "If denotation were limited to words, this belief would be called *linguistic determinism;* this view, usually associated with the linguist

B. L. Whorf, has been much discussed and generally rejected in cognitive psychology, primarily because people can be shown experimentally to make perceptual distinctions which they cannot communicate verbally" (1987:47–48). Similarly, a psychoanalyst (Bucci 1985:576–77) refers to the "linguistic determinism of Whorf," and critic Christopher Norris also associates Whorf with "relativism in its more extreme and unguarded forms" (1985:193ff.). All cite Carroll 1956 as canonical source.

Even this brief history of the way Whorf's writing has been received raises a host of questions. Is it correct to emphasize Whorf's "scientism" (à la Longacre, Carroll, and Murray) and downplay his "mysticism"? Or is it correct to acknowledge the mysticism and downplay the scientific achievements (à la Rollins)? Or is it more appropriate to choose a middle path (à la Friedrich) which acknowledges the value of Whorf's mystical side insofar as this allow for openness to the play of aesthetics, but repudiates Whorf's alleged belief in totalizing aesthetic harmony as more suitable for religion than art? Friedrich rejects religion in favor of art, indeed in favor of the verbal art of the individual poet, convinced as he is that "a deep philosophical skepticism is most appropriate for linguists today, when we have little cause for optimism and few grounds for belief in any perfection in the world" (1986:139).

Indeed, the discourses of science, religion, and art do not exhaust the possible ways of making Whorf's writings consistent and meaningful. Joshua Fishman has long stressed that it is in the domain of ethics, within a discourse of moral concern, that Whorf's contribution is best considered: "Precisely because Whorf can be interpreted as believing that there are only a limited number of language-based perspectives available to mankind he must also be interpreted as basically arguing for the benefits of language pluralism: the world will be a better place and humanity will be more successful in solving its ever more serious problems if we all master more (and more dissimilar) languages, because then we can share perspectives and shift perspectives more appropriately. The height of rationality, for Whorf, is the ability to select from among many language-dependent perspectives and to combine them productively" (1980:27).

Of course, concentrating on Whorf's ethical messages can lead one to gloss over some of the more intractable issues his linguistic analyses raise. For example, in his enthusiasm to promote Whorf the moralist, Fishman is led to argue that technical criticisms and attempts to test Whorf's scientific claims are inappropriate, successful only in "vulgarizing Whorf rather than testing (let alone disconfirming) him. What is needed from this point of view, is not so much to experimentally separate language from culture . . . but an even richer realization of the intricate and endless intertwining of the two" (1980:35).

While Fishman's final exhortation is admirable, and may indeed be the way to fruitful insight, his exposition suggests that Whorf himself did not seek to separate language from culture and, in fact, urged that we concentrate on the "intricate and endless intertwining" of language and culture. While such a suggestion is implicit in Fishman, it becomes quite explicit in the work of Danny Alford, who, of all contemporary linguists, may be the most dedicated to producing a consistent, monological, scientifically respectable reading of Whorf.[2] In a series of articles beginning in 1978, Alford argues that previous scholars have misinterpreted "the real Whorf," and accuses many of them—with some justice—of failing to return to what Whorf actually wrote before forming opinions about the validity of his ideas. Alford offers a close reading of Whorf (based on Carroll 1956) in which he proposes to clarify once and for all what Whorf really said, and to demonstrate thereby Whorf's scientific respectability and contemporary relevance.

Alford points out, quite rightly, that Whorf himself was not responsible for "the Whorf hypothesis"; this was the result of commentary by others. (See, for example, Carroll [1956:23; emphasis added], who writes, "what [Whorf] called the principle of linguistic relativity, which states, *at least as a hypothesis,* that the structure of a human being's language influences the manner in which he understands reality and behaves with respect to it.") Indeed, Carroll's rephrasing of the linguistic relativity principle corresponds to what has been called the "weak version of the Whorf hypothesis." It illustrates Carroll's attempt to wrest from Whorf a scientifically respectable (and presumably testable) principle that could not be equated with linguistic determinism. Yet the "strong version of the Whorf hypothesis"—linguistic determinism—was exactly what critics other than Carroll found when they read Whorf (and what they still find, assuming they are actually reading Whorf for themselves and not repeating the arguments of others: see the references to Arnheim, Arrell, Bucci, and Norris, above).

Again, Alford rightly points out that there is no explicit statement of linguistic determinism to be found in Whorf's writings (1978:489). He then goes on to argue, however, that "Whorf always defines language as a cultural phenomenon—two inseparable sides of a single coin, as it were" (1978:489–90). Alford offers three passages from the Carroll canon to support this assertion. Unfortunately, however, all three passages harbor serious ambiguities.

The first passage is from "A Linguistic Consideration of Thinking in Primitive Communities," published in the Carroll volume for the first time:

> The problem of thought and thinking in the native community is not purely and simply a psychological problem. It is quite largely cultural. It is moreover largely a matter of one especially cohesive aggregate of cultural phenomena that we call a language. (Whorf 3:65)

This passage serves as well as any as an introduction to the elusive quality of Whorf's prose. It begins unproblematically enough, suggesting that primitive thought is not shaped by innate psychological features of "primitive peoples," but is rather something learned. This seems a straightforward Boasian assertion of the distinction between race and culture. But what about language? Language is a part of culture—an "especially cohesive aggregate of cultural phenomena." This suggests that language, though part of culture, is yet more important and powerful than other parts of culture. And, indeed, Whorf goes on to state that this important influence of culture on thought "is approachable through linguistics," the scientific study of language in particular. Language is but part of culture, and yet language is the only part of culture with any marked effect on thought!

Alford's second passage is from the Sapir festschrift article, "The Relation of Habitual Thought and Behavior to Language" (Whorf 4:156). The passage Alford cites reads as follows:

> Which was first: the language patterns or the cultural norms? In main, they have grown up together, constantly influencing each other.

This seems completely unproblematic. It remains so, however, only because Alford neglected to cite the two sentences which immediately follow. Whorf continues: "But in this partnership the nature of the language is the factor that limits free plasticity and rigidifies channels of development in the more autocratic way. This is so because language is a system, not just an assemblage of norms" (Whorf 4:156). When we consider the passage in its entirety, the equal partnership of culture and language is called into question. *Language* is the factor that limits, rigidifies, is more autocratic. And this is because language is a *system,* and "culture" is "just an assemblage of norms" (an insider's reference to Lowie's famous statement that culture is "a thing of shreds and patches?"). Of course, Whorf does not state explicitly that *culture* is just an assemblage of norms; he merely states that language is *not* just an assemblage of norms. The reader is left to infer the nature of culture, while the text itself leaves the issue strictly undecidable.

We seem to have here an example of what Bakhtin, in discussing Dostoevsky's style in the story "The Double," calls a "microdialogue". A microdialogue is "not yet polyphony, but no longer homophony. One and the same word, idea, phenomenon is passed through three voices and in each voice sounds differently" (1984[1929]:220). A microdialogue is a kind of hybrid construction in which more than one voice sounds through what appears to be the mouth of a single speaker—and the voices address and respond to one another. Bakhtin emphasizes the way in which Dostoevsky's style in the story highlights "the intraatomic counterpoint of voices, their combination solely within the bounds of a single dismantled consciousness" (1984[1929]:220–21). In Whorf's text, the "word, idea, phenomenon" in question is first culture, then language. In one voice, culture and language *co*determine—but this voice is interrupted immediately by the other voice in which language is "more autocratic" because it is a "system." And yet the first voice is not entirely muffled because the second voice stops short of (or is prevented from) asserting explicitly that culture is *not* a system, and thus not as determinative as language. The extent to which the consciousness within which these voices combine is "dismantled", and by whom, and for what purposes, is an interesting question. One should take care, however, before dismissing the argument as an instance of nothing more than naive contradiction, let alone as an absence of contradiction altogether, which is what Alford tries to do.

One cannot accuse Alford of total bad faith in this instance, since he does include the omitted sentences in a footnote. However, even here, he fails to cite the damaging final clause, "not just an assemblage of norms" (1978:498). Even if Whorf's text does leave the nature of culture unspecified, and the microdialogue unfinalized, the rhetorical force of this clause favors the determinative power of language, which apparently makes Alford uneasy enough to eliminate it altogether.

Alford's final passage is from the "mystical" posthumously published article "Language, Mind, and Reality" (Whorf 9:252):

> And every language is a vast pattern system, different from others, in which are culturally ordained the forms and categories by which the personality not only communicates, but also analyzes nature, notices or neglects types of relationship and phenomena, channels his reasoning, and builds the house of his consciousness.

This passage, much like the first one, describes the interpenetration of language and culture. But what is the nature of this interpenetration? Is language part of culture or culture part of language? The first sentence (the first voice) suggests that culture is "within" language, because language is a "pattern system," and it is this patterned, systemic nature of language which gives it the upper hand. We heard this voice in the previous quotation. Language, as a system, orders the "assemblage of norms," placing them into "forms and categories" which "ordain" how the personality communicates, analyzes, notices or neglects, channels, and builds. But the passage does not state explicitly that *language* ordains, channels, and controls in this way; the subject of "ordain" is *culture* (the other voice responds!). But culture can ordain only *within* the pattern system of language! Or so the previous voice retorts, and apparently has the last word. The rhetorical shape of the passage leads us to conclude that language is more powerful than culture. But perhaps this is not the last word after all, for the text itself, again, does not allow the matter to be finalized.

To his credit, Alford wrestles with the stickiness of this passage. He says, "Whorf sensed something 'chicken-and-egg-y' about the language-culture interaction problem. He sensed its paradoxical unity and attempted to maintain a very difficult stance which would respect the paradox by not choosing one over the other as preexisting or causal" (1978:499 [*sic*]). But, as we have seen, Whorf's desire to "respect the paradox" is anything but straightforward. Why did he not just come out and *say*, "I sense something 'chicken-and-egg-y' about the language-culture interaction problem," or, "I believe that language and culture are two sides of the same coin whose paradoxical unity must be respected without reducing one to the other"? Whorf appears to *see* the paradox, yet he *wants* to favor language, at the same time sensing that the favoritism is misplaced. This is tension-ridden prose! The voice of holism and the voice of reductionism are battling for supremacy.

So it is too easy to speak, as Alford does, of "Whorf's acausal views" (1978:491 [*sic*]), or to interpret such difficult passages as containing clear-cut "yes-yes statements" of a holistic or gestalt nature which unsympathetic scientistic interpreters have systematically distorted (Alford 1981:17). While not exactly wrong, such a conclusion is in its own way reductionistic. It drains the lifeblood from Whorf's utterances, making him sound merely consistent, commonplace, finished off, dead. Again, if this were all Whorf had to say, he would hardly remain so controversial. It is as if Alford were seduced by Whorf's prose style—a graceful, charming style that seems spontaneous, friendly, and above all sincere.

Surely such a smooth individual style must indicate a smooth single-voiced content, especially if one begins with the assumption that authors normally speak in a single voice! And yet we have seen how Alford is forced to do violence to that style even as he quotes Whorf to defend him.

Alford criticizes those who accuse Whorf of inconsistency and remarks, "It is curious how . . . the holistically balanced insights of one generation become, in the next, plundered for their analytic regularities" (1981:17). Again, while one cannot totally disagree with this observation, it is inadequate to the complexity of Whorf's texts. Alford seems to be suggesting that Whorf's "holistic balance" is unproblematic, straightforward, explicit, sincere. A balance without tension, without doubt. If these passages exhibit "balance," however, it is a precarious balance that threatens continually to collapse. This is the outcome, I would argue, of Whorf's attempt to cast holistic insights in the language of positivist science. The tension in these passages is not simply due to Whorf's indecision over which phenomenon—language or culture—is the true determining force to which all else must be reduced. It is equally a result of Whorf's attempt to speak holistically using a mode of discourse whose forms require a mechanical-materialist reductionism. Positivistic discourse requires that he choose one factor to which the others can mechanically be reduced. And yet his own experience resists any such reduction. Because Whorf respects science and the language of science, he finds himself trying to express ideas—noncanonical ideas—for which the language of positivist science is inadequate. He pushes that language as far as it will go without losing its identity as the language of science, and the results are tension-ridden passages like the ones above.

The "distortions" which Alford decries point directly to this struggle between modes of discourse, indeed a struggle *to create* a new mode of discourse that can encompass holistic insights without betraying science. It is a struggle, however, which Alford does not acknowledge. He fails to recognize that to argue holistically within the discourse of positivist science can *only* be interpreted as inconsistency.

Yet, consistency from the point of view of positivist science is not the only kind of consistency that may be sought. As we saw with Paul Friedrich, Whorf may be valued precisely to the extent that he can be interpreted as *rejecting* scientism. And although Friedrich hardly views Whorf's writings as free of contradiction, this is not the case with Ranjit Chatterjee who, in a comparison of Whorf and Wittgenstein, asserts that "by the company it keeps, Whorf's linguistic thought is seen to be not eccentric or deviant, but in its basic insights akin to both the wisdom of the ancients and the conclusions of a great modern philosopher" (1985:60). Far from finding Whorf's "mysticism" off-putting, Chatterjee finds in it the key to consistent interpretation, and hence, the key to what is most valuable in Whorf. Commenting on the "mystical" article, "Language, Mind, and Reality," Chatterjee observes that "Whorf's texts are seen to point *beyond* the seemingly explicit statements that are generally taken to represent his thought. They are part of a *via negativa* that leads to the abiding involvement both Whorf and Wittgenstein had with critical linguistic philosophies akin to those of Madhyamika Buddhism (as expounded by Murti and Conze) and Taoism (as expounded by Hansen)" (1985:57). Chatterjee further suggests that "poststructuralism points in the same direction" (1985:60).

Thus, there is clearly more going on in Whorf's texts than most interpreters are normally willing to acknowledge. Nevertheless, a few readers have suggested that Whorf might be playing games with us. Longacre, explicating Whorf's statement of the linguistic relativity principle ("We are thus introduced to a new principle of relativity, which holds that all observers are not led by the same physical evidence to the same picture of the universe, unless their linguistic backgrounds are similar or can in some way be calibrated" [Whorf, 6:214]), urges us to "note the possibility of a joker in the last phrase; could it be that in spite of the great diversity of the world's languages, they may all be at least partially capable of translation?" (1956:300). Dillon (1982:75) accuses "Whorf and his followers" of practicing "rhetorical sleight of hand" as they match up linguistic practices and cultural norms, a practice of which, in his view, stylisticians are equally guilty, and which may not be as innocent as it seems. In an unpublished Whorf manuscript entitled "The Newtonian Room and the Christian Rosebush," Rollins detects signs of "puckish glee" in Whorf's account of the dismantling of nineteenth-century sensationalist psychology (1980:34–35). And Silverstein detects glee mixed with terror: "To be sure, Whorf proposes that scientific linguistics . . . will be no little aid both in understanding the implications of the relativity and uncertainty principles, and in overcoming them. To what extent this is all tongue-in-cheek is an interesting question, since, like most positivists (or those whose scientific training was in that tradition), Whorf had a mystic inside screaming to get out" (1979:238). I propose, in the pages that follow, to face this perverse and unsettling side of Whorf head on. In doing so, I am bringing to bear upon Whorf's writings a poststructuralist perspective, specifically that elaborated by Mikhail Bakhtin and his circle.

1 Bakhtin and Whorf

Several features of the work of Bakhtin and Whorf suggest that the two might be fruitfully compared with one another. In a footnote, Michael Holquist groups Bahktin with those thinkers identified with linguistic relativity in the West, stating that "for Bakhtin, as for von Humboldt, the diversity of languages *is of itself of philosophical significance,* for if thought and speech are one, does not each language embody a unique way of thinking? It is there that Bakhtin also comes very close to the work of Sapir, and, especially, of Whorf" (1986:101). Holquist makes explicit reference to two of Whorf's articles, "Science and Linguistics" and "Languages and Logic." It is perhaps noteworthy, given what we have seen already about the subtlety of Whorf's style, that Holquist here presents his version of the linguistic relativity principle in the form of a rhetorical question, refraining from claiming outright that, for Bakhtin or for Whorf, language determines thought. In fact, occasional statements of Bakhtin's compare with Whorf's in terms of stylistic subtlety on this very point. For example, in the following passage, the unconscious power of speech genres to shape our thought sounds every bit as relentless as the power of grammatical forms described by Whorf:

> Like Molière's Monsieur Jourdain who, when speaking in prose, had no idea that was what he was doing, we speak in diverse genres without suspecting that they exist. Even in the most free, the most unconstrained conversation, we cast our speech in definite generic forms, sometimes rigid and trite ones, sometimes more flexible, plastic, and creative ones. . . . We are given these speech genres in almost the same way that we are given our native language. . . .
> (1986[1952–53]:78)

In addition, even as Whorf saw a special role for the linguist in bringing the unconscious pressures of grammar to conscious awareness, thus freeing us from its constraint, Bakhtin assigned the literary critic a special role in freeing readers and writers from the bonds of spoken and written literary genres that culture and history impose on each generation.

> The author himself and his contemporaries see, recognize, and evaluate primarily that which is close to their own day. The author is a captive of his epoch, of his own present. Subsequent times liberate him from this captivity, and literary scholarship is called upon to assist in this liberation. (1986[1970]:5)

Although Whorf and Bakhtin seem to be vibrating on the same wavelengths, it is nevertheless the case that the tactics they employ in exploring linguistic relativity are not identical. To begin with, Whorf's substantive focus was on grammar, rather than discourse: Michael Silverstein avers that "he developed the sharpest tools for describing the grammatical categories of propositional language we have yet seen, of which the emergence of transformational-generative grammar is merely a notational refinement" (1979:198). Bakhtin's substantive focus, by contrast, was on discourse rather than grammar, and he provided an innovative analysis of forms of discourse—written and spoken genres—which make use of, but are not reducible to, grammar. For Bakhtin and his colleagues, grammar was properly the subject of linguistics, but a study of grammar did not exhaust all that was of importance about language. Equally worthy of study was discourse, that is, "language in its concrete living totality"; and discourse was properly the subject of what he called metalinguistics (1984[1929]:181). Once one paid attention to discourse, language-in-the-concrete, one could not avoid recognizing that such language involves using words in utterances, that is, to address other people and to respond to them in specific, unrepeatable contexts. Thus, the study of discourse was simultaneously a study of dialogical relationships (1984[1929]:182).

Bakhtin gave a separate identity to phenomena of a metalinguistic nature that Whorf struggled to subsume under the rubric of grammar. Thus Bakhtin's concepts not only help make sense of what he and his colleagues were doing; they help us understand what Whorf was doing as well. Claims that each was doing "metalinguistics" are in fact accurate: each in his own way dealt with matters that went beyond the traditional concerns of linguistics as practiced in the first third of the twentieth century. The differences between them, however, are what make them such good dialogic partners. To read one in terms of the other is most illuminating.

In particular, to compare Whorf with Bakhtin provides a powerful confirmation of the Bakhtinian appreciation of the need to interpret a writer's works as utterances whose meaning cannot be fully understood without knowing the dialogizing background against which they were uttered. While the dialogizing background in terms of which Bakhtin wrote has been elucidated by Holquist and others, the dialogizing background against which Whorf wrote has never been fully explored by most of his critics. It is even true to say that the very existence of such a background has not been recognized by most critics. As we have seen, most have assumed that Whorf spoke with a single voice, and that his work, therefore, could be assimilated to one or another conventional monologic disciplinary perspective, even if nobody could agree on exactly which one.

Thus, if a first step in understanding Whorf requires us to recognize the different voices that speak from his texts, a second step requires us to evaluate his voices in terms of those other voices which he addressed. This second step leads directly to a focus on Whorf's style, which was shaped for particular audiences and hoped to elicit particular responses from them.

Our understanding of Whorf's dialogizing background can be sharpened, I believe, by comparing it with Bakhtin's. That is to say, although both Whorf and Bakhtin shared a similar understanding of language and appreciation for linguistic diversity, they found themselves having to convey that understanding to different kinds of audiences living under widely different social, cultural, and political circumstances. Each could assume (indeed, had to assume) things about his readers and their world which the other could not assume, simply because the readers and the worlds in question were so different from one another. These differences were especially striking as regards each society's experience and understanding of language, which involved at least the following elements:

1. In America, people are free to speak their minds: this is the central folk understanding about language held by most Americans. Institutionalized censorship on the scale practiced in the Soviet Union during the Stalin era is unknown and un-American. The American ideology of free speech fosters the sense that it is we who control language, and not the reverse; indeed, that each individual controls his or her own language and bends it to his or her own purposes.

Not only is there no *state* censorship, in America there is no *group* censorship of language at any level below the state. At least, this is what most middle-class Americans believe. America is the land of the rugged atomistic individual to an extent that boggles the minds even of other Western observers who defend individual agency (see Taylor 1985b(1979):187–210). Popular common sense in America has always presumed individuals to be fully formed, autonomous beings who make their own way in the world, directed by the choices of an inner consciousness that is fully transparent to itself. Individual subjectivity is taken for granted "as an inherent characteristic of human beings, not in need of explication . . . [and] not open to any kind of social analysis" (Giddens 1979:120). During the years Whorf was writing, social scientists in America were attempting to develop theories that were precisely concerned with opening individual human action to explication and social analysis. But they faced steadfast opposition in their attempts to persuade the American public of the validity of those theories.[1]

Americans resist strongly the idea that ethnicity or class membership, for example, does or should affect *anything* Americans choose to do in life, including how they choose to speak. Paradoxically, this is the reason why Americans think everyone in America should speak English. This is what is American about America, as opposed to the Old World (including Russia) where class and religion and national origins restricted action and speech. Even more strongly in Whorf's day than today, linguistic diversity was seen as a problem to be solved. The motto seemed to be: Become monoglot in the dominant language and be free! Sociolinguists and linguistic anthropologists have fought an uphill battle to convince even academic colleagues that this may not always be either possible or desirable.

Related to this, of course, is the American experience of *other languages,* as opposed to the experience of many Western and Eastern Europeans, and of the Russians for whom Bakhtin wrote. Most white middle-class Americans live in a world "muffled by a dense monoglossia" (Bakhtin 1981b[1940]:63). Only a select few learn second languages, and then only in the classroom. Even immigrants who spoke other languages ordinarily were not proud of the fact, and certainly were not encouraged to continue to do so once they arrived in this country. The language of the Old Country represented another of those illegitimate ties, restrictions on individual liberty, that needed to be eliminated in the New World, where all were to have equal access to the language of the rulers. Complacent American monolingualism is, in fact, perhaps the single most powerful background factor accounting for the impact of

Whorf's texts on American audiences, especially the impact of those texts in which the grammatical refinements of a native American language are celebrated and deemed superior to English.

2. In America there is the sense that people using the standard forms of a common language can freely say what they mean and mean what they say. White middle-class Americans rarely feel they must choose their words carefully in order to avoid punishment by the censors—or, if they do, they feel this pressure as illegitimate and in no way constitutive of the language policies of the society as a whole.

In Bakhtin's Russia, however, one finds the opposite situation: bi- or multilingualism was far from unknown in ordinary life, but diversity—particularly diversity of *content*—was forcibly restricted by rulers who controlled what might be said by anybody in any language. If the standard forms have been appropriated by the rulers, those who wish to speak on forbidden topics must resort to various forms of verbal subterfuge to communicate with one another. The resources of language must be plundered for paraphrase, figuration, and other alternatives to the standard forms. Far more meaning must be carried by context if saying what you mean in no uncertain terms can land you in prison or exile or worse. And so Bakhtin (and his fellow Russians) seem to have developed an acute awareness of the potentials *within* any particular language for saying the same thing in different ways, or different things in the same way, as a survival skill. This being the case, it is all the more remarkable that Bakhtin and his colleagues were as willing as they were to speak openly about the means to subterfuge. Even so, of course, Bakhtin's two most famous colleagues, Voloshinov and Medvedev, perished under Stalin, and he himself was arrested. Part of the fascination of his work is the stylistic cunning he used to get past the censors and communicate on dangerous topics. Whorf also used stylistic cunning of his own, but for different purposes. Rather than maneuvering to get past censors whose existence nobody could deny, he found himself having to convince his readers that they engaged in a kind of self-censorship when they blithely assumed that the categories of English bore some unique correspondence to reality.

3. The only understanding of "form" in language which Americans find credible relates to "grammar." This was clearly the case for the linguists of Whorf's day, who focused on phonemes and morphemes to the virtual exclusion of all else. How this preoccupation is to be understood is ambiguous, since, on the one hand, it could in principle be seen as a positivistic attempt to reduce syntax, semantics, and every other

aspect of language to the unconscious controlling mechanisms of sound patterns and other patterns closely dependent upon these (e.g., morphophonemics). On the other hand, by restricting the rigid rules to sound and word formation rules, it might equally be possible to argue that in every other aspect of language, freedom prevailed and individuals could do what they wished. And this was certainly the official Saussurean position which prevailed during the same period in Europe.

What do you do if you want to point out not only that linguistic diversity exists but that it is a good thing? If you are Bakhtin, you will not deny that restriction on speech exists, something in any case which is all too plain to your readers. Being a careful scholar, you will even document linguistic forms previously unnoticed: namely, forms of utterances, called speech genres, which take the forms of grammar and categorize them for use in culturally specific speech situations. However, if you are Bakhtin, you also want to give hope to those who live under restrictive linguistic circumstances by emphasizing those areas of language where freedom can be claimed even under censorship. You will therefore emphasize the immensely varied resources that exist *within* any particular language (not to mention in other languages) for saying the same thing in different ways, or different things in the same way. And you will demonstrate that even if linguistic forms, and forms for the use of forms, are "always already there," the decision to follow the rules for the use of forms is always up to the speaker, who can manipulate them in pursuit or his or her own authentic word.

If you are Whorf, however, you must first convince your readers that censorship exists. You must break through their "false consciousness" of absolute linguistic liberty by showing them that they are, in fact, restricted to the forms of a single language. Thus, their liberty is relative to that language. And to hammer home the lesson, you emphasize the constraints of grammatical form, the only kind of linguistic form Americans are willing to pay attention to. Even though you believe, like Bakhtin, that openings for relatively free expression exist in language, to begin your argument by conceding this would be to lose the interest of your American audience, for whom free expression is an article of faith. You must therefore bury your concession in complex prose, in marginal expositions, or in the compositional form (rather than the overt content) of your text. This, I hope to show, is exactly what Whorf did.

Paradoxically, Bakhtin emerges for many readers as an apostle of hope and freedom in language, while Whorf is treated as a prophet of doom and determinism. Yet if my thesis is correct, both portraits are caricatures based on the authorial images each writer constructed for his own particular audience. Thus Holquist is correct when he remarks about Bakhtin's essay on speech genres that "given its emphasis on normative restraints that control even our most intimate speech, the essay should at the very least sound a cautionary note for those who wish to invoke Bakhtin in the service of a boundless libertarianism" (1986:xvii; see also xix). What I hope to show is that a similar cautionary note should be sounded for those who wish to invoke Whorf in the service of a relentless reductionism.

A Dialogue Between Whorf and Bakhtin

We have been introduced to some of the puzzles and promise of Whorf's writings on linguistic relativity. Before pursuing them further, it is necessary to speak in more detail about what Bakhtin had to say on these same topics. This is important, to begin with, in order to document fully the similarities between Whorf and Bakhtin which have been claimed. We will also be allowed to examine those crucial areas into which Bakhtin and his colleagues ventured openly, but on which Whorf remained silent. In addition, however, it is necessary to make plain some of Bakhtin's broader concepts about language and social life which can aid our understanding of Whorf's texts.

Thus, in the following section I propose to do the following:
1. to compare statements by Whorf and by Bakhtin or Voloshinov in which the basic precepts of linguistic relativity are most fully developed.
2. to devote attention to a particular topic on which Whorf is virtually silent, but which is hinted at in Voloshinov and most fully developed by Bakhtin: the linguistic diversity *within* any particular language, or *heteroglossia*.
3. to examine the broader concepts about language and social life which Bakhtin derives from his analysis of literary texts. In particular, we will focus on that form of writing in which, according to Bakhtin, an author is most free to exploit the multiple resources of grammar and genre in pursuit of his own ends, namely, *artistic* (or *novelistic*) *prose*. While presenting sophisticated views about the ways language can be used, Bakhtin provides at the same time a series of literary-critical tools which may be used to analyze what an actual author, such as Whorf (or Bakhtin himself), is up to in a particular text. This section will therefore prepare the way for the one which follows, in which Whorf's artistic prose is subjected to Bakhtinian critical analysis. In particular, the apparatus Bakhtin develops in his analysis of Dostoevsky's prose will be applied to Whorf's writing with, I hope, illuminating results.

Linguistic Relativity in Whorf and Bakhtin

As we saw earlier, many of Whorf's critics have interpreted his linguistic relativity principle as a statement of linguistic determinism: the categories of language are said to determine categories of thought and perception. If it be agreed that this is indeed what Whorf is claiming about language, then many critics believe they have an unbeatable means of refuting Whorf's claim. They argue that linguistic determinism is undone by the paradox of translatability.

The translatability paradox arises as soon as one considers Whorf's defense of the linguistic relativity principle together with his substantive studies of Native American languages such as Hopi. If the linguistic relativity principle is true, so the argument goes, it should be impossible for anyone, Whorf included, to break out of the categories of his or her own native language to learn the categories of another, very different language. Yet, in order for Whorf to have been able to write such articles as "The Punctual and Segmentative Aspects of Verbs in Hopi," he must have been able to learn Hopi categories and find ways of expressing them in English that made them accessible to his readers. Thus, his own categories from English did not stand in the way of learning or translating Hopi, and therefore, linguistic relativity is an illusion.

The translatability paradox has been used by early critics (e.g., Longacre 1956, Black 1962[1959]) and recent critics (e.g., Putnam 1981, D. Davidson 1984) in order to refute linguistic relativity. At a later point, we will consider such articles as "The Punctual and Segmentative Aspects of Verbs in Hopi" and ask whether interpretations of that article by Whorf's critics are fully adequate in capturing what Whorf accomplished and how he accomplished it. For the moment, however, let us simply note that, despite criticism of Whorf, Davidson is willing to grant that he succeeds in giving his readers a "feel for" the exoticism of Hopi grammar, which amounts to recognition of, at least, the "weak version" of linguistic relativity.

In his clearest statements of the linguistic relativity principle, Whorf seems to be arguing that speakers of different languages do *not* all share identical forms and categories of thought simply by virtue of the fact that they are all human beings. At the same time, Whorf refrains from suggesting that all human beings possess, *within the boundaries of their native tongue,* vast resources for categorizing experience in a variety of ways, and hence the capacity to debate the advantages and disadvantages of the alternatives they invent.

Consider again the classic statement of the linguistic relativity principle cited earlier: "We are thus introduced to a new principle of relativity, which holds that all observers are not led by the same physical evidence to the same picture of the universe, unless their linguistic backgrounds are similar or can in some way be calibrated" (Whorf 6:214). The assumption of Whorf's critics, upon reading this passage, has been that similarity of linguistic background refers to the observers' all speaking the same native language (or "national language," in Bakhtin's terms). Whorf says nothing, moreover, to disabuse them of this assumption, although, again, he does *not* state explicitly that observers *must* be native speakers of the same language in order to come to the same picture of the universe! If readers ignore this curious silence, and are swept away by the deterministic phraseology ("all observers are not led . . . unless their linguistic backgrounds are similar . . ."), they are virtually bound to conclude that Whorf is proposing that all human beings who speak a particular language share the same *relatively absolute* categories of thought.

Were this the case, Whorf would be vulnerable to the translatability refutation, since his own ability to learn exotic languages testifies to the fact that the categories of English did not stand in his way. Critics may also pick up on the significant loophole left by Whorf's silence concerning *intra*linguistic variety. Feuer (1953) did this, pointing out that Western philosophers speaking Standard Average European languages have, for centuries, been able to devise a variety of worldviews and argue about them using the same grammatical categories. He therefore doubts that study of the grammar of Hopi is likely to suggest to SAE speakers anything that they could not have figured out on their own. Similarly, Lakoff has recently concluded that "Whorf seemed to think conceptual systems were monolithic . . . it is as though there were no room for alternatives *within* a language and a conceptual system" (1987:239). That is, Whorf is taken to have claimed that, relative to the limited universe of their own speech community, shared linguistic categories exert absolute and universal control over the thought processes of the people who use them.[2]

Some passages in a 1926 text by Voloshinov, "Discourse in Life and Discourse in Art," give off a similar relative-absolutistic aura. To be sure, Voloshinov begins from a different starting point. He discusses the *utterance,* that central concept of the Bakhtin circle, which cannot be reduced to the language of grammar books and dictionaries, but instead refers to what language becomes when it issues from one person's mouth, directed to a specific listener in a specific context with a particular intonation. For language used in this way to be understood, it is never enough to know grammar and the dictionary meanings of words. One must be able to grasp the *theme* of the utterance—what it means *for this speaker and this listener in this situation in this tone of voice.* Grasping the theme of an utterance thus requires a complex understanding of *context.*

Voloshinov suggests that three factors make up the extraverbal context of the utterance: "(1) the *common spatial purview* of the interlocutors (the unity of the visible . . .), (2) the interlocutors' *common knowledge and understanding of the situation,* and (3) their *common evaluation* of that situation" (1987[1926]:99). Note that certain experiences and background knowledge must *already* be held in common by the interlocutors if they are to understand one another fully: unless you are already part of the group, living its life, speaking its language fluently, you will not understand what is being said. Put another way, you will not be led by the same physical evidence to the same picture of the universe unless the linguistic backgrounds of you and your interlocutor are similar, or can in some way be calibrated. Voloshinov makes the point emphatically:

> Whatever kind it be, the behavioral utterance always joins the participants in the situation together as *co-participants* who know, understand, and evaluate the situation in like manner. *The utterance,* consequently, *depends on their real, material appurtenance to one and the same segment of being and gives this material commonness ideological expression and further ideological development.* (1987[1926]:100)

Let us compare the loopholes in Whorf's text with those in Voloshinov's text. Whorf, on the one hand, never tells us just what he means by "linguistic background." Although the rhetorical intent, given the context provided by the rest of his work, apparently is to convey the idea that he means "background in the same language as formally defined by linguistics, e.g., English, or Hopi," he does not explicitly rule out a class-based or ethnicity-based background rooted in but a single variety of one or another such language. He does not even rule out explicitly the similar linguistic background of two interlocutors bilingual in the same (or even different) languages.

Voloshinov, on the other hand, is trying to construct a marxian sociological poetics, and he wants to make it plain that the linguistic matters of which he speaks are not metaphysical chimeras, but are rooted in the objective material and social conditions of life. Every behavioral utterance has two parts: the part which is made up of words and the part which is assumed. Both parts, moreover, are objective and socially constituted. Language, of course, is given to people by their society, not invented anew by each person; and the assumed context, Voloshinov argues, is equally given, equally social and objective: "What *I* know, see, want, love, and so on cannot be assumed. Only what all of us speakers know, see, love, recognize—only those points on which we are all united can become the assumed part of an utterance" (1987[1926]:100). And again, "every utterance in the business of life is an objective social enthymeme. It is something like a 'password' known only to those who belong to the same social purview. . . . Once severed from that context, [utterances] lose almost all their import—a person ignorant of the immediate pragmatic context will not understand these utterances" (1987[1926]:101).

Thus, for Voloshinov, it is not just the categories of language, but also the categories of context and the linguistic forms appropriate to them, which are socially determined and, hence, determine the meaning of our speech. The individual seems little more than a puppet of these forces: "*Individual* emotions can come into play only as *overtones* accompanying the *basic tone of social evaluation.* 'I' can realize itself verbally only on the basis of 'we' " (1987[1926]:100). And again, "A creatively productive, assured, and rich intonation is possible only on the basis of presupposed 'choral support.' Where such support is lacking, the voice falters and its intonational richness is reduced, as happens, for instance, when a person laughing suddenly realizes that he is laughing alone. . . . *The commonness of assumed basic value judgments contitutes the canvas upon which living human speech embroiders the designs of intonation*" (1987[1926]:103).

The rhetorical flavor of these passages suggests neatly bounded and highly unified social groups, not unlike self-conscious marxian social classes. The members of such groups apparently can safely assume a great deal about their world and about one another, and are apparently untroubled by any hint of ambiguity. And this is seemingly the way it should be:

> A healthy social value judgment remains within life and from that position organizes the very form of an utterance and its intonation, but it does not at all aim to find suitable expression in the content side of discourse. Once a value judgment shifts from formal factors to content, we may be sure that a reevalution is in the offing. (1987[1926]:101–2)

Membership in a healthy social group is unproblematic; it is easy to say what you mean and mean what you say and be understood perfectly. It is only when one deals with outsiders that problems arise. To leave the group is to become inauthentic, to sicken.

The more a poet is cut off from the social unity of his group, the more likely he is to take into account the *external* demands of a *particular reading public*. Only a social group alien to the poet can determine his creative work from outside. One's *own* needs no such external definition. It exists in the poet's voice, in the basic tone and intonations of that voice—whether the poet intends this or not. (1987[1926]:114)

It is here that the loophole widens. Everything said so far suggests that poets can speak authentically only in the voice of their group, only using the language and common assumptions they share with that group. If this were true, it would be as crippling as Whorf's supposed linguistic determinism. But in fact, poets (and people in general, we assume) need not lead such monochromatic, monological, monoglot lives. For after painting such a deterministic picture, Voloshinov tells us that this "immediate context" that determines so much in such an unambiguous fashion

> may be of varying scope. In our example, the context is extremely narrow: It is *circumscribed by the room and the moment of occurence,* and the utterance makes an intelligible statement only for the two persons involved. However, the unified purview on which an utterance depends can expand in both space and time. *The "assumed" may be that of the family, clan, nation, class and may encompass days or years or whole epochs.* The wider the overall purview and its corresponding social group, the more *constant* the assumed factors in an utterance become. (1987[1926]:101)

It is perhaps plausible that members of a smallish, closely knit group living under the same material and social conditions could share a "restricted code" that was extremely coherent and largely free of ambiguity. But this picture becomes less and less plausible the wider Voloshinov casts the net of the group and the time depth for which it is supposed to exist. If the assumed understandings of a social group be called its "tradition," it becomes increasingly difficult to decide what that "tradition" is as more and more people and subgroups are included and allowed to offer their opinion over longer and longer stretches of time. So what can Voloshinov possibly mean by these "assumed factors" which become more "constant" as the "overall purview and its corresponding social group" increase? Since social variability (and ambiguity and disagreement) are bound to increase as the group gets larger and more of its history is considered, that which remains constant would be reduced to material features and processes of the physical surroundings and human bodies of interlocutors, and the relationships between them. And it is not just the diversity of what may be assumed as common tradition that introduces a loophole into Voloshinov's carefully constructed, relative absolutistic worldview. There is also the diversity of experience of the poet (or any individual person) over the course of his or her lifetime. "The poet," he tells us, "acquires his words and learns to intone them *over the course of his entire life* in the process of his everysided contact with his environment. . . . A poet's style is engendered from *the style of his inner speech,* which does not lend itself to control, and his inner speech is itself the product of his entire social life" (1987 [1926]:114). The rhetorical force of this and the previously quoted passages conspires to form the picture of individuals molded completely by experience of life and culture and language *within the bounds* of their close-knit group. But the more widely these individuals travel, the greater their experience of other peoples and places and languages, the older they get, the more their "entire social life" will *include* elements originating *outside* the group in which they first belonged. "Style," Voloshinov continues, "is at least two persons, or, more accurately, one person plus his social group in the form of its authoritative representative, the listener— the constant participant in a person's inner and outward speech" (1987[1926]:114). But a person, over the course of his or her entire social life, is bound to be involved with many social groups in different ways, thus having to keep straight a variety of listeners and needing to develop a complex inner and outward speech capable of addressing *all* of them.

Up to this point, the relative-absolute paradox in Voloshinov is very similar to the one in Whorf. But Voloshinov does what Whorf avoids doing: namely, discuss explicitly some of the varied linguistic resources upon which different speakers may draw in suiting their speech to different listeners. In the same article from which the previous quotations were drawn, Voloshinov begins, in a characteristically Whorfian manner, to describe how the pronominal forms of languages such as Japanese enable speakers to specify precisely their social position and that of the person addressed. However, far from allowing his readers to draw the conclusion (as Whorf might have done) that Russian speakers are crippled in their efforts to make such social distinctions because their language lacks these pronominal forms, Voloshinov takes a different tack. "In European languages these and similar interrelationships between speakers have no special grammatical expression. . . . However, interrelationships between speakers do find expression in these languages—and expression of far greater subtlety and diversity—*in the style and intonation of utterances*" (1987[1926]:111).

Grammar can do a lot, but style and intonation can do more. The same position is repeated by Bakhtin in an article written almost thirty years later:

> Language as a system has an immense supply of purely linguistic means for expressing formal addresses. . . . But they acquire addressivity only in the whole of a concrete utterance. *And the expression of this actual addressivity is never exhausted, of course, by these special language (grammatical) means. They can even be completely lacking, and the utterance can still reflect very clearly the influence of the addressee and his anticipated responsive reaction.* (1986[1952–53]:99; emphasis added)

Elsewhere, Bakhtin defines style as "the fundamental and creative [triple] relationship of discourse to its object, to the speaker himself and to another's discourse; style strives organically to assimilate material into language and language into material" (1981c[1940]:378). Style and intonation break us out of the trap of grammar. Of course, styles and intonations are themselves culturally patterned linguistic phenomena. The escape would seem merely out of one prison cell and into another, but in fact there remains a tiny margin of freedom. All speakers can draw upon their knowledge of the patterns of grammar and genre and intonation to construct *particular* utterances in *particular* circumstances directed to *particular* individuals in a *particular* tone of voice, thereby manipulating these forms in pursuit of their own interests—interests which may contradict the culturally approved canons of usage. "Words belong to nobody, and in themselves they evaluate nothing. But they can serve any speaker and be used for the most varied and directly contradictory evaluations on the part of the speakers" (Bakhtin 1986[1952–53]:85).

In this way, having established in no uncertain terms the power of socially shaped forms of language over individual speakers, Voloshinov and Bakhtin then proceed to demonstrate how these same speakers are not passively molded by language, but in fact actively resist and manipulate obligatory forms in pursuit of their own authentic voices. And, it turns out, speakers have far more resources at their disposal than the single set of forms and stylistic conventions of a single "language." In fact, every national language is teeming with sublanguages, each with its own conventions. Wherever significant social differentiation occurs in life, there too will begin to form a new sublanguage. In any society of any complexity, therefore, numerous such sublanguages always coexist, challenge one another, and become grist for the verbal mill of those who master their conventions. What we are describing, of course, is the state of *heteroglossia,* which Bakhtin takes to be the primordial linguistic state for human beings in society.

Bakhtin takes delight in heteroglossia. He openly admits his "love for variations and for a diversity of terms for a single phenomenon. The multiplicity of focuses. Bringing distant things closer without indicating the intermediate links" (1986[1970–71]:155). And these diverse ways of speaking are not isolated from one another, mute to one another like a silent collection of artifacts in a museum. On the contrary, the sublanguages of heteroglossia are used by real people to address and respond to one another. Bakhtin is sensitive to and stimulated by this exchange: "I hear *voices* in everything and dialogic relations among them" (1986[1974]:169). This is far from an incoherent babble. For Bakhtin, it is not texts which speak themselves through people, but people who wrestle with texts (words, stylistic genres, intonations) in an effort to speak for themselves to other people. And awareness of the dialogue is an enriching experience. "The one-sided and limited nature of a viewpoint (the position of the observer) can always be corrected, augmented, transformed (transferred) with the help of like observations from others' viewpoints. Bare viewpoints (without living and new observations) are fruitless" (1986[n.d.]:124).

The tone of these observations by Bakhtin, written at the end of his life, is that of contented, even joyful, serenity. Though heteroglossia was dangerous, he did not fear it and learned to delight in it. The dialectic of freedom and constraint, which was far from theoretical for him and his friends under Stalin, did not appear to cause him deep personal anguish. At least, personal anguish is not visible in the authorial image he presents. But the same cannot be said for Whorf, at least if the authorial image in his texts can be taken to indicate something about his personal state of mind. Whorf never explicitly denies the existence of what Bakhtin calls heteroglossia within a single national language. He comes closest to affirming its existence when he posits the existence of "fashions of speaking" which cut "across the typical grammatical classifications" (Whorf 4:158). But it was not a topic that he pursued at length in any of his own substantive studies. Rather than celebrating *intra*linguistic variety (which, apart from losing the interest of his readers, might have stirred up unpleasant political problems involving supposedly assimilated minority groups in American society), Whorf focused on *cross*-linguistic variation. And rather than stressing the way forms could be manipulated, he stressed the way forms constrain. Although this was a rhetorical ploy in part, expressing his glee at exposing prejudicial thinking, it was also part of his struggle to reconcile the monological language of science with linguistic diversity. And he posed the problem dramatically.

For Bakhtin and his colleagues the monological discourse of state censorship was bad, and needed to be undermined. For Whorf, the monological discourse of science was not bad. But it was clearly limited and could not deal with alternative discourses (cf. Silverstein 1979:194). It was obliged to see such discourses as primitive or irrational or illogical, and could never take them seriously until they had been translated (assimilated) into its own language. Whorf's dilemma began when he found himself having to take seriously the alternative discourses, in the form of alternative grammars in alien languages, which his sophisticated linguistic studies revealed to him. How could one affirm the language of science without deforming these alternative languages? He devoted much attention to the problem, trying to hammer out for himself a mode of discourse in which he could be faithful both to Scientific Truth and to the particular truths of particular languages. This mode of discourse was, as we have seen, tension ridden and ambiguous. It allowed his critics to accuse him of "relativism" (when they focused on the passages, like the one cited earlier, in which he seemed to be arguing for relative absolutism). But it also allowed them to accuse him of *rejecting* "relativism," insofar as they detected his desire to defend science. This is what allowed Rollins to claim that "Whorf could hardly accept the relativism implicit in Kuhn's picture of scientific development. . . . [He was] certain that ultimate truths could be unveiled" (1980:23).

The dilemma, and the distress it generated for Whorf, is evident in one of his earliest texts on language, "On the Connection of Ideas," written in 1927, but not published until it appeared in Carroll 1956. In this short text, Whorf speaks in a highly suggestive way about associations linking people's ideas—the overall relatedness among the categories of their thought and language—and proposes ways of differentiating experimentally between "true" associations and "accidental" associations. He asserts the Aristotelian distinction between essence and accident somewhat defensively, however. Seemingly sensing the chaotic possibility of an endless, uncontrollable dissemination of meaning, Whorf flatly decrees that "the subject must not jump at the first idea that comes to mind as in a 'free association' experiment; hence the experiment might be considered a form of 'controlled association'; yet it might be quite 'free' in its own sphere, for any connection may be permitted" (Whorf 1:36).

How can associations between ideas be controlled and free at the same time? Whorf's formulation suggests something of the "rule-governed creativity" said by a later generation of linguists to characterize the grammars of natural languages. Both formulations, moreover, share the same paradoxical quality, which derives from the attempt to reduce freedom to constraint. Our language allows us to say anything we want to say, the argument goes, as long as we follow the rules. And the argument seems plausible as long as we find it reasonable to suppose that interlocutors begin with knowledge of the *same* rules. In Whorf's case, this supposition is phrased in terms of "communicability" between speakers of the same language, which is assumed a priori. From this perspective, if people do not understand one another perfectly, it is because they failed to code or decode the perfectly adequate forms of their shared language; there is no room for the possibility that *language itself* may be contradictory or ambiguous, or *might deliberately be made so by features of the context in which it was uttered by one particular individual to another particular individual.* Thus Whorf continues,

> One of the necessary criteria of a connection is that it be intelligible to others, and therefore the individuality of the subject cannot enter to the extent that it does in free association, while a correspondingly greater part is played by the stock of conceptions common to people. The very existence of such a common stock of conceptions . . . seems to be a necessary concomitant of the communicability of ideas by language . . . and is in a sense the universal language, to which the various specific languages give entrance. (Whorf 1:36)

But his nervousness is evident in the way he qualifies the extent to which individuality and the common stock of conceptions may or may not play a role in controlled association: "the individuality of the subject cannot enter to the extent that it does in free association" *but is not totally excluded.* And "a correspondingly greater part is played by the stock of conceptions common to people," *but not a totally determinative part.*

Whorf's readiness to lay down the law about what is "necessary" suggests that he may be worried that his distinction between "true" and "accidental" connections may not stand up to close scrutiny (cf. Waterman 1957:209). He is as eager as Saussure or Chomsky to attribute deviations from "true" associations only to purely arbitrary, idiosyncratic factors peculiar to the biographies or current mental states of his experimental subjects. And he is revealingly vague when he identifies "the stock of conceptions common to people" as "a necessary concomitant of the communicability of ideas by language," which, in turn, is "in a sense the universal language, to which the various specific languages give entrance." By speaking of the stock of conceptions *common* to people, he seems to be suggesting something that all people share. Communicability, for him, depends on a shared stock of conceptions. However, when Whorf goes on to suggest that "the stock of conceptions common to people" is "in a sense" the "universal" language, we are forced to ask, In *what* sense? At least three possibilities suggest themselves: (1) universal in the sense of "relatively universal," i.e., universal relative to the community formed by all the speakers of a particular language; (2) universal in the sense of "absolutely universal," i.e., shared by all speakers of all languages, by the human race; or (3) "absolutely universal" in the sense of *potentially accessible* to all speakers of all languages (or *some* speakers of *all*—or some—languages: an elite, perhaps?), since "the various specific languages give entrance" to this universal language.

It is the possibility of this third kind of universality which is most intriguing, especially when we compare Whorf with Bakhtin. Whorf seems to be straining to write about truth in a way that would not require the language of science to demolish every other form of discourse in order for truth to be established. In fact, truth so conceived might even *depend on* modes of discourse other than that of positivist science, if it is to be established in the first place. Truth so conceived would be similar to what Bahktin called "unified truth," and which requires a plurality of different consciousnesses to be realized (e.g., Bakhtin 1984:81). This dialogical, polyphonic, unified truth he opposes to "single, impersonal truth," which is monological and requires all other modes of discourse to be assimilated to it or effaced before it (Bakhtin 1984:95). Single, impersonal truth is the truth of positivist science, which Whorf finds as inadequate as Bakhtin. But notice that for Bakhtin, the alternative to single, impersonal truth is not some kind of single, *personal* truth, i.e., individual subjectivism or solipsism. For Bakhtin, there can be no such thing as a single (universal) personal truth, because every person occupies a different position, views life from a different point of view. Individual, personal views can never coincide, and thus can never constitute a single truth valid for all.

What Bakhtin seeks is a formulation of truth which *transcends without destroying* the points of view of particular single consciousnesses, and this seems to be Whorf's goal as well. Many formulations in later texts reflect Whorf's tense struggle to broaden and deepen the discourse of positivist science in order to make it an adequate vehicle for his new understanding of truth. These formulations are, as a result, often even more maddeningly ambiguous than the foregoing fragment. Indeed, some of the best-known passages from Whorf's works, in which the rhetoric of determinism is in full flood, become, upon closer analysis, something other than they have traditionally been taken to be. Consider the following:

> When linguists became able to examine critically and scientifically a large number of languages of widely different patterns, their base of reference was expanded; they experienced an interruption of phenomena hitherto held universal, and a whole new order of significances came into their ken. It was found that the background linguistic system (in other words, the grammar) of each language is not merely a reproducing instrument for voicing ideas but rather is itself the shaper of ideas, the program and guide for the individual's mental activity, for his analysis of impressions, for his synthesis of his mental stock in trade. Formulation of ideas is not an independent process, strictly rational in the old sense, but is part of a particular grammar, and differs, from slightly to greatly, between different grammars. We dissect nature along lines laid down by our native languages. The categories and types that we isolate from the world of phenomena we do not find there because they stare every observer in the face; on the contrary, the world is presented in a kaleidoscopic flux of impressions which has to be organized by our minds—and this means largely by the linguistic systems in our minds. We cut nature up, organize it into concepts, and ascribe significances as we do, largely because we are parties to an agreement to organize it in this way—an agreement that holds throughout our speech community and is codified in the patterns of our language. The agreement is, of course, an implicit and unstated one, BUT ITS TERMS ARE ABSOLUTELY OBLIGATORY; we cannot talk at all except by subscribing to the organization and classification which the agreement decrees. (Whorf 6:212–14; from the article "Science and Linguistics")

This passage is one of those which Holquist (1986:101) cites to compare Whorf with Bakhtin. It has also often been taken as a key Whorfian text in defense of linguistic determinism (or relative absolutism), and no wonder: Whorf asserts that "the background linguistic system (in other words, the grammar) of each language" is "the shaper of ideas," the "program and guide" for all thought. "Formulation of ideas" is "part of a particular grammar." Most famously, "We dissect nature along lines laid down by our native languages." The "kaleidoscopic flux of impressions which has to be organized by our minds" is organized "largely by the linguistic systems in our minds," and this is "largely because we are parties to an agreement to organize it in this way," an agreement whose terms are "ABSOLUTELY OBLIGATORY; we cannot talk at all except by subscribing to the organization and classification of data which the agreement decrees."

And yet, the categories and types laid down by the linguistic systems in our minds only "largely" organize the kaleidoscopic flux of impressions. Such a qualification gives rise to a host of questions. How large a part of the flux of impressions is organized by linguistic systems? What is responsible for organizing the rest? Or does the rest remain unorganized, chaotic? The text does not tell us. We are forced, Whorf asserts, to cut nature up, organize it into concepts, and ascribe significances "largely" because we are parties to an agreement whose terms are "ABSOLUTELY OBLIGATORY." His capital letters allow no refusal to face the full impact of language's power over us. And yet, what can it mean to be "largely" parties to an agreement whose terms are absolutely obligatory? If we are not wholly parties to the agreement, how can its absolutely obligatory terms exert deterministic force upon us? And if we can *partly* escape the absolutely obligatory terms of the agreement, what makes this possible?

Whorf suggests one possibility in the very first sentence in this passage, when he refers to the time when "linguists became able to examine critically and scientifically a large number of languages." At this moment, linguists discovered simultaneously both how they had been bound by their own linguistic prejudices and how they might break free of them. The key must lie in the power of criticism, scientific criticism, which is connected to knowledge of many languages. This gave linguists in particular the perspective they needed to compare their own linguistic system with others and to gain awareness of "a whole new order of significances." Yet, if language is the shaper of ideas, how can ideas critical of the ideas language shapes emerge?

Although Whorf is silent on the origins of critical thought, Bakhtin, who addressed the same question, suggests an explanation which depends on the very forces Whorf refuses to discuss openly. For Bakhtin, the "critical interanimation of languages"—that is, heteroglossia and polyphony—is the force which makes all people (not just linguists) sit up and stop taking their language, and their way of life, for granted. Critical awareness is born in people who encounter a welter of different languages coexisting in the world around them. A person's consciousness finds itself "inevitably facing the necessity of *having to choose a lan-*

guage," having actively "to orient itself amidst heteroglossia. Only by remaining in a closed environment, one without writing or thought, completely off the maps of socio-ideological becoming, could a man fail to sense this activity of selecting a language and rest assured of the inviolability of his own language, the conviction that his language is predetermined" (Bakhtin 1981c[1940]:295).

If, however, heteroglossia is basic to the human condition, is it plausible that *any* people, anywhere, at any time have ever been free of the obligation to choose a language? Perhaps the Primitive Man of anthropological lore, who "lives according to rigid rules, in total harmony with the environment, and is not cursed with a glimmer of self-consciousness" (Rabinow 1977:151)? Perhaps the Illiterate Peasant, another stock figure of comparative social science? Bakhtin, in fact, offers the peasant as an example of someone who, under traditional circumstances, was not forced to choose a language. But notice how different this peasant is from the monological (and presumably monoglot) primitive enshrined in Western thought:

> Thus an illiterate peasant, miles away from any urban center, naively immersed in an unmoving and for him unshakeable everyday world, nevertheless lived in several language systems: he prayed to God in one language [Church Slavonic], sang songs in another, spoke to his family in a third and, when he began to dictate petitions to the local authorities through a scribe, he tried speaking yet a fourth language (the official-literate language, "paper" language). All these are *different languages,* even from the point of view of abstract socio-dialectological markers. But these languages were not dialogically coordinated in the linguistic consciousness of the peasant; he passed from one to the other without thinking, automatically: each was indisputably in its own place, and the place of each was indisputable. He was not yet able to regard one language (and the verbal world corresponding to it) through the eyes of another language (that is, the language of everyday life and the everyday world with the language of prayer or song, or vice versa). (1981[1940b]:296)

Such a characterization of unregenerate complacent consciousness can hardly be topped by Whorf. But this remarkable passage by Bakhtin ends with a footnote reading, "We are of course deliberately simplifying: the real-life peasant could and did do this to a certain extent" (1981c[1940]:296; cf. 1981b[1940]:66). And the very next sentence in the text reads as follows: "As soon as a critical interanimation of languages began to occur in the consciousness of our peasant . . . then the inviolability and predetermined quality of these languages came to an end, and the necessity of actively choosing one's orientation among them began" (1981b:66). So perhaps scientific and literary consciousnesses are not the only ones capable of critical deliberation and choice; perhaps it is not linguists alone who "examine critically a large number of languages."

Similar ambiguities crop up in another famous passage from "Linguistics as an Exact Science" (Whorf 7:221):

> The obligatory phenomena within the apparently free flow of talk are so completely autocratic that speaker and listener are bound unconsciously as though in the grip of a law of nature. The phenomena of language are background phenomena, of which the talkers are unaware or, at the most, very dimly aware—as they are of the motes of dust in the air of a room, though the linguistic phenomena govern the talkers more as gravitation than as dust would. These automatic, involuntary patterns of language are not the same for all men but are specific for each language and constitute the formalized side of the language, or its "grammar"—a term that includes much more than the grammar we learned in the textbooks of our schooldays.

This passage, too, abounds with the vocabulary of determinism: "obligatory," "completely autocratic," "bound unconsciously as though in the grip of a law of nature," "automatic, involuntary." But *what is it* that is obligatory, autocratic, and so forth? Mostly, Whorf tells us, "phenomena"—"the phenomena of language." There is something oxymoronic about obligatory phenomena. How can anything so vague and hard to identify be so coercive? Later in the passage, Whorf equates the "phenomena" of language with the "automatic, involutary patterns" of language, and with "the formalized side of the language, or its 'grammar,' " Yet what seems like a satisfactory concretizing of the phenomena of language is immediately called into question, as Whorf tells us that the linguist's grammar is not the lay person's grammar. Although he assures us that it includes "much more" than the grammar we learned in school, we are not told, precisely, how much more or what kind of "more."

Part of what is interesting about Whorf in this passage is precisely his eagerness to go beyond traditional notions of grammar to locate the vital patterns of linguistic usage among as yet imperfectly understood "phenomena of language." Again, one thinks immediately of the suggestive passage (in a different article) in which he contrasts the concept of grammar with that of "fashions of speaking" that cut "across the typical grammatical classifications" (Whorf 4:158; see also Whorf 6:222). Yet Whorf never developed theoretically or substantively what he meant by fashions of speaking.

Bakhtin and his colleagues, however, did exactly this in their theory of the utterance. They recognized, as many Western linguists and linguistic anthropologists have not, that, in Sherzer's words, "conflation of grammar and discourse . . . confuses the issue" (1987:302). Indeed they explicitly separated theories about language-in-the-abstract (theories of grammar, devised by linguists preoccupied with sound patterns and syntax and lexicography) from theories about language-in-the-concrete (theories of discourse, devised by scholars—literary critics and others—who deal with words as they issue from people's mouths in the fullness of everyday life). They distinguish the abstract *meaning* disclosed by linguistic semanticians in their study of language forms, from the concrete *theme* disclosed by social scientists or literary critics who study the way in which abstract language forms are put to work in actual utterances in real social situations, often with the effect of undermining their formal grammatical or dictionary meanings.

Bakhtin and his colleagues succeeded in opening up a theoretical space that allowed them to talk more precisely and persuasively about factors whose existence Whorf recognizes but is still struggling to find adequate language for. His difficulty is complicated by the nature of the audience he is addressing. The passage cited above comes from an article addressed to MIT alumni, and he makes no mention of "fashions of speaking" (although in a different article addressed to the same audience [Whorf 6:222], he does refer briefly to "*façons de parler,*" without, however, developing theoretically what he means by this phrase). A rhetorical motive may thus underlie his silence: he knows that his audience of nonlinguists believes in grammar but nothing more. He therefore ascribes all patterns in language to "grammar." His loophole, however, is to make this a "linguist's grammar" in which language patterns unsuspected by English teachers or lay readers may find a place.[3]

At the same time, however, nowhere in this article does he state explicitly just how far beyond "traditional" grammar his linguist's grammar goes. Most of his examples from other languages are traditionally "grammatical," dealing, for example, with patterns of verbal conjugation, or sentence structure. He wants his grammar to involve the formalized side of language, the patterned side. But what about patterns (cryptotypes, for example) that are not formally marked? Indeed, according to what criteria is "formalization" identifiable? Whorf stretches the concept of "grammar" as far as it can be stretched, and at the limits calls into question the very notion of "grammar" as an adequate concept for describing the phenomena of language of interest to him.

How, then, is one to interpret the struggle in Whorf's work between the Official Standard Average European language of science and all the unofficial languages (of the Hopi, of the Shawnee, of theosophists) whose points of view Whorf cannot dismiss? For those who subscribe to the language of science, as we have seen, the simplest solution is to accuse Whorf of contradiction, to find him guilty of arguing for two mutually exclusive absolutisms at the same time, trying to defend the (universally absolute, single) truth of science while defending at the same time the (relatively absolute, particular, diverse) truths of alternative discourses. Because he writes using the forms of scientific discourse, and attempts to sound deterministic and reductionistic in order not to lose his audience, many listeners only hear him saying, "The absolute, universal, single truth is that there are *only* relative, particular, diverse truths." Unfortunately, the only points of view positivists recognize are (1) universal impersonal truth and (2) individual error. If Whorf is not with them on the side of universal, impersonal truth, he must therefore be a defender of relative, particular, diverse forms of individual error.

The attempt to offer a third alternative—a polyphonic truth which avoids both the "anything-goes" form of "relativism" (i.e., individual subjectivism) *and* the monolithic form of official (dogmatic) scientific ideology—is disallowed. This third alternative is precisely what Bakhtin is trying to formulate: "We see no special need to point out that the polyphonic approach has nothing in common with relativism (or with dogmatism). But it should be noted that both relativism and dogmatism equally exclude all argumentation, all authentic dialogue, by making it either unnecessary (relativism) or impossible (dogmatism). Polyphony as an *artistic* method lies in an entirely different plane" (1984:69).

So, too, Whorf's method lies in an entirely different plane. For the theme of his utterances concerning linguistic relativity is *precisely* designed to draw his listeners into dialogue (cf. Bakhtin 1984[1929]:18). His play with the deterministic language of science is designed to undermine determinism, to expose dogmatism and censorship. But his critics refuse to rise to this new plane. It is difficult to convince those who believe positivist science has unveiled the single, impersonal truth about the universe that they are guilty of dogmatism or censorship. And what right-minded seeker after truth could object to the repression of error?

The positivists have defined the rules of the game, and Whorf has agreed to try to play by them. He has chosen his language, and it is fateful for him, because the language he has chosen does not allow him to speak directly in his own authentic voice. If he waffles, or resorts to parody, or tries to bend the rules of scientific discourse to mitigate the consequences of his choice, his positivist listeners deem him incoherent or frivolous or mystical and refuse to listen any longer.

Even sympathetic scientific listeners seem bound by their own commitment to scientific discourse, and therefore struggle to interpret Whorf dualistically. Lakoff, for instance, has proposed that Whorf was a relativist with respect to fact, but an objectivist with respect to value (1987:324). "Objectivism" is defined by Lakoff as the assumption "that reality is *correctly* and *completely* structured in a way that can be modeled by set-theoretical models—that is, in terms of entities, properties, and relations. On the objectivist view, reality comes with a unique, correct, complete structure in terms of entities, properties, and relations. This structure exists, independent of any human understanding" (1987:159). As Lakoff reads him, Whorf "believed that there was an objectivist reality and he thought that some but not other conceptual systems built into language were capable of fitting it with reasonable preciseness" (1987:324).

While Lakoff's reading is better than most at facing and coping with the tensions in Whorf's work, it is too easy to try to resolve them by assimilating them to a fact-value dichotomy which, in itself, is highly problematic. Certainly Whorf's texts do not explicitly suggest that he subscribed to such a dichotomy; one could argue, in fact, that the moral dimension to his work depends directly upon the facts of relativity revealed by his linguistic research. To his credit, Lakoff does not attempt to tidy up all the loose ends he finds in Whorf's work, and is constrained to observe that "Whorf was a complex thinker. It should be borne in mind throughout the following discussion that his stands on these issues by no means exhaust his views, nor convey their subtlety" (1987:328).

That Lakoff should characterize the tension in Whorf's work as one between "relativism" and "objectivism," however, calls for further comment. Lakoff's definition of "objectivism" corresponds very well to Bakhtin's definition of "single, impersonal truth," discussed earlier. Lakoff seems unable to make the distinction which Bakhtin makes (and which I believe Whorf is trying to make) between single, impersonal (objective) truth and a unified, dialogic, polyphonic truth. To the extent that Whorf spoke as a scientist and deployed the discourse of science to explicate and defend his own work—particularly when he pointed to the possible future synthesis and breakthrough in understanding which the science of linguistics might achieve—he sounds like someone in search of truth that will elicit the assent of all observers, regardless of the point of view from which they view the world. A proper understanding of language, provided by linguists like himself, will lay the groundwork for such a breakthrough, linking up perspectives that previously were isolated. But which perspectives (or whose perspectives) will be linked? Lakoff would have it that the link will be between some (but not all) elements of some (but not all) grammars/conceptual systems—as it were, a single supergrammar resembling a patchwork quilt or Frankenstein's monster, constructed by stitching together those parts of natural language that turned out to be right after all—and the unique, correct, complete structure of reality posited by objectivist science which that supergrammar mirrors. The reality so structured would be the reality of physics, and the grammatical structures that mirror this reality would deal with reference and description of objects and processes in the material world.

But it is more than likely, given Whorf's impatience with traditional scientific discourse, and in light of his comment about the way particular languages "give access to" the universal language, that he has something else in mind.

> It should be pointed out that the single and unified consciousness is by no means an inevitable consequence of the concept of a unified truth. It is quite possible to imagine and postulate a unified truth that requires a plurality of consciousnesses, one that cannot in principle be fitted into the bounds of a single consciousness, one that is, so to speak, by its very nature *full of event potential* and is born at a point of contact among various consciousnesses.

The voice is Bakhtin's (1984[1929]:81), but the utterance sounds very much like something Whorf might have said, had he been able to find his own direct word.

Such a view of the relationship between truth and particular worldviews (or the languages that embody them) is rather far from traditional positivistic thinking. There is a nitty-gritty, trial-and-error feel about it, the suggestion that there are no giant leaps from any single particular perspective to universal truth. Instead, there is only patient, incremental growth in understanding as one concrete, particular language/worldview after another is encountered, acknowledged, and grappled with. There is, for conventional positivists, the appalling suggestion that what passes as universal correctness is just the best possible degree of relative correctness we can devise at the moment, given the limited variety of viewpoints that have currently been recognized and struggled with. In addition there is the nagging suspicion that, if this much is conceded, there is nothing to prevent the seeker after truth from going beyond the traditional scientific preoccupation with reference and description of the material world to consider, say, linguistically embodied views of social relations. What if each point of view to be considered has an opinion, not only about how many basic categories of color or kinds of movement there are, but also about what kinds of creatures human beings are and what their needs are and how they might best live together? For scientists to get involved in all this would call into question the traditional understanding of what science is all about.

Getting involved in all this is, however, highly plausible as an interpretation of Whorf's thinking, for calling into question the traditional understanding of what science is all about was his primary aim. For him as a scientific linguist, coming to "a proper understanding of language" did not involve just the methods of positivist science of just the methods of analytic philosophy. Objectivist scientists and philosophers, for him, could never achieve their aim (or his) because they unwittingly subjected themselves to self-censorship and dogmatism. They were bogged down by the limitations of the forms and categories of SAE, a system of language and thought which he considered to have been "worked to death," to be "out of focus for observing what may be very significant aspects of reality, upon the due observation of which all further progress in understanding the universe may hinge" (Whorf 9:247). This assessment of science was shared by Bakhtin: "Science (and cultural consciousness) of the nineteenth century singled out only a miniature world (and we have narrowed it even more). . . . included almost nothing of the East. . . . We have narrowed it terribly by selecting and by modernizing what has been selected. We impoverish the past and do not enrich ourselves. We are suffocating in the captivity of narrow and homogeneous interpretations" (1986[1970–71]:140).

It is this need Whorf expressed to make science *see more* than it has allowed itself to see up till now that leads Whorf's critics to accuse him of "mysticism." It is responsible for Rollins' claim that Whorf's primary motivation was to reconcile science with religion. But this claim assumes that if one goes beyond traditional science, the only place to go is to traditional religion. Western dualism has hammered this lesson home for a long time. But Whorf's work would hardly have remained so controversial for so long if he were just another distressed modern trying to reconcile the irreconcilable. Whorf himself saw more and wanted to say more than the language of science permitted, and his texts reveal the battle he waged to turn the discourse of materialist reductionism to his own subversive purposes. We saw earlier how this appears in the form of microdialogues in certain key passages. If my thesis is correct, however, Whorf's aim and achievements are far more radical and unsettling precisely because what he offered as an alternative to positivist science was *not* a return to any traditional form of "old dogma."

I have argued that those of Whorf's statements taken to demonstrate his espousal of conventional linguistic determinism or conventional objectivism are full of loopholes. Such loopholes can be, and have been, interpreted as defects in his writing, betraying serious lapses in logic. But this is not the only way to understand loopholes. Bakhtin (whose own writing abounds in loopholes) points out that "the word with a loophole has enormous significance in Dostoevsky's works in general." Far from being the result of carelessness or lapses in logic, Bakhtin interprets "this loophole of consciousness and of the word" as "the retention for oneself of the possibility for altering the ultimate, final meaning of one's own words" (1984[1929]:232–33). Loopholes are necessary if one is unable to articulate one's direct authorial word straightforwardly, if one is constrained to use double-voiced discourse. Loopholes protect an author against such distortion. On the other hand, to construct loopholes is not without consequences for the consciousness that does so: such a person is bound to become "ambiguous and elusive even for himself" (1984:234).

But it is not just these loopholes—these negative instances, so to speak—that I wish to invoke to support my argument. There are positive data as well which demonstrate Whorf's ability to see more, and his desire to help his readers to see more, to rise above the complacent linguistic prejudice that had been handed down to them. The most powerful evidence consists of those texts where he makes explicit cross-linguistic comparisons, especially the *Technology Review* articles. In these texts he finds a direct authorial word for himself, less in terms of content than in terms of composition. But the content is hardly irrelevant. Rather, in these texts he artfully employs double-voiced discourse, using content both for itself and for his own purposes, which are to force his readers to become critically self-conscious, to force them to argue with the examples he presents from Hopi or Shawnee, to force them to grapple with alien grammars whose sophistication he will not permit them to deny. And, in accomplishing this last—by creating images of alien grammars (and thus, indirectly, of alien speakers) whose sophistication and full humanity his most skeptical readers cannot gainsay—he creates a polyphonic text. By drawing his readers into a dialogue in spite of themselves, he is able to stimulate them into working out for themselves the kind of unified truth that depends on multiple consciousnesses (or, in this case, multiple languages). He makes few direct claims and draws few direct conclusions in support of this position. Instead, he relies on style and intonation to force his readers to draw the conclusions for themselves, to admit in spite of everything that there are more things in heaven and in earth than are dreamt of in their positivistic science.

2 The Politics of Style
Whorfian Verbal Rhetoric

Bakhtin writes, "The internal politics of style (how the elements are put together) is determined by its external politics (its relationship to alien discourse). Discourse lives, as it were, on the boundary between its own context and another, alien context" (1981c[1940]:284). What were the alien discourses which determined the internal politics of style in Whorf's writing? Where were the contextual boundaries on which Whorf's discourse lived? For Bakhtin, the boundaries between one's own and another's context are usefully understood as the boundaries between one's own and another's language. For Whorf, the languages that were most significant were the language of positivist science and the language of his various Native American informants. To some extent all these languages were alien languages for him, and Whorf's texts reveal his struggle to wrest out of them (and perhaps also out of the languages of art and religion) his own authentic word.

From a Bakhtinian perspective, then, Whorf was surrounded by heteroglossia, and the roots of this linguistic diversity should be traceable to social and historical developments. In his study of transitional periods in European history, Bakhtin attributed the creativity of such periods as the early Renaissance to the "actively polyglot world" in which people lived at such times:

> The world becomes polyglot, once and for all and irreversibly. The period of national languages, coexisting but closed and deaf to each other, comes to an end. Languages throw light on each other: one language can, after all, see itself only in the light of another language. The naive and stubborn coexistence of "languages" within a given national language also comes to an end—that is, there is no more peaceful coexistence between territorial dialects, social and

professional dialects and jargons, literary language, generic languages within literary language, epochs in language, and so forth. (1981d[1941]:12)

The world in which Whorf lived was actively polyglot. The end of the nineteenth century and the early twentieth century in America witnessed the final "pacification" of Native American populations and a flood tide of new immigrants from Europe and Asia who swelled the working classes. In the society in which Whorf came of age (as a member of the privileged Yankee elite), the "interillumination of languages" set in motion by these events was threatening. Dissident groups, be they outside or inside the "nation," indeed were not willing to remain closed and deaf to one another; there was the opposite of peaceful coexistence. In Europe, this struggle by unofficial voices to make themselves heard would culminate in the rise of fascism and the Holocaust, but many elements of the struggle were equally present in America.

One can cope with heteroglossia either by repression (the fascist solution) or by developing what Bakhtin called a "Galilean language consciousness" which is broad and deep enough to accommodate change and diversity (1981c[1940]:415). Bakhtin suggests that, in the early Renaissance, Galilean language consciousness found its voice in artistic (or novelistic) prose, the work of Rabelais being its finest example. He also argues that, at a later time of intense social dislocation—that occasioned by the penetration of capitalism into Russian society in the nineteenth century—such artistic, novelistic prose reached new heights in the polyphonic novels of Dostoevsky (1984:19–20).

A Galilean language consciousness is one in which many coexisting languages and traditions are encompassed and enter into dialogue with one another, mutually illuminating one another. According to Bakhtin, artistic prose is prose in which an author makes use of compositional forms that allow these coexisting, dialogically engaged languages to achieve verbal expression. As Bakhtin documents in his study of Rabelais, Goethe, and the history of novelistic discourse in the West, such compositional forms have not always been available. Rather, they were invented over centuries, beginning with the carnivalesque low comic and fantasy genres of antiquity that were considered beyond the pale of "serious" literature. As these low genres gradually became refined and accepted as canonical literary genres, they became resources on which writers of later eras could draw, in order to create images of the diverse languages coexisting in the society of their own day.

Bakhtin's task was, in part, to document the historical creation and emergence of such forms which, once constituted, could be used by writers for their own purposes. Another part of his task was to look closely at the work of particular writers who, in his opinion, put these forms to work in unprecedented new ways, transforming them in the process. But presupposed in both these tasks was Bakhtin's lively awareness of the influence of *social experience* on those writers who created both the forms and the artistic products that the forms made possible. These writers could not ignore the consequences of heteroglossia and were stimulated to devise literary means for dealing with it. Thus, Dostoevsky used in his novels literary forms (e.g., Socratic dialogue, Menippean satire) which originated in antiquity. If he chose to use these forms and not others, however, it was because they alone seemed adequate for expressing the heteroglossia he experienced in the concrete nineteenth-century Russian social world in which he lived.

> Dostoevsky found and was capable of perceiving multi-leveledness and contradictoriness not in the spirit, but in the objective social world. In this social world, planes were not stages but *opposing camps* . . . and the contradictory relationships among them were not the rising or descending course of an individual personality, but the *condition of society*. The multi-leveledness and contradictoriness of social reality was present as an objective fact of the epoch. (1984[1929]:27)

Indeed, to make these received compositional forms adequate to his own Galilean (revolutionary? marxian?) language consciousness, he had further to transform them, and in the process, according to Bakhtin, he created the polyphonic novel.

That Whorf developed a Galilean language consciousness of this kind is suggested by those interpretations of his work (e.g., Fishman, Lakoff) which stress the moral stand it takes against the repression of minorities at a time in history when such a stand was increasingly unfashionable in America and positively dangerous in parts of Western Europe. What leads these readers to draw such moral conclusions from Whorf's work? I wish to suggest it is his style and intonation. I believe that, although Whorf was not writing novels, he was using artistic/novelistic prose techniques in his most famous and controversial articles. I would argue further that his techniques bear a family resemblance to the techniques developed by Dostoevsky and analyzed by Bakhtin. To substantiate this argument, of course, it is necessary to analyze Whorf the way Bakhtin analyzes Dostoevsky.

The first point of similarity in the artistic styles of Dostoevsky and

Whorf is the emphasis on *relativity*. The low genres originating in popular carnival in antiquity, but eventually adopted into serious literature (thus creating a carnivalesque literary tradition on which later writers might draw) had the precise role of destabilizing a monolithic, monologic world: "By *relativizing* all that was externally stable, set and ready-made, carnivalization with its pathos of change and renewal permitted Dostoevsky to penetrate into the deepest layers of man and human relationships. It proved remarkably productive as means for capturing in art the developing relationships under Capitalism" (1984[1929]:166). This is because capitalism, "similar to that 'pander' Socrates on the market square of Athens, brings together people and ideas" (1984:167). This is itself a carnival-like activity, for "the structural characteristics of the carnival image" require that "opposites come together, look at one another, are reflected in one another, know and understand one another" (1984:176).

How do writers create an image of the social and linguistic relativity which surrounds them in everyday life? According to Bakhtin, the "single adequate form for *verbally expressing* authentic human life is the *open-ended dialogue* (1984[1961]:293; emphasis in original). The writer of artistic prose must find a way to represent the voices taking part in that dialogue, find a way to create an authentic image of the languages which the dialogic partners speak. Voices belong to individual human beings, but they are shaped by the language practices that all of us encounter in life, which preexist us and with which we must grapple if we are to speak at all. Each set of language practices a person encounters in a heteroglot world constitutes, for Bakhtin, a *social language:* "a concrete socio-linguistic belief system that defines a distinct identity for itself within the boundaries of a language that is unitary only in the abstract . . . it is a potential dialect. . . . Language in its historical life . . . is full of such potential dialects" (1981c[1940]:356). Individual speakers must then struggle to create a personal *voice* out of the resources of the social languages they come to learn. Voice "includes height, range, timbre, aesthetic category (lyric, dramatic, etc.). It also includes a person's worldview and fate. A person enters into dialogue as an integral voice. He participates in it not only with his thoughts, but with his fate and with his entire individuality" (1984[1929]:293).

In order to cope with heteroglossia as a novelist or as a social scientist, one must, of course, recognize its existence and take it seriously. This means going beyond "language-in-the-abstract," the traditional focus of linguistics and stylistics, and paying attention to "discourse-in-the-concrete," that is, to the various social languages and to the voices of those who make use of them. To do so, according to Bakhtin, leads one to consider certain previously ignored phenomena (Whorf's "phenomena of language"?) "that are present in discourse and that are determined by its dialogic orientation, first amid others' utterances inside a *single* language (the primordial dialogism of discourse), then amid other "social languages" within a single *national* language and finally amid different national languages within the same *culture,* that is, the same socio-ideological conceptual horizon" (1981c[1940]:275).

To these phenomena anthropologists might want to add a fourth mode of dialogic orientation: amid different national languages belonging to *different* cultures, that is, to *different socio-ideological conceptual horizons.* This, of course, is what seems most characteristic of the fieldwork encounters that are central to anthropological inquiry. Indeed, the fieldwork encounter pushes to the limit the strains on dialogue. If Bakhtin is correct, and "dialectic is the abstract product of dialogue" (1984[1961]:293), then the initial encounter between a Western, SAE-speaking fieldworker and the representative of a non-Western, non-SAE-speaking society would be a dialogue verging on dialectic. All that would remain within the common purview of these two individuals would be the material features of their surroundings and their own bodies. Rabinow's decision (1977:38) to refer to anthropological fieldwork as a dialectic rather than a dialogue (at least in its initial stages) would receive additional justification.

Dostoevsky seems to have been, for the most part, content to document the various forms of otherness, and the dialogues between voices speaking from these diverse points of view, as they coexisted within his own society (although his story "The Gambler" reads like a parable of Fieldwork as Hell). Whorf's task was to try to capture verbally the experience of cross-cultural, cross-linguistic dialogue, dialogue at the margins. He himself appears to have found the experience to be profoundly unsettling and profoundly liberating at the same time. And he made repeated attempts to proselytize among skeptics in his own world, represented by the MIT alumni for which he wrote three of his most controversial pieces. Such readers believed that free speech was unproblematic, especially for them. If Whorf had showered them with examples of heteroglossia within American English, in an effort to prove to them that their own presumed complete control over a unitary language was a myth, they would most likely have remained unimpressed. They would undoubtedly have been as hostile as later generations of their spiritual descendants, who have rejected positive analyses of Black English, for example, as nothing but a political ploy by speakers of defective "broken" English who are trying to make a virtue out of a defect.

So Whorf had to raise the stakes. Not heteroglossia but polyglossia would be his focus. He would expose instead the myth that their language was the *only* language (cf. Bakhtin 1981b[1940]:68). Drawing on his own multilingual consciousness, he could shift the ground of argument from one in which his listeners believed themselves in control to one in which he alone would be in control. He would show them, by means of examples from languages vastly different from English or any other Standard Average European language, that their linguistic complacency was founded on ignorance: this was the overt content of his text. But he would go further than this: he would structure his text in such a way that his readers would be *helpless to avoid being drawn into dialogue with the points of view represented by his exotic linguistic examples.* He would force them *by sheer artistry* to develop a kind of multilingual consciousness of their own. And once they developed it, Whorf would have them in the palm of his hand. They could not deny their new consciousness except in bad faith. They would be unable to avoid considering the possibility, as Bakhtin put it, that "language, no longer conceived as a sacrosanct and solitary embodiment of meaning and truth, becomes merely one of many possible ways to hypothesize truth" (1981c[1940]:370).

Whorf's strategy apparently succeeded with its original audience of engineers (Carroll 1956:20); only scientifically oriented academics seem to have been offended, or to find Whorf's texts controversial, as we saw earlier. It remains a brilliant strategy. But it was not easy for Whorf to achieve. He might have shifted the ground of the dialogue into territory that was his, but he still had to use the language of the enemy if he wished to keep the dialogue going. And, as we have documented, Whorf had great difficulty making that language speak in his voice. He therefore resorted to what Bakhtin calls *double-voiced discourse:* "Where there is no adequate form for the unmediated expression of an author's thoughts, he must resort to refracting them in someone else's discourse. Sometimes the artistic tasks are such that they can be realized only by means of double-voiced discourse (as we shall see, such exactly was the case with Dostoevsky)" (1984[1929]:192). And double-voiced discourse is "parodistic discourse in all its varieties, or a special type of semi-conventionalized, semi-ironic discourse (that of late Classicism, for example). In such epochs, and especially in epochs dominated by conventionalized discourse, the direct, unconditional, unrefracted word appears barbaric, raw, wild"

(1984:202). Whorf could not risk appearing barbaric, raw, or wild before those he wished to convert. Nor, indeed, could those whose languages he was using as grist for the conversion. The kind of writing he eventually produced was indeed "semi-conventionalized, semi-ironic discourse." This is why so many conventional readers have grown so impatient with him: they begin by taking him seriously and finish with the uneasy sense that he has just made fun of them.

According to Bakhtin, double-voiced discourse as an artistic technique depends on the writer's skill at *stylization*. "Stylization forces another person's referential (artistically referential) intention to serve its own purposes, that is, its new intentions. . . . Conditional discourse is always double-voiced discourse. Only that which was at one time unconditional, in earnest, can become conditional. . . . This is what distinguishes stylization from imitation. Imitation . . . takes the imitated material seriously, makes it its own. . . . What happens in that case is a complete merging of voices" (1984[1929]:189–90). Stylization is often revealed in a *hybrid construction,* "an utterance that belongs, by its grammatical (syntactic) and compositional markers, to a single speaker, but that actually contains mixed within it two utterances, two speech manners, two styles, two "languages," two semantic and axiological belief systems. [There is no formal boundary] between these utterances . . . even one and the same word will belong simultaneously to two languages" (1981c[1940]:304). But in this hybrid mixture, the two utterances are not closed and deaf to one another: "What is a hybridization? It is a mixture of two social languages within the limits of a single utterance, *an encounter within the arena of an utterance, between two different linguistic consciousnesses, separated from one another by an epoch, by social differentiation or by some other factor*" (1981c:358; emphasis added).

"Prose consciousness" is another way to describe Galilean language consciousness, or bilingual/multilingual consciousness, or polyphonic consciousness. Bakhtin focuses primarily on what happens to literature when prose consciousness takes over, but clearly it is not only novelists who possess prose consciousness. Anyone who makes it his or her business to document diversity and give each diverse point of view its full measure of attention shows the same consciousness. Anthropologists and field linguists (at least) ought to be actively engaged in broadening and deepening this kind of critical self-consciousness as they carry out their professional work. This is why anthropologists (and anthropological linguists especially) should find nothing shocking in what Bakhtin has to say about the experience of the novelist. "For the novelist working in prose, the object is always entangled in someone else's discourse about it, it is already present with qualifications, an object of dispute that is conceptualized and evaluated variously, inseparable from the heteroglot social apperception of it" (1981c[1940]:330). Poets and positivists, in this view, turn out to be monomaniacal censors, Stalinists, who refuse to acknowledge just how partial their understanding and control really are. Prose artists and anthropologists, by contrast, are (ideally) sensitive to the relativity of each particular voice in the dialogue, and are therefore, it would seem, better custodians of the truth precisely because they know their limitations and are willing to learn from others.

A number of Bakhtin's characterizations of the ideal writer of prose, in fact, might be said to characterize the ideal ethnographer as well: "Prose consciousness feels cramped when it is confined to only *one* out of a multitude of heteroglot languages, for one linguistic timbre is inadequate to it" (1981c:324). "The writer is a person who is able to work in a language while standing outside language, who has the gift of indirect speaking" (1986[n.d.]:110). "A prose writer can distance himself . . . he can make use of language without wholly giving himself up to it, he may treat it as semi-alien or completely alien to himself, while compelling language ultimately to serve his own ends . . . he speaks, as it were, *through* language" (1981c[1940]:299).

This is possible, for novelist and ethnographer alike, because of the diverse concrete social and linguistic practices they actively seek to experience: "A deeply involved participation in alien cultures and languages (one is impossible without the other) inevitably leads to an awareness of the disassociation between language and intentions, language and thought, language and expression. By 'disassociation' we have in mind here a destruction of any absolute bonding of ideological meaning to language, which is *the* defining factor of mythological or magical thought" (1981c:369). Prose writers and anthropologists both come to discover that forms, linguistic and otherwise, are not obligatorily connected with a single impersonal meaning (see Bakhtin 1984[1929]:193).

Simultaneously, however, they also learn "to become sensitive to the 'internal form' (in the Humboldtian sense) of an alien language, and to the 'internal form' of one's own language as an alien form." Bakhtin urges writers to "learn how to develop a sensitivity toward the brute materiality, the typicality . . . in how the world is seen and felt, ways that are organically part and parcel with the language that expresses them." Such a formulation seems to fall afoul of the translatability paradox, for Bakhtin seems to be binding worldview (and therefore thought) to language. But such a criticism would in fact be misplaced here, for it could be valid only if we accept that each individual consciousness may possess but a *single* monolithically structured language. And Bakhtin explicitly rejects this: "Such a perception is possible only for a consciousness organically participating in the *universum* of mutually illuminating languages. What is wanted for this to happen is a fundamental intersecting of languages in a single given consciousness, one that participates equally in several languages" (1981[1940b]:367). Whorf's critics do not recognize multilingual consciousness, but it is precisely because Whorf's consciousness *is* multilingual that he can achieve the "sublimity of free perspectives" (to use Wayne Booth's phrase [1984:xx]), which is the goal of linguistic relativity.

For Bakhtin, therefore, there is a deep connection between heteroglossia, linguistic relativity, prose consciousness, and the carnivalesque (or comic) literary tradition. "Heteroglossia, once incorporated into the novel, is *another's speech in another's language,* serving to express authorial intentions but in a refracted way. Such speech constitutes a special type of *double-voiced discourse.* It serves two speakers at the same time. . . . And all the while these two voices are dialogically interrelated, they—as it were—know about each other" (1981[1940b]:324). Double-voiced hybrid constructions thus allow a writer of prose to give verbal expression to heteroglossia in a manner unavailable to the poet. This is because poetry, as classically conceived, is a matter of a single consciousness fitting impersonal words to the world. By contrast, "For the prose artist the world is full of other people's words. . . . He must introduce them into the plane of his own discourse, but in such a way that this plane is not destroyed" (1984[1929]:200). Poetry therefore excludes dialogue. But it equally excludes irony and parody, which require a second consciousness and a second voice: "To understand the difference between ambiguity in poetry and double-voicedness in prose, it is sufficient to take any symbol and give it an ironic accent. . . . in the space between the word and its object another's word, another's accent intrudes" (Bakhtin 1981c[1940]:328–29). And, of course, hybrid constructions based on stylization are, for Bakhtin, "especially characteristic of comic style" (1981c:305).[1]

It is heteroglossia as an attribute of the individual consciousness, multilingualism rather than monolingualism, that is the necessary ground condition. This is what makes irony, parody, comedy possible. And since it is impossible to imagine human beings anywhere who are immune to humor in some form, it must be the case that heteroglossia in some form is basic to the human condition. That, in turn, means that any particular "language" within an individual's repertoire is inevitably relative to all the other such languages *which will always be found there.* While many literary genres (e.g., poetry, analytic philosophy?) and speech genres (e.g., the authoritative word of the ruling class?) try to deny or obliterate heteroglossia and relativity in defense of one or another "standard," comic forms encourage the questioning of standards. They "permit languages to be used in ways that are indirect, conditional, distanced. They all signify a relativizing of linguistic consciousness in the perception of language borders—borders created by history and society, and even the most fundamental borders (i.e., those between languages as such)—and permit expression of a feeling for the materiality of language that defines such a relativized consciousness" (1981c[1940]:323–24).

Bakhtin's ideal of the novelist (and the novel) might almost be a blueprint for the ideal ethnography: "The author participates in the novel (he is omnipresent in it) with *almost no direct language of his own.* The language of the novel is a *system* of languages that mutually and ideologically interanimate each other. It is impossible to describe and analyze it as a single unitary language" (1981c[1940]:47). And indeed, for Bakhtin, multilingual prose consciousness is not limited to novelists: "It seems to us that one could speak directly of a special *polyphonic artistic thinking* extending beyond the bounds of the novel as a genre. This mode of thinking makes available those sides of a human being, and above all the *thinking human consciousness and dialogic sphere of its existence,* which are not subject to *artistic* assimilation from *monologic positions*" (1984[1929]:270). My thesis is that Whorf exhibited just this kind of polyphonic artistic thinking in his most controversial writing. We have already noted Whorf's use of hybrid constructions in certain critical passages in his work: recall the way in which "language" and "culture" belong simultaneously to "two semantic and axiological belief systems" even as they appear to belong formally to a single speaker, the author. In those passages, broad parody is absent. But the passages tease readers, play cat and mouse with them, suggesting a semi-ironic intent that has not gone unnoticed. This becomes apparent as soon as the reader tries to identify the author with one or another of the points of view he is elaborating. At this point, the loopholes appear. Whorf will not allow his direct authorial word to be subsumed by any of the conventional levels of discourse that a conventional reader might identify. And this is exactly what we should expect, if Whorf is writing polyphonic prose: "The author . . . is to be found at the center of organization where all levels intersect. The different levels are to varying degrees distant from this authorial center" (1981b[1940]:48–49). Put another way, "the writer of prose does not meld completely with any of these words, but rather accents each of them in a particular way—humorously, ironically, parodically and so forth" (1981c[1940]:299).

It is necessary, at this point, to examine Whorf's writing more closely for evidence of his comic prose style. In doing this, we will be using categories developed by Voloshinov and Bakhtin. To begin with, we need to recognized that any piece of writing must be conceived of as an utterance. This means that it cannot be understood, as New Critics might understand it, as something existing in and for itself, with no significant ties to either its author or its audience. On the contrary, an utterance is *always* seen as language directed by a particular speaker to a particular listener about a particular topic, and each of these three elements needs to be understood if that utterance is to be understood. As Voloshinov put it, "every instance of intonation is oriented *in two directions* with respect to the listener as ally or witness and with respect to the object of the utterance as the third, living participant whom the intonation scolds [etc.]" (1987[1926]:104). As a result, analysis of utterances requires that (1) the author's position be examined (as revealed in his intonation, his style); that (2) the author's understanding of his listener be examined (ally, witness, or enemy?); and that (3) the object (theme, topic, "hero") of the utterance be examined. None of these aspects of the utterance can be understood fully without taking into consideration the other aspects. This means that we are concerned to interpret not just referential meaning (i.e., regarding the object of the utterance), but also contextual meaning (i.e., regarding the listener and the world he or she represents *as related to* the object of the utterance *and* the speaker of the utterance).

If we look for counterparts to these three aspects of the utterance in Whorf's work, we find them without difficulty. We discover, as it were, a drama with three characters. These are (1) the character of the author, the Scientific Linguist; (2) the character of the listener, Mr. Everyman; and (3) the character of the Hero, the speaker(s) of the Amerindian languages Whorf discusses. Were we dealing here with a "serious" exposition, we might expect each of these characters to appear, as do characters in epic style, without flaw and neither more nor less than they are officially supposed to be. But since Whorf is interested in demonstrating just how inaccurate official suppositions are, epic style does not suit him. And he will employ parody to show not only that the listener, Mr. Everyman, is *less* than the official, "impersonal, going opinion" (i.e., his own) recognizes, but also that the heroes, the Hopi, are *more* than this official, impersonal, going opinion recognizes. More specifically, it is the *languages* of Mr. Everyman and the Hopi that will be compared and brought into dialogue in Whorf's utterance. And since he, as author, is monitoring that dialogue from a comic point of view, the result will be that the latter will get the better of the former. This is achieved by Whorf's parodic stylizations of the languages both of Mr. Everyman and of the Hopi (see Bakhtin 1981c[1940]:302).

But what about the Scientific Linguist? If Bakhtin is correct, then we should not expect Whorf's position to coincide with that of the Scientific Linguist. And in fact, parody infects the way the Scientific Linguist is portrayed as well; this is why Silverstein could ask (as we saw earlier) whether Whorf's pronouncements about the significant role linguistics could play in clearing up cross-cultural misunderstanding should be taken tongue-in-cheek. If Whorf himself is anywhere in his text, therefore, he is *not* embodied in one of his characters. In comic style, after all, "it is as if the author has no language of his own, but does possess his own style, his own organic and unitary law governing the way he plays with languages" (Bakhtin 1981c[1940]:311). To succeed artistically, however, this "play with languages" must have the outward appearance of sober exposition. Thus, each incorporated language will be presented "in an impersonal form, 'from the author,' alternating with direct authorial discourse" (1981c:311). Once this has been accomplished, "the incorporated languages . . . are unmasked and destroyed . . . what predominates . . . are various forms and degrees of *parodic stylization* of incorporated languages [which can] verge on a rejection of any straightforward and unmediated seriousness" (1981c:312).

Bakhtin's analysis of the forms of parodic stylization in prose is fullest in his discussion of Rabelais. Parodic stylization is a form of utterance, and thus must be understood as dialogic, depending for its effect on object and listener, as well as author. Analysis of Rabelais' writings revealed to Bakhtin three categories of parodic stylization, each of which he identified with a role adopted by the author who carries it out. These are (1) the *rogue,* whose "gay deception parodies high language"; (2) the *clown,* who "maliciously distorts" high language; and (3) the *fool,* who shows "naive incomprehension" of high language (1981c[1940]:405). Each of these forms of parodic stylization is thus destructive, bound to provoke listeners who identify with the language being parodied. At the same time, in Whorf as in Rabelais, "the truth that might oppose such falsity receives almost no direct intentional and verbal expression . . . does not receive its *own* word—it reverberates only in the parodic and unmasking accents in which the lie is present. Truth is restored by reducing the lie to an absurdity, but truth itself does not seek words; she is afraid to entangle herself in the word, to soil herself in verbal pathos" (1981c:309).

The Image of the Author in Whorf's Prose

If Whorf is writing comic prose, then it would be a serious mistake to take the narrative voice in his works as Whorf's own. Rather, the image of the Scientific Linguist would be a posited narrator, like the posited narrators in novelistic fiction. Such a tack, of course, opens up for an author "the possibility of never having to define oneself in language, the possibility of translating one's own intentions from one linguistic system to another, of fusing 'the language of truth' with 'the language of the everyday,' of saying 'I am me' in someone else's language, and in my own language, 'I am other' (Bakhtin 1981c[1940]:314). This, it seems to me, sums up beautifully exactly what Whorf is trying to do. His own problematic identity cannot be resolved by reducing it to his identity as a scientific linguist, or by his identifying with other positivist scientists, or even by his identifying with the Hopi. And so "the author utilizes now one language, now another, in order to avoid giving himself up wholly to either of them . . . in order that he might remain as it were neutral with regard to language, a third party in a quarrel between two people (although he might be a *biased* third party)" (1981c:314). Whorf is clearly a biased third party, which is the source of the sometimes abusive hyperbole in his writing. According to Bakhtin, "hyperbole is always festive (including abusive hyperbole)" (1986[1970–71]:154). This does not mean, however, that it leaves no damage in its wake. In Whorf's case, the damage was not inconsiderable, on himself as well as on his listeners and heroes, and restitution was difficult in coming.

This is why it is so difficult to find out "what Whorf really said," that is, to identify, in Bakhtinian terms, his *direct authorial word*. The direct authorial word of a novelist is found in that part of his writing "which directly embodies (without any refracting) semantic and axiological intentions of the author" (1981c[1940]:301). In comic prose, however, such passages are rare or nonexistent. Writing of the *parodia sacra* of the Middle Ages (which might be compared with Whorf's parody of "sacred" science in his own day), Bakhtin observes that "it is often very difficult to establish precisely where reverence ends and ridicule begins. It is exactly like the modern novel, where one often does not know where the direct authorial word ends and where a parodic or stylized playing with the characters' language begins" (1981c:77). Part of the agony one detects underlying Whorf's texts is due to the fact that reverence and ridicule are simultaneous. He reveres and ridicules science; he reveres and distorts the languages of his Indian informants; and, knowing full well what he has done, and suffering for it, he reveres and ridicules himself. Like Rabelais he pokes fun at the various voices he brings into dialogue. At the same time, like Dostoevsky, he wants to show his respect for these voices, to permit them "to unfold to their maximal fullness and independence" (Bakhtin 1984[1929]:67–68). The parodic intentions and the respectful intentions undercut each other, engendering a comic violence that Whorf is able to repair only indirectly.

We need, therefore, to investigate what texts like "The Punctual and Segmentative Aspects of Verbs in Hopi" succeed in *doing* to their readers. The rhetorical construction and rhetorical accomplishments of such texts are at least as important as anything Whorf succeeds in saying explicitly within them. This investigation will reveal the ways in which, contrary to the linguistically determined framework he so often appears to defend, Whorf points beyond language to shareable, potentially universal experiences of a nonlinguistic kind, which make possible those conditions favorable for cross-linguistic and cross-cultural understanding. For it is here, if anywhere, that his direct authorial word breaks through. It is here, if anywhere, that he is able to make restitution to those, listener and hero alike, whom he has just savaged. Indeed, it is more a direct authorial gesture than a spoken word, as we will see when we consider his nonverbal rhetoric. Whorf *points* to the openings in our experience that take us beyond the horizon of what has been handed down to us and permit us to examine it critically. These openings occur whenever speakers of different languages share nonlinguistic experience which may form the focus of talk. They occur whenever speakers of the same language use rhetorical devices such as parody to estrange one another from their taken-for-granted forms of talk, or taken-for-granted contexts, in order to draw attention to them, open them up for debate.

Let us examine, therefore, the images of listener and hero which Whorf created, and the way each enters into dialogue with the author. We will examine Whorf's textual strategy, considering the way he sets up the arena of argumentation (or sets his trap) and draws listener and hero into it. Three aspects of this strategy in particular will be emphasized:

1. Since his listeners are people of positivist scientific background, he needs to persuade them that he shares their point of view and is, in fact, presenting an acceptable scientific account. This means creating for his listeners the *artistic image of a monological, deterministic, reductionistic argument about the way language molds thought*.

2. To the extent, however, that Whorf wishes to suggest that the mold can be broken, he needs to undercut this deterministic image by offering

his listeners an *artistic counterimage* that demonstrates the means by which openness can be wrested from closure, freedom from determinism, relativity from absolutism. This counterimage is constructed in part by the vivid *image of a new hero, "primitive man"* (Shawnee or Hopi, for example). This image is conveyed metonymically, by means of the *image of the "primitive" language* (again, usually Hopi), a non-SAE language which he contrasts with the English of his listener. All this is part, as it were, of the content of Whorf's text.

3. But the artistic counterimage is completed, not in terms of content, but in terms of form—the stylistic form of the text itself. And style points back at *the image of the author,* which nowhere openly shows a face, but whose nature is defined by the *multilingual prose consciousness* that could bring together English and Hopi in the first place and make them argue with one another; and that could, in the second place, draw the speakers of these languages, by implication, into dialogue as well.

Let us examine each aspect in turn.

The Image of the Listener: Mr. Everyman, the Natural Logician

Whorf is writing for "scientists"; they make up the listener/readers for his utterances. There are the social scientists, professional linguists, and anthropologists; and there are the scientifically trained readers of his articles for the MIT *Technology Review.* And he has chosen to communicate with them in their "language": the accepted positivistic discourse appropriate to a physicalist, no-nonsense, empirical point of view.

Since Whorf was himself trained as a scientist, a chemical engineer, alongside his fellow MIT graduates, his readers might suppose that in speaking their language he is demonstrating solidarity with their perspective. Yet the perspective he defends, while sharing common ground with that of science, nevertheless is critical of science as currently practiced. And so solidarity turns into opposition. Voloshinov asks, "How does the author sense his listener?" Although usually author and listener stand "side by side" as allies and together examine the "hero," this is not the case in such genres as satire or confession (1987[1926]:112). And Bakhtin suggests, "in the comic novel . . . 'common language' . . . is taken by the author precisely as the *common view. . . .* To one degree or another, the author distances himself from this common language" which is gradually seen to represent a position that is "always superficial and frequently hypocritical" (1981c[1940]:301–2). And in fact what Whorf has prepared for his unsuspecting listeners is a satire on themselves. Whorf begins in ostensible solidarity with his listeners, as together they criticize the apparent "hero" of the text: "Mr. Everyman, the natural logician," as Whorf calls him in the article "Languages and Logic" (Whorf 8:233). The twist of the blade occurs when his listeners discover that the buffoon they have been laughing at is made in their image. Whorf lets it be known that scientists are Mr. Everymen of the worst sort—and he distances himself from all such scientists.

How does Whorf initially go about persuading his readers that he views them as allies? The most obvious tactic is the use he makes of the discourse of science; that is, the stylistic means he employs to create the image of a hard-hitting, no-nonsense, reductionist argument which might be summarized: "language determines thought." That it is the *image* of a reductionist argument, rather than the genuine article, should be clear by now, since, as we have seen, he never says anywhere straightforwardly, in so many words, that language determines thought. Rather he hopes to persuade us rhetorically that this is the case, all the while leaving himself a loophole.

The figure of Mr. Everyman is a second tactic Whorf employs. Mr. Everyman is—presumably—the monolingual speaker of any particular language. Whorf uses humor and hyperbole to cajole us into agreeing that Mr. Everyman's language controls his "natural logic" far more than his natural logic controls his language. Perhaps the most sustained discussion of Mr. Everyman's "natural logic" occurs in the article "Science and Linguistics" (Carroll 1956:207–19). Whorf begins by suggesting:

> Every normal person in the world, past infancy in years, can and does talk. By virtue of that fact, every person—civilized or uncivilized—carries through life certain naive but deeply rooted ideas about talking and its relation to thinking. Because of their firm connection with speech habits that have become unconscious and automatic, these notions tend to be rather intolerant of opposition. They are by no means entirely personal and haphazard; their basis is definitely systematic, so that we are justified in calling them a system of natural logic—a term that seems to me preferable to the term common sense, often used for the same thing. (Whorf 6:207)

The concept of "natural logic" described by Whorf seems to be based upon the "metaphysics of presence" which Derrida and his followers have done so much to disclose and debunk:

> According to natural logic, the fact that every person has talked fluently since infancy makes every man his own authority on the process by which he formulates and communicates. . . . Talking, or

the use of language, is supposed only to "express" what is essentially already formulated nonlinguistically. Formulation is an independent process, called thought or thinking . . . supposed to be largely indifferent to the nature of particular languages. Languages have grammars which are assumed to be merely norms of conventional and social correctness, but the use of language is supposed to be guided not so much by them as by correct, rational, or intelligent thought. . . . Natural logic holds that different languages are essentially parallel methods of expressing this one-and-the-same rationale of thought and, hence, differ really in but minor ways which may seem important only because they are seen at close range. It holds that mathematics, symbolic logic, philosophy, and so on are systems contrasted with language which deal directly with this realm of thought, not that they are themselves specialized extensions of language. (Whorf 6:207–8)

Derrida moves to undercut his readers' faith in the metaphysics of presence by focusing on the radical alterity of linguistic signs and the consequent uncontrollable dissemination of meaning. Whorf, by contrast, chooses to undercut his readers' faith in natural logic by focusing on the relative absolutism of particular grammars and the consequent grammatical control of meaning when speakers and thinkers believe themselves most free. Both moves are equally absolutistic, involving festive, abusive hyperbole. Whorf tells us that natural logic contains two fallacies, the first of which is that natural logic

does not see that the phenomena of a language are to its own speakers largely of a background character and so outside the critical consciousness and control of the speaker who is expounding natural logic. Hence when anyone, as a natural logician, is talking about reason, logic, and the laws of correct thinking, he is apt to be simply marching in step with purely grammatical facts. . . . by no means universal in all languages and in no sense a common substratum of reason. (Whorf 6:211)

The foregoing passage resembles other passages in Whorf that we have examined, passages which have ordinarily been interpreted as statements of linguistic determinism. If, however, we note that here, as in those other passages, Whorf leaves loopholes, such a naive reading cannot be sustained. Note, for example, that those hard-to-pin-down "phenomena of language" are referred to as the determining factors, which seem to be equated with "purely grammatical facts." But recall that for Whorf, the grammar of the linguist must not be equated with the layman's notion of grammar; that the linguist's grammar includes much more than the textbooks would admit.

Note, too, that these supposedly controlling phenomena of language are "largely of a background character and so outside the critical consciousness and control of the speaker." If the phenomena of language are only "largely" of a background character, does this mean that some of these phenomena are always, or sometimes (or all of them are sometimes?), of a *foregrounded* character, that is to say *present* to critical consciousness and control of the speaker? If so, when, and under what circumstances? Furthermore, Whorf falls short of claiming that reason, logic and the laws of correct thinking are always reducible to "purely grammatical facts." What he does say is that anyone talking about reason, logic, and the laws of correct thinking "is apt to be simply marching in step with purely grammatical facts." Is "apt to be," but is not necessarily doing so? How can we tell the difference?

These tantalizing ambiguities continue in Whorf's discussion of what he calls the second fallacy of natural logic, the fact that "natural logic confuses agreement about subject matter, attained through use of language, with knowledge of the linguistic process by which agreement is attained: i.e., with the province of the despised (and to its notion superfluous) grammarian" (Whorf 6:211). Note first of all the presupposition of "agreement about subject matter" which Whorf builds into his argument. As in his early text about true connections in language, he assumes that talk cannot occur without some sort of preexisting consensus among interlocutors. The problem is to find the source of that agreement. Natural logicians assume that the source of agreement lies in some universal logic, or reason, or laws of correct thinking, to which they have unproblematic access and to which the rules of their particular language are superfluous. And yet the linguist knows, Whorf continues, that agreement is not naturally given and sufficient to itself; rather, it is attained by a process, a linguistic process which the linguist can describe, but of which the natural logicians are blissfully unaware.

This passage is a particularly tricky one. For Whorf comes as close as he ever does to explicitly affirming a dialogic point of view. "Agreement about subject matter, attained through use of language" sounds exactly like dialogue: making use of the resources available in any language to attack or argue for particular points of view. Except, of course, Whorf says nothing about *disagreement*. He writes as if the attainment of agreement were a foregone conclusion, the only conclusion. And as long as nobody calls him on this point, he can legitimately claim that it is "naive" to assume, as natural logicians do, that they agree with one another because *nothing*—neither grammar, nor language, nor culture, nor political interest—comes between their several rational minds and the objective structure of the universe.

Whorf is concerned to demonstrate that, in fact, logic and rationality *are* refracted by something: namely, by the "background phenomena of language." And by suggesting that these background phenomena "are the province of the grammarian—or of the linguist, to give him his more modern name as a scientist" (Whorf 6:211), he seems to want his readers to draw the conclusion that grammarian/linguist/scientists are the *only* ones who may speak knowledgeably about such phenomena. Scientifically minded readers might even be inclined to accept such an assertion without question, familiar as they are with disciplinary specialization, and the perils of pretending to pass as an expert in a scientific field which is not your own.

But Whorf is clearly on dangerous ground. He cannot admit openly that agreement *and* disagreement—both sides of the dialogic coin—are possible using one and the same language: given his audience, this would be interpreted as just a fancy way of reaffirming the freedom of speech they assumed they had all along. By stressing, therefore, only their *freedom to agree,* and linking that freedom to language practices they share and that make agreement possible, Whorf can raise in them the suspicion that perhaps they are *not free to disagree.* Once doubt about freedom of expression is sown, scientifically minded readers might be more likely to turn to the one scientific expert who promises to liberate them from the bonds of language: namely, the scientific linguist.

But even now, Whorf is not home clear. Even if he convinces his readers that they need to be liberated, they may yet suspect that they can do it on their own. After all, these readers are educated men. Most of them probably studied foreign languages in school; perhaps some are even fluent in one or more European languages. Surely their ability to learn languages and even perhaps speak them is evidence that they are not crippled by the rules of any particular grammar?

Whorf's response to this anticipated riposte is twofold. On the one hand, he reduces the significance of multilingualism in other European languages (the kind his readers are most likely to have) by lumping all of them together with English and treating them as if they constituted another language with its own restrictive rules of grammar. In the same article we have been analyzing, "Science and Linguistics," Whorf does not explicitly use the term he coined elsewhere to refer to this superlanguage: Standard Average European, or SAE. He states in no uncertain terms, however, that "our modern European languages, with perhaps Latin and Greek thrown in for good measure," display "a unanimity of pattern which at first seems to bear out natural logic," but only as long as we avoid looking at non-Western languages.

> When Semitic, Chinese, Tibetan, or African languages are contrasted with our own, the divergence in analysis of the world becomes more apparent; and when we bring in the native languages of the Americas, where speech communities for many millenniums have gone their ways independently of each other and of the Old World, the fact that languages dissect nature in many different ways becomes patent. (Whorf 6:214)

Multilingual knowledge at this level goes beyond the experience of virtually all his readers, and seriously undermines any defense they might offer. Their defense is further undermined, in any case, since Whorf also claims that the mere fluency of a lay multilingual cannot confer the kind of linguistic knowledge needed to break the bonds of linguistic determinism: "Scientific linguists have long understood that ability to speak a language fluently does not necessarily confer a linguistic knowledge of it, i.e., understanding of its background phenomena and its systematic processes and structure, any more than ability to play a good game of billiards confers or requires any knowledge of the laws of mechanics that operate upon the billiard table" (Whorf 6:211).

This passage is extraordinarily crafty. While carrying a deterministic rhetorical force, it nevertheless abounds in loopholes. For instance, ability to speak a language "does not necessarily" confer linguistic knowledge—yet the possibility that it *might* confer such knowledge is not firmly ruled out. Perhaps polyglots already possess the tools they need (or *some* may possess these tools? or *all* may possess *some* of these tools?) to escape the prison of determinism? Before readers become overconfident, however, they need to be a bit more clear on just what the tools in question are. If mere multilingualism cannot confer "linguistic knowledge," what kind of understanding of many languages can confer it? Indeed, what kind of knowledge is it? Whorf tells us that linguistic knowledge is understanding of a language's "background phenomena and its systematic processes and structure." We have already seen, however, that Whorf's "background phenomena" of language are notoriously difficult to specify. But since they are, as he told us a few sentences earlier, "the province of the grammarian," we are left to conclude once again that it is *grammar* that the scientific linguist understands and the polyglot layperson does not.

For Whorf immediately tells us that the linguist is more than merely someone who knows many languages. Or, more exactly, he distinguishes the scientific linguist from the "polyglot or multilingual" whom he defines as "a person who can quickly attain agreement about subject matter with different people speaking a number of different languages" (Whorf 6:211). But again Whorf is sly, for a polyglot so defined is not exactly the same thing as a person who speaks several different languages fluently. In fact, the style of the definitional sentence even makes it unclear *who* speaks the different languages: the "person who can quickly attain agreement about subject matter" or the "different people speaking a number of different languages" with whom agreement is attained? And to top it off, the sentence in which the multilingual's attainments are called into question makes no mention of multilingualism at all! Whorf simply says that scientific linguists "have long understood that ability to speak a language fluently does not necessarily confer a linguistic knowledge of it"—and this could apply as easily to monolinguals as to multilinguals. It is only the surrounding context that allows us to apply it to multilinguals; thus, the sentence itself creates another loophole.

In this way Whorf tortuously avoids having to state explicitly the possibility that fluent multilinguals might gain the kind of language consciousness sufficient for breaking the bonds of grammar. Such an admission would allow a Ph.D. philologist, or an MIT graduate fluent in German, to exempt himself from anything else Whorf had to say. So Whorf insists that it is not fluency in other languages, but knowledge of the grammar of other languages, as revealed by scientific linguistic investigation, that counts. And, in Whorf's day, this meant descriptivist accounts in which fluency was almost something to apologize for, something that would blind you to the intricacies of an alien language rather than reveal them to you. Fluency also suggested that one might speak unscientifically with informants on a wide range of topics in the course of everyday life, thus tainting the data. In a passage which must make defenders of the "ethical" Whorf shudder, Whorf tells us:

> The experimental linguist, like the biologist, uses and must have experimental animals. Only, his "animals" are human. They are his informants and must be paid for working with him. Sometimes he must make trips to Indian reservations or African villages where his informants live; at other times it is more economical to transport them to him. They provide the field for experimental investigation. They are apparatus, not teachers. (Whorf 7:231)

For scientific purposes, informants exist only to answer a restricted set of systematic questions about their language and nothing more. Treating informants as dialogic partners with equal rights is unscientific (although the means by which the "scientific" informant-linguist data-gathering interaction ever comes about at all raises questions which ought to plague the conscience of any linguist oblivious of context and scornful of multilingual fluency).

The rhetorical force of the exceedingly complex passage we have been discussing urges us to draw the conclusion that it is the inflexible rules of grammar that guide lay people who speak the same language to the same conclusions about the world, thus giving them the illusion of rational freedom. And Whorf caps his argument in the final sentence of the passage with the metaphor of the billiard game. The Newtonian overtones of this metaphor (references to billiard balls and the mechanics that operate on the billiard table) suggest that the systematic processes and structures of language deploy themselves according to their own laws, exactly like objects in a Newtonian universe. There is something rather odd about summoning up the image of a Newtonian linguistic universe in an argument defending linguistic relativity, but it is the same oddness—paradox—we find in the notion of relative absolutism: each linguistic universe is Newtonian, though if we compare a series of such closed Newtonian linguistic universes, we discover that each operates according to laws that are only absolute relative to the particular universe in which they are found.

However, given the pains Whorf has taken to provide himself with loopholes out of strict relative absolutism, we may question the aptness of this metaphor. Although he invokes it for the rhetorical purpose of driving the lesson of relative absolutism home, it does not really square with the partial consciousness and control over language (at least part of the time) for which he leaves room in the immediately preceding discussion. It is almost as though he were diverting attention away from that aspect of the billiard game which *would* be apt (that is, the rules of the game; the meanings assigned by the rules to the various possible mechanical outcomes the balls may experience on the billiard table; even possible disputes over which rules apply to which mechanical outcomes, or whether the rules apply at all in some cases). He would like the metaphor to perform the rhetorical service of reducing the rules of billiards to the laws of mechanics, so that if one knew the latter, one could unambiguously deduce the former. If the metaphor persuades, then the reader should be equally willing to concede that reason, logic, and the laws of correct thinking can be unambiguously deduced from the

laws of a particular grammar. But again, Whorf never claims straightforwardly that such unambiguous deduction is possible.

To summarize, in several articles (e.g., "Science and Linguistics,"
"Languages and Logic," "Language, Mind, and Reality") Whorf's favor-
ite rhetorical means of persuading readers of the powerful way in which
language shapes thought is to resort to a discussion of natural logic and/
or to set up the stock figure of Mr. Everyman. Mr. Everyman is a comic
counterpart to Saussure's Talking Heads and their offspring, such as
Chomsky's Ideal Speaker-Hearer. All are "ideal types," but since Whorf
is writing parody, he emphasizes the way in which ideal figures are in
fact exaggerated and distorted versions of the ordinary folk whose
speech and reasoning they were invented to clarify. Mr. Everyman is a
send-up of Chomsky's Ideal Speaker-Hearer, for while the latter is sol-
emnly presumed to know all the rules of his language by virtue of some
innate mechanism operating according to universal linguistic principles,
Whorf's Mr. Everyman only *thinks* he knows, and mistakes the relatively absolute rules of his native tongue for universally absolute rules of
reason, logic, or correct thinking. Or, if we take Whorf's hedging seriously, Mr. Everyman *can never be sure* when the linguistic structure that
controls his thought and speech is marching in step with the patterns of
universal principles and when it is not; he simply assumes that it is, and it
never occurs to him to ask critical questions.

In fact, Mr. Everyman is a remarkably obtuse fellow. Mr. Everyman
can understand nothing if it is not put to him in the syntactic forms and
familiar words of his native tongue. This suggests, although Whorf does
not explicitly claim it, that figurative language and metaphorical insight
are beyond Mr. Everyman's capabilities. He looks, in fact, a lot like the
fool of parodic prose described by Bakhtin: "A fool introduced by the
author for purposes of 'making strange' the world of conventional pathos
may himself, as a fool, be the object of the author's scorn. The author
need not necessarily express a complete solidarity with such a character.
Mocking these figures as fools may even become paramount. But the
author needs the fool: by his very uncomprehending presence he makes
strange the world of social conventionality. By representing stupidity, the
novel teaches prose intelligence, prose wisdom" (1981c[1940]:404). In
this role, Mr. Everyman bears a strong family resemblance to two other
stereotypical "fools": the Primitive Man and Illiterate Peasant we discussed earlier. Unfortunately for Whorf's readers, however, Mr. Everyman the fool can also be a *Scientist!*

Whorf implies the equation indirectly in his article "Science and Linguistics," when he offers a hypothetical scenario involving scientists

from two different cultures, speaking different native languages, who attempt to arrive at an "agreement on subject matter" when one possesses a physics dependent upon "a concept of dimensional time" (i.e., SAE) and another lacks this concept (i.e., Hopi). Mr. Everyman's mulish lack of imagination is exposed (though not explicitly labeled) as soon as Hopi physicists and SAE physicists begin to talk to one another (characteristically, Whorf doesn't indicate which language they are speaking, or whether they are employing the services of an interpreter!):

> A scientist from another culture that used time and velocity would have great difficulty in getting us to understand these concepts. We should talk about the intensity of a chemical reaction; he would speak of its velocity or its rate, which words we should at first think were simply words for intensity in his language. Likewise, he at first would think that intensity was simply our own word for velocity. At first we should agree, later we should begin to disagree, and it might dawn upon both sides that different systems of rationalization were being used. He would find it very hard to make us understand what he really meant by velocity of a chemical reaction. We should have no words that would fit. He would try to explain it by likening it to a running horse, to the difference between a good horse and a lazy horse. We should try to show him, with a superior laugh, that his analogy also was a matter of different intensities, aside from which there was little similarity between a horse and a chemical reaction in a beaker. We should point out that a running horse is moving relative to the ground, whereas the material in the beaker is at rest. (Whorf 6:218)

This passage occurs as the penultimate paragraph in the article. It leads us to expect that Whorf will demonstrate in the final paragraph how a linguist would go about resolving the dialogical impasse in which our two Mr. Everyman scientists find themselves, but he does not. Indeed, there is a highly disturbing logical gap between the foregoing passage and the sentence immediately following it, namely: "One significant contribution to science from the linguistic point of view may be the greater development of our sense of perspective." One is left wondering how anyone could engender a tolerant sense of perspective in the literal minds of Mr. Everymen who lack the capacity to imagine alternatives, and thus are bound to interpret any they are offered as category mistakes.

No doubt this little scenario with the physicists would cause less anxiety to scientific readers if Whorf made it clear somewhere that "Mr. Everyman" really represented only the "primitive" unenlightened (illiterate, monolingual, peasant) masses. Indeed, commentators on Whorf have often implicitly or explicitly assumed that such was the case. Gipper (1977:226), for example, says:

> In a "primitive" or original culture like that of the Hopis a scientific Weltbild has not yet developed. The Hopi cosmography—if there is any—closely linked with the Hopi *Weltanschauung*, that is their religious beliefs. Hopi thinking has not yet reached a critical distance towards language. The confidence in the "truth values," so to speak, of the mother tongue is therefore greater than in our societies. Thus the Hopi language can be said to be an authentic key to the understanding of the Hopi *Weltanschauung*.

Alford makes a similar assumption, arguing that Whorf was able to break out of the circle of determinism because he was "a comparative linguist cognizant of the traps of habitual language by his awareness of alternate language world-views—something quite beyond the average monolingual" (1978:494).

T. D. Crawford, undertaking a Whorfian analysis of Plato's dialogues, makes a similar argument for the ancient Greeks:

> As we see from the conclusion of the "Cratylus," Plato held that names had originally been given to objects because of a supposed correspondence between the form of each word and its meaning. To one who held this belief, ambiguity was much less easy to come to terms with than it is for us, for whom "le signe linguistique est arbitraire." (1982:225–26)

And he concludes, "If the structures of the Greek language could impose their influence upon one of the most acute minds in the classical world, to what extent must we assume that the structures of the languages of Western civilization in general have influenced its development?" (1982:226).

Crawford (like Holquist 1986:101) is shrewd to couch his conclusion about linguistic determinism in the form of a rhetorical question. For his analysis of Plato suggests that the great philosopher's "belief" in the correspondence between the form of a word and its meaning may not be so innocent and unself-conscious as it appears. Indeed, his analysis suggests that Plato *wanted* to be able to demonstrate the correspondence between form and meaning, but that his efforts to do so were undercut by linguistic ambiguities he could not ignore. As a result, Plato often takes identity of form "to imply identity of function where in fact the structure was functionally ambiguous" (1982:222). Crawford is at pains to give Plato the benefit of the doubt: "Plato never seems to have understood fully the role of ambiguity in language" (1982:223). Yet he suggests at the same time that Plato "exploited" underlying ambiguities when it served his purposes (1982:224). One wonders if Plato, in fact, understood quite well the role of ambiguity in language, and feared it, and set about to domesticate it, using subterfuge when necessary. And if this were true for Plato, it might also be true for "average monolinguals" and members of "primitive or original cultures." In fact, it might be true for everyone.

Indeed, other comments by Whorf make it plain that, for him, Mr. Everyman is hardly limited to "primitives." "Natural man, whether simpleton or scientist, knows no more of the linguistic forces that bear upon him than the savage knows of gravitational forces" (Whorf 9:251). Even more disconcertingly, "scientist and yokel, scholar and tribesman, all use their personal consciousness in the same dim-witted sort of way, and get into similar kinds of logical impasse. They are as unaware of the beautiful and inexorable systems that control them as a cowherd is of cosmic rays" (Whorf 9:257). In passages like these, Whorf turns on the readers whom he had seduced into a false sense of solidarity with him. In so doing, he also turns on himself, or that part of himself, that voice within him, that is still a "scientist." Yet even here he is cunning, he leaves himself a loophole. For if Whorf is a scientist who has been able to break free of linguistic determinism, and the reader find his arguments plausible, then the reader may be one of those happy few who, like Whorf, belong to the elite who can view belief systems from the perspective of linguistic relativity. And it is always possible to think of examples of scholarly colleagues whose dim-wittedness is unquestionable.

Yet the reader's bewilderment can only increase (and the loophole widen) when Whorf goes on to proclaim *in the same sentence* that "the higher mind or 'unconscious' of a Papuan headhunter can mathematize quite as well as that of Einstein" (Whorf 9:257)! Whorf insists on elevating "primitives" to the level of scientists (or downgrading scientists to the level of "primitives") in a manner which cannot fail to disconcert complacent scientific-minded readers. However, the final element of Whorf's textual strategy revolves precisely around the image of the "primitive" which he creates. If his initial hero, Mr. Everyman, is discovered to be a double for his listener, employed to destroy the listener's complacent self-image, then the second hero he introduces—"primitive man"—is utilized to help the listener rebuild his self-image in a new form.

The Image of the Hero: "Primitive Man"

Many of Whorf's readers, like Joshua Fishman, have praised the ethical position implied by linguistic relativity. They see it as according, to oppressed or minority peoples and languages, an important measure of respect and dignity which various kinds of absolutist ideologies have withheld. They have made this evaluation, in no small part, because they recognize that the Hopi, or Shawnee, or other Amerindian peoples, are the heroes of Whorf's work. We need, however, to explore a bit more fully what being a "hero" might mean. Bakhtin's observations about Dostoevsky's heroes can help us to pinpoint what it is about Whorf's images of native Americans that readers find so moving.

Bakhtin argues that "the hero interests Dostoevsky . . . as a *particular point of view on the world and on oneself*" (1984[1929]:47). "In a monologic design, the hero . . . cannot exceed the limits of his own character. Dostoevsky renounces all these monologic premises. Everything that the author-monologist kept for himself . . . Dostoevsky turns over to his hero. . . . There is literally nothing we can say about the hero of 'Notes from Underground' that he does not already know himself. . . . *Any point of view from without is rendered powerless in advance and denied the finalizing word*" (1984:52; emphasis added).

For Whorf, the Hopi do indeed represent a particular point of view on the world. Whorf uses his knowledge of their language, in particular of its grammar, to elucidate that point of view as fully as he can for his readers. And this effort is shocking to some readers precisely because Whorf's image of the Hopi does exceed "the limits of [their] own character" as the readers have understood it. For the portrait of the Hopi which emerges from his analyses of their language is anything but a stock Primitive or Illiterate Peasant or Fool. The linguistic weapons Whorf uses to destroy this stereotype are carefully chosen and presented: Whorf renders Standard Average European "powerless in advance" to explain the originality of Hopi, thus denying to SAE and its speakers the finalizing word about the Hopi (and, by extention, about all speakers of so-called "primitive" languages).

Whorf accomplishes this gracefully, with a genial smile on his face (or on the surface of his prose). And yet the deed is filled with tension. Just as he did damage to the scientist in himself when he attacked positivistic scientific excess, he does damage to the Hopi even as he elevates them as examples of wisdom whom erstwhile positivists should respect. For although Whorf is eager to present the Hopi and their particular point of view on the world, he fears to allow them a particular point of view—or worse, *points of view—on themselves.* The voice of the monological positivist in him struggles with the voice of dialogic awareness. He wants his SAE readers to enter into dialogue with the Hopi, to develop with them the kind of multilingual consciousness that will allow science to transcend its sterile parochialism. And yet he places restrictions on the nature of that dialogue: the "voices" that enter into it must struggle to make themselves heard.

If Whorf has exaggerated the dim-wittedness and passivity of his SAE listeners in order to persuade them that dialogue is necessary, he has also exaggerated the unanimity of the Hopi voice that will respond in that dialogue. Bakhtin warns us of the dangers of allowing this to happen when dealing with alien languages: "the entire language—as a consequence of our distance from it—seems to lie on one and the same plane." "Historico-linguistic research," a reconstruction of "each language's social-ideological meaning and an exact knowledge of the social distribution and ordering of all the other ideological voices of the era" are needed to provide the required "third dimension" (1981c[1940]:416). Much of this is impossible to recover for extinct societies with scanty records. But with living societies, such as those Whorf knew, the needed information could have been supplied *and wasn't.* This is the source of the tension underlying Whorf's portrayal of the Hopi as hero. They speak freely, but only through an interpreter—Whorf himself. They are allowed a "voice," but it is a "group voice": individual Hopi remain voiceless. And although the Hopi group voice may speak "freely," that free speech is kept tightly within a particular sphere: that of denotation and reference. No "free-associating" that might allow talk to stray onto topics of reservation life or portraits of the white man: this will be a "controlled association" from beginning to end.

Such restrictions seem necessary on pragmatic as well as personal terms for Whorf. He needs to retain the interest of his readers, and so he must deal with topics (such as the way words link up with the world) that positivistic science finds significant. At the same time, his desire is not to destroy science completely; rather he wants to enrich it with Hopi insights. Bakhtin observes, "In the presence of the monologic principle, ideology . . . inevitably transforms the represented world into a *voiceless object of deduction.* . . . The accents of ideological deduction must not contradict the form-shaping accents of the representation itself. If such a contradiction exists it is felt to be a flaw, for within the limits of a monologic world contradictory accents collide within a single voice" (1984[1929]:83). The collision is muffled by Whorf's artistry, but the strain shows as he struggles to speak dialogically with a single monologic accent. This leads him to risk creating a distorted image of the Hopi, to omit from his image of them aspects of their lives which might interfere with his scientific goals, even if such aspects would contribute to a richer portrait of Hopi humanity.

Whorf's fateful decision is to allow the Hopi language to represent Hopi humanity, and then to restrict his discussion of that language to matters of grammar. This is the series of reductions he employs to get from complex Hopi heteroglossia to a single Hopi voice which enters into dialogue with the single voice of SAE. Both voices are misleading distortions, even as the dialogue in which they are asked to participate is significant and necessary. This is the painful compromise Whorf is able to fashion between the monologic and dialogic principles. He encourages cross-linguistic dialogue with all the art he can muster—but on the condition that it be abstract, single grammars that "speak," rather than human persons (cf. Voloshinov 1926:97). Bakhtin reminds us that the monologic notion of unified consciousness can be detected whenever an author speaks of "the spirit of a nation, the spirit of a people, the spirit of history, and so forth" (1984[1929]:82). In Whorf, this monologic notion might be phrased "the spirit of a grammar." Grammar is as close as Whorf will allow himself to come to the human beings whose language provides him with the data to describe it. He is simultaneously attracted to Hopi humanity in the abstract and, seemingly, repelled by it in the concrete. Perhaps this is one reason why he never became a full-time professional linguist and spent so little time in the field. It is almost as if closer contact would have threatened beyond repair the delicate truce Whorf had achieved between the various voices raging within him.

As a result, Whorf walks on a narrow tightrope in his dealings with the Hopi. He seems only too aware of—and frightened by—the insight Bakhtin offers in his discussion of Dostoevsky: "The consciousness of other people cannot be perceived, analyzed, defined as objects or as things—one can only *relate to them dialogically*. To think about them means to *talk with them: otherwise they immediately turn to us their objectivized side;* they fall silent, close up, and congeal into finished, objectivized images" (1984[1929]:68). He seems dogged by the realization that "the truth about a man in the mouths of others, not directed to him dialogically and therefore a *secondhand* truth, becomes a *lie* degrading and deadening him if it touches upon his 'holy of holies,' that is, 'the man in man' " (1984:59). In making himself the official spokesman for the Hopi, Whorf has therefore condemned himself to offering secondhand truth about them, and to degrading them in the process, even as he wants to use this opportunity to elevate them, to make them appear more human in the eyes of his non-Hopi readers.

Bakhtin argues that "in Dostoevsky's novels, the author's discourse about a character is organized as discourse about *someone actually present,* someone who hears him (the author) and is *capable of answering him*" (1984:64). One may well ask, therefore, if the Hopi, whose full humanity Whorf works so hard to delineate, are capable of answering Whorf or Whorf's readers. And the answer, I believe, is "No—and yes." Whorf gets very nervous if the Hopi—or any informants—are allowed to do more than provide data. The rigors of scientific linguistics are in fact, at one and the same time, the rigors of a kind of political repression. The Hopi are allowed to speak only so long as they agree to speak on topics approved by the censor (cf. Bakhtin 1981c[1940]:280–81).

And yet, it is as if Whorf's conscience bothers him. Destructive parody is not sufficient. Whorf is not content to leave Mr. Everyman and the Hopi without hope. Examine, for example, the following passage:

> Consider how the world appears to any man, however wise and experienced in human life, who has never heard one word of what science has discovered about the Cosmos. To him the earth is flat. . . . It will be impossible to reason him out of these beliefs. He will assert them as plain, hard-headed common sense; which means that they satisfy him because they are completely adequate as a SYSTEM OF COMMUNICATION between him and his fellow men. That is, they are adequate LINGUISTICALLY to his social needs, and will remain so until an additional group of needs is felt and is worked out in language. (Whorf 9:250–51)

What can it possibly mean to "feel" an "additional group of needs" and "work them out in language"? To do such a thing would imply above all an ability to break out of servitude to what has been handed down, to perceive new needs and to develop new social practices (or the reverse), and to whip language into a shape that makes it possible to talk about them. If the man enslaved to natural logic nevertheless possesses the capacity to recognize new social needs and work them out in language, then neither the Hopi nor positivist scientists need be restricted to inherited linguistic forms. If positivist science is moribund, perhaps it can be given new life if scientists learn how to address the Hopi and other non-Western peoples in dialogue, with the aim of learning from them. They will find areas of understanding where their traditions intersect, but they will also be exposed to new points of view unsuspected and unanticipated by their old perspective. To engage in such dialogue would be to

repeat, for all scientists, the development of a multilingual consciousness which Whorf himself experienced as his linguistic knowledge grew.
And so Whorf takes care to provide additional loopholes through which both the derided reader and the distorted hero may regain their just proportions. And he uses double-voiced discourse to do so. His Hopi data, even in restricted form, are encouraged to speak *for themselves* in testimony to Hopi humanity, in an effort to make doubtful readers accept that humanity. But these data are also made to speak *for Whorf*, both to expose the prejudice of complacent readers and to provide an example of the kind of multilingual consciousness his readers must develop if science is to be saved. He *demonstrates* this in his compositional structure, he *points* to it, rather than state it in so many words. And that is why we will analyze the voices both of the Hopi and of Whorf at the same time.

The Image of a Multilingual Consciousness: The Linguist as Seer

Mr. Everyman is a rhetorical construct designed to persuade readers of the absolutistic control over thought exercised by language. The scientific linguist is another such construct who accomplishes what Mr. Everyman seems unable to achieve: the freedom of a relativistic perspective on language. Yet Whorf also allows his readers to construct for themselves the image of a third figure who remains unnamed, but who sees more than conventional scientists or conventional linguists (e.g., philologists). Whorf's image of the scientific linguist provides the starting point for the image of this third figure, but only a starting point. The figure is completed in the consciousness of each reader as a result of the effect on that reader of the stylistic composition of Whorf's text. This third image is that of a multilingual consciousness. Its prototype is the scientific linguist. But every reader of Whorf's texts who is drawn into dialogue with them develops such a consciousness for himself or herself, and so the multilingual consciousness is shown not to be the property of scientific linguists alone.

In according the freedom of a relativistic perspective to a scientist, Whorf is expressing his respect for the scientific enterprise. At the same time, a "scientific linguist" cannot be classed with other scientists. This is because the linguist is the only kind of scientist whose practical activity naturally leads him to surmount the barriers of relative absolutism. We have already seen some of the difficulties Whorf encountered in his effort to isolate the "bad" scientist and to disarm him. He had to persuade his readers that linguistics was *scientific* to a degree which they would find beyond reproach. At the same time, he had to convince them that any linguistic knowledge they possessed was insufficient for the purposes of the scientific *linguist*. Ultimately, however, linguistic relativity could be attained only by a scientific linguist who *sees more* than conventional scientists or conventional linguists. Such a figure, whom we will call the scientific-linguist-as-seer, embodies a multilingual consciousness.

In his article "Linguistics as an Exact Science," Whorf seeks to demonstrate the scientific respectability of linguistics by likening it to a laboratory science such as experimental biology. As we saw earlier, Whorf told his readers that scientific linguistic investigation requires rigor, requires the linguist to relate to informants as apparatus, not as people. Whorf does not emphasize participant-observation and the study of language in context as essential for the *scientific* investigation of language (although, characteristically, he does not rule it out). He makes it clear, however, that the informants' role is to answer the linguists' questions and provide texts, not to engage them in conversation or debate.

But other kinds of scientists are not qualified to debate the linguist either. Knowledge about the underlying phenomena of language is exacted by a form of systematic questioning—rather like dissection—which only scientific *linguists* are competent to carry out. As a result, lay persons, and even other scientists, cannot accomplish what the linguist can accomplish. In this way Whorf is able rather neatly to disqualify in advance any criticism of his analyses that might be offered by either his heroes (i.e., his Native American informants) or his readers (i.e., other scientists).

It is therefore in his "scientific" voice that Whorf claims a privileged role for the linguist. But when he speaks of the role linguists can play in the discovery of scientific truths, we hear Whorf's "mystical" voice, the voice that desires to *see more* than traditional positivistic science (or descriptive linguistics) allows. The linguist's work, he tells us, will bring to light a "prodigal wealth of new truth" (Whorf 3:81). Indeed, the future of the human species must be envisioned in terms of mental growth, and this will be fostered by the scientific study of preliterate languages which demonstrate "much more precise and finely elaborated" systems of relationships "on the mental or intellectual plane" than does SAE (1956:83–84). This would seem to suggest that scientific and spiritual growth depend upon growth of our knowledge of languages. Apparently the "new truth" is but old truth, inhabiting the grammatical forms of languages other than our own. Mr. Everyman confronts this truth as through a glass, darkly, but the scientific linguist sees it face to face.

For Whorf, linguists have the potential to occupy the most exalted of scientific positions: although "no individual is free to describe nature with absolute impartiality . . . the person most nearly free in such respects would be a linguist familiar with very many widely different linguistic systems. As yet no linguist is in any such position" (Whorf 6:214). Yet linguists are further along the path to enlightenment, it would seem, than most ordinary mortals, for "only the science of linguistics has begun to penetrate a little into this realm [of language], its findings still largely unknown to the other disciplines" (Whorf 9:251).

There is a definite "elitist aura" surrounding Whorf's view of the linguist as one who discloses ultimate truths, not unlike, for example, the aura surrounding the practitioners of *phronesis* whom Gadamer so admires. Richard Bernstein claims that Gadamer "softens this elitist aura by blending his discussion of phronesis with his analysis of a type of dialogue and conversation that presupposes mutual respect, recognition, and understanding" (1983:165). Whether or not Gadamer achieves such a softening, I believe that Whorf definitely and deliberately undercuts the elitist aura surrounding the the scientific-linguist-as-seer in texts which suggest that both his readers and his hero-informants are more capable of "dialogue and conversation that presupposes mutual respect, recognition, and understanding" than we might otherwise have supposed. This is significant, given Whorf's parodic antagonism toward Mr. Everyman-as-scientist, and his willingness to view informants as "apparatus" whose role as experimental animals places them in the same category as "good phonographic reproducing devices" and "business machines" (Whorf 7:232).

And it is also necessary if Whorf is to persuade his readers of the value of multilingual consciousness. That is, before they will accept the value of a multilingual consciousness, they need to be convinced that alien languages offer something radically different from, but equal or greater in value than, what their own language offers them. And this means that Whorf must create an image of the alien language (and, by implication, of its speakers) which portrays it as equal or superior to the readers' native tongue. Only such a language—fully equal to one's own in sophistication, but offering radically different or improved perspectives on common experience—would seem worth learning. And only if an alien language seems worth learning would Whorf's readers take the trouble to learn it, and thus to acquire for themselves a multilingual consciousness.

This is why Whorf's image of informant-as-hero is so closely tied to his image of linguist-as-seer, and why both images make sense only if interpreted in terms of the image of their dialogic partner, Mr. Everyman-as-reader. Whorf uses the informant's language in two ways: first, to illustrate its intrinsic human and scientific value; and second, to show the wonderful things that happen when that language intersects with English in the consciousness of a single human being. This to-and-fro movement of double-voiced discourse is always *addressed* to Whorf's scientific readers, in one article after another, and is not a mere exercise in linguistic pyrotechnics. Whorf would not keep trying to communicate with his readers if he were not convinced that they too possessed the capacity for developing a multilingual consciousness. And if his readers possess such a capacity, so too must Whorf's hero-informants, since Whorf has just shown their language to be of equal or superior status to the language of his readers.

It is by such convoluted actions that Whorf works to restore full humanity both to reader and to hero. Evidence for this activity, however, is hardly highlighted in Whorf's comic prose, which is designed to grab his readers' attention through parodic distortion. Rather one needs to look for evidence at the margins of his works, and in the composition (rather than content) of these works.

Let us begin by considering Whorf's 1941 article "Languages and Logic." Although it was one of the original four articles on metalinguistics published in 1949 and reappears in Carroll, and though it is a late text (1941), it is rarely mentioned in critical discussion of Whorf, which tend to focus on better-known pieces such as "The Relation of Habitual Thought and Behavior to Language" or "Language, Mind, and Reality." Even when it is cited, however (as by Holquist [1986:101]), only the explicit theoretical statements are attended to. I believe, however, that paying close attention to the *stylistic composition* of this article—which makes use of, but is not reducible to, the explicit theoretical statements it contains—allows us to see Whorf's restitutive activity as it unfolds.

Fishman voices a common criticism of Whorf when he argues that "we are far more valiant, nimble, experienced and successful strugglers and jugglers with language-and-communication problems than Whorf realized" (1980:33). In "Languages and Logic," however, Whorf recognizes and allows for these skills, even as he begins his presentation by invoking the unimaginative Mr. Everyman. Whorf presents his readers with two sentences: "I pull the branch aside" and "I have an extra toe on my foot." With dramatic exaggeration, he insists that in English these two sentences

> have little similarity . . . we may say that no similarity exists. Common, even scientific, parlance would say that the sentences are

unlike because they are talking about things which are intrinsically unlike. So Mr. Everyman, the natural logician, would be inclined to argue. Formal logic of an older type would perhaps agree with him. If, moreover, we appeal to an impartial scientific English-speaking observer . . . he will be more than likely to confirm the dicta of Mr. Everyman and the logician. (Whorf 8:233)

These initial assertions by Whorf are designed to set up the framework for the demonstration which follows. Indeed, one could argue that the intense hyperbole of the first two paragraphs of this article amounts to "protesting too much." He feels obliged to insist so strongly and steadily on the intrinsic differences between the two sentences because otherwise a thoughtful reader might have time to ponder them at greater length. Whorf's rhetorical strategy in the article—his rhetorical sleight of hand—involves bamboozling his readers into adopting the uncritical, unimaginative attitude of Mr. Everyman, for whom things belong to clear-cut categories based on intrinsic similarity and difference, and for whom there are no gray areas, no ambiguities of classification.

Having, at least provisionally, persuaded readers to adopt this attitude, Whorf then turns to data from Shawnee, which he uses to demonstrate that in this language, the two statements "are closely similar; in fact, they differ only at the tail end" (Whorf 8:234). He breaks the Shawnee sentences down into their component morphemes, they key one of which is *l'θawa,* "a common Shawnee term, denoting a forked outline." At this point (at least for me the first time I read the article, and for my students every time I assign it) sudden insight dawns, the smokescreen of arguments about Mr. Everyman's opinions evaporates, and readers are not surprised to discover, by the end of the paragraph, that "the first sentence means 'I pull it (something like branch of tree) more open or apart where it forks,' " and that the second sentence "can mean only 'I have an extra toe forking out like a branch from a normal toe' " (Whorf 8:234). The shock of insight is intensified by the fact that, in the Carroll volume, we must turn the page to find the discussion of the Shawnee sentences, together with a sketch of forked outlines (see Figure 3, p. 103).

Building on this shock of insight whose intensity his style has done so much to encourage, Whorf goes on to remark, "Shawnee logicians and observers would class the two phenomena as intrinsically similar." Again, he seems to be suggesting that English speakers and Shawnee speakers, by virtue of the grammar of their respective languages, are forced to make relative-absolutistic judgments as to similarities and differences between phenomena, and that, as a consequence, neither is able to detect or articulate the point of view recognized by the other. This, of course, is well in keeping with linguistic determinism. But then, what are we to make of the very next sentence? "Our own observer, to whom we tell all this, focuses his instruments again upon the two phenomena and to his joy sees at once a manifest resemblance" (Whorf 8:235).

Mr. Everyman, the dull, unimaginative, uncritical slave to his own grammar, has only to be presented with an alternative way of viewing trees and toes, and he sees "at once" a resemblance between them! One is bound to ask how strong a hold his English grammar had on his thought processes for such instantaneous insight to be possible. To be sure, in Whorf's scenario, it took a linguist to provide him with evidence from Shawnee before the insight could occur. However, one may ask whether such insight depends on intervention by linguists, or whether ordinary folk might be capable of it on their own. Are "average monolinguals," for example, so passive in their thinking that they must be prodded from the outside before they can entertain an alternative view of the world? Whorf's Mr. Everyman represents just such a passive figure. His characteristics were undoubtedly influenced by the behavioristic psychology in vogue at the time Whorf wrote, whose views the positivist in him wanted to endorse. In such a scientific climate, making Mr. Everyman the passive recipient of stimuli beyond his control no doubt contributed scientific respectability to Whorf's account of the relationship between language and thought.

And yet, the rhetorical structure of this text depends for its effect on readers who are not passive. Whorf's intense argument in defense of a passive, unquestioning Mr. Everyman is designed to bank the critical imagination in his readers, all the better to rekindle it when he decides to dazzle them with his Shawnee evidence. To be sure, Whorf goes on to state, in the discourse of relative absolutism, that the "point of view of linguistic relativity changes Mr. Everyman's dictum: Instead of saying, 'Sentences are unlike because they tell about unlike facts,' he now reasons: 'Facts are unlike to speakers whose language background provides for unlike formulation of them' (Whorf 8:235). And yet the readers' *experience* in reading this text, and grasping instantaneously the Shawnee speaker's point of view, flatly disallows any such narrow, relatively absolutistic conclusion! For English speakers with no knowledge of Shawnee, equipped only with a simple sketch of a forked outline and the barest of glosses on two Shawnee sentences, have been able to grasp instantaneously that trees and toes are like and unlike at the same time.

Moreover, without Whorf's initial attempt to persuade them otherwise, it is highly likely that these same readers, on their own, would immediately have begun looking for similarities between the phenomena represented in the two English sentences as soon as they were alerted to the possibility that such resemblances might exist.

Whorf's implicit faith in the imaginative powers of Mr. Everyman, despite his explicit denials of such powers, also appears in his article "Linguistics as an Exact Science," in a discussion of second-language learning. In this context, he argues that when a "youth begins to learn a foreign language" the sound patterns of his native tongue inhibit his learning the sound patterns of a second language, and "constantly block" his attempts to speak fluently. However, Whorf assures us, these blocks could be removed if the foreign language were taught by a "theoretic linguist," who will explain the patterns of English phonology to him "in such a way [in what way, exactly?] that they become semiconscious, with the result that they lose the binding power over him which custom has given them, though they remain automatic as far as English is concerned. Then he acquires the French patterns without inner opposition, and the time for attaining command of the language is cut to a fraction" (Whorf 7:225).

Here again, the second-language learner, another Mr. Everyman, is presented as passively enslaved to the sound patterns of his native tongue until the theoretic linguist shows him that they are only learned patterns, and that French has different patterns. As with the Shawnee example, so too in this case the reader/learner has but to be presented with the evidence of an alternative pattern to grasp its significance so completely that, in Whorf's optimistic phrase, "he acquires the French patterns without inner opposition."

It is worth noting in this case that for Whorf the unmentioned but assumed locus of second-language learning is the classroom, and the learner is assumed to be a monolingual English speaker. That is to say, Whorf allows us to make these middle-class American assumptions (based on the experience of his assumed readers) without suggesting second-language learning might be different for people in different social and cultural circumstances. The rhetorical justification for his doing so might be that, as in the Shawnee case, it allows him to intensify the shock of insight achieved under circumstances which would severely militate against it. But, if in these restricted and highly artificial circumstances, instantaneous insight into the patterns of another language is still possible, how much more likely would such insight be in situations where the second language was learned not in the classroom with a linguist as instructor, but among native speakers who might serve as both teachers and sources of data; not via drills on vocabulary and syntax, but through conversation and practical activity? Whorf is characteristically silent on such possibilities, but he never explicitly denies that they could occur.

It is also worth noting Whorf's characteristic reliance on *grasping intellectually* the alien grammatical pattern. To any English-speaking reader who has actually studied French, Whorf's account of the way in which mastery of the French sound system is acquired is laughable. It is *not* enough merely to understand *mentally* the principles behind French sound patterns. Students need also to practice producing them *physically,* and mastery is frequently a long time coming. Again, Whorf studiously avoids messy encounters with languages as they are actually used by their flesh-and-blood speakers. He seems most comfortable in a classroom setting, where grammar seems to pass cleanly from mind to mind, totally bypassing actual practical encounters between student and native speaker as concrete human beings. This seems especially true when language learning requires contact between a learner and an informant who are divided by acute political and social differences, as Whorf and his Native American informants were divided. Whorf's preference is for spiritual communion without physical contact. He seems most comfortable when languages relate to one another Platonically, as opposed to the rough and ready "cohabitation" of languages which Bakhtin connects with polyglossia and heteroglossia (1981c[1940]:291; 1981b[1940]:67). This preference, of course, provides ammunition for those who would charge Whorf with "mysticism."

Perhaps the most sustained attempt by Whorf to cultivate in his readers the shock of discovery occurs in one of his most famous and controversial articles, "The Punctual and Segmentative Aspects of Verbs in Hopi." Unlike "Languages and Logic" with its simple Shawnee example, or "Linguistics as an Exact Science" with its sketchy discussion of French, this article presents the reader with a rich corpus of Hopi data, together with Whorf's grammatical analysis.

In this article, Whorf does not begin by invoking Mr. Everyman. Perhaps because this article was published in a professional journal, that rhetorical strategy was inappropriate. However, for modern readers (particularly students or nonlinguists), the difficulty of mastering Hopi grammar is powerfully suggested in the first few paragraphs of the article, where Whorf discusses Hopi's nine voices and nine aspects in a daunting professional jargon. Just, however, as the readers' brains are about to seize up from attempting to figure out what the distinction between "passive," "semipassive," and "extended passive" voice might mean, and their eyes are beginning to glaze over as they attempt to decipher Whorf's description of the formation of the segmentative aspect ("the phenomenon denoted in the root, shown in the punctual aspect as manifested about a point, becomes manifested as a series of repeated interconnected segments of one large phenomenon of a stretched-out segmental character, its extension usually being predominantly in one dimension, indifferently of space or time or both"), he presents us with concrete examples—and insight is immediate.

Not only do we grasp instantly the pattern of formation of the segmentative aspect; Whorf's glosses also allow us instantly to see connections between punctual phenomena and the segmentative phenomena built on the same verb forms. And, as in the Shawnee example from "Languages and Logic," whereas the paired Hopi punctual-segmentative expressions demonstrate the *similarity Hopi recognizes* between punctual and segmentative phenomena, Whorf's English glosses for these expressions seem designed to demonstrate the *differences English recognizes* between the same phenomena: e.g., "It is bent in a rounded angle" (punctual) contrasted with "It lies in a meandering line, making successive rounded angles" (segmentative); or "It forms a sharp acute angle" (punctual) contrasted with "It is zigzag" (segmentative); or "It is notched" (punctual) contrasted with "It is serrated" (segmentative).

It would have been perfectly possible to draw upon the resources of English to gloss these expressions in a manner which would have emphasized Hopi-English similarities: e.g., "It is curved" and "It forms a curvy line," or "It forms a sharp acute angle" and "It forms a sequence of sharp acute angles," or "It is notched" and "It forms a series of notches along an edge," or something of the sort. Yet Whorf chose instead to use English expressions which, though faithful to Hopi meanings, were rendered in a fashion that would obscure the possibility that English speakers might also be able to recognize and describe in their own tongue the same similarities the Hopi recognize and express in theirs.

Again, I would like to suggest that Whorf chose to gloss the Hopi expressions as he did, and to preface his presentation of the Hopi data with impenetrable linguistic jargon, not only in order to highlight the contrast between the way Hopi speakers and English speakers describe the "same" recognizable phenomena. He also wanted to emphasize the complex, technical vocabulary (controllable, one presumes, only by scientific linguists) needed to capture in English those distinctions which, in Hopi, can be made simply and effortlessly by ordinary speakers. And though this maneuver succeeds brilliantly as a rhetorical strategy, making "The Punctual and Segmentative Aspects of Verbs in Hopi" one of the best texts introductory students of anthropological linguistics can be assigned, it also leads one to question whether, apart from the classroom situation, the linguist's contribution is more hindrance than help. One wonders whether ordinary English speakers, living with the Hopi and learning the Hopi language in the context of everyday life, might not come to grasp the punctual and segmentative aspects of verbs more quickly and with much less fanfare.

To sum up, the elitist statements Whorf makes about the scientific linguist's privileged insight into linguistic relativity are belied by the presupposition—evident on stylistic grounds—that his readers can be trusted to possess and exercise the same critical faculties he possesses. In this connection, it is important to remember that four of his articles (including "Linguistics as an Exact Science" and "Languages and Logic") were written for nonlinguists. This fact, rather than being taken as evidence that such articles belong outside the Whorfian canon, might just as well be taken as evidence of Whorf's faith in the imaginative capacities of lay people. And even if the lay audience for which he usually wrote consisted of graduates of MIT, a rather elite group, these were nevertheless technologically minded types, who might indeed be viewed as a particularly resistant group of natural logicians, Mr. Everymen of the most sophisticated kind.

In the texts we have just examined, Whorf moves back and forth between Native American languages and English in an effort to demonstrate experientially, without defining verbally, what a multilingual consciousness is like. Only for his theosophical audience does he try to describe explicitly the essence of multilingual consciousness, in the article, "Language, Mind, and Reality." Yet he must mix the languages of science, art, and religion in his attempt to construct his direct authorial word.

> To very few is it granted to attain such consciousness as a durable state; yet many mathematicians and scientific linguists must have had the experience of "seeing" in one fugitive flash, a whole system of relationships never before suspected of forming a unity, [an experience which] momentarily overwhelms one in a flood of aesthetic delight. (Whorf 9:254)

Rollins (1980) has emphasized more than any of Whorf's critics the systematic effort Whorf makes in this article to translate his insights about language into, as Whorf himself puts it, "philosophical Sanskrit terms" (Whorf 9:252). In doing so, Whorf does not repudiate science. At the same time he risks failing to convey his respect for science. Indeed, just as scientific audiences are alienated by his "mystical" voice, he risks alienating a theosophical audience if he uses his "scientific" voice. He must therefore adopt double-voiced discourse in addressing them as well.

An example of this discourse occurs in the following discussion of idiomatic usage in science and logic:

> When a word like "group" can refer either to a sequence of phases in time or a pile of articles on the floor, its element of reference is minor. Referents of scientific words are often conveniently vague, markedly under the sway of the patterns in which they occur. It is very suggestive that this trait, so far from being a hallmark of Babbittry, is most marked in intellectual talk, and—*mirabile dictu*—in the language of poetry and love. And this needs must be so, for science, poetry, and love are alike in being "flights" above and away from the slave-world of literal reference and humdrum prosaic details, attempts to widen the petty narrowness of the personal self's outlook, liftings toward *Arupa,* toward that world of infinite harmony, sympathy and order, of unchanging truths and eternal things. . . . reference is the lesser part of meaning, patternment is the greater. (Whorf 9:260–61)

A key concept in this passage is *patternment.* Whorf's fullest definition of this concept can be found in "Linguistics as an Exact Science" (Whorf 7:226):

> the formula for the English monosyllabic word. . . . looks mathematical, but it isn't. It is an expression of pattern symbolics, an analytical method that grows out of linguistics and bears to linguistics a relation not unlike that of higher mathematics to physics. . . . the operations here are not addition, multiplication, and so on, but are meanings that apply to linguistic contexts. From these operations, conclusions can be drawn and experimental attacks directed intelligently at the really crucial points in the welter of data presented by the language under investigation. . . . Pattern-symbolic expressions are exact, as mathematics is, but are not quantitative. They do no refer ultimately to number and dimension, as mathematics does, but to pattern and structure. Nor are they to be confused

with theory of groups or with symbolic logic, though they may be in some ways akin.

Patternment is as exact as mathematics, but it is not mathematics. Nor is it identical with symbolic logic. Both mathematics and symbolic logic, however, have been taken by formal linguists as models for the analysis of language. Grammar is orderly for Whorf, but this is the order of patternment, not the order of mathematics or logic. And yet he wants patternment to be as subtle, flexible, complete, and noncontradictory as mathematics or logic. His scenario of linguistic research suggests this: the scientific linguist devises elegant, consistent patterns which are then tested against the data gathered, of are offered to an informant, whose role is to confirm or deny their acceptability. But this is acceptability in a narrow sense—grammatical acceptability. Whorf asks nothing about social acceptability in various sociolinguistic contexts, nor does he allow his informants to comment on such matters. As long as such commentary is censored, Whorf can preserve the image of language as a noncontradictory set of subtle patterns—orderly and harmonious. He can allow his mystical-minded readers to associate this "patternment" with their own nonscientific concept of cosmic order.

But mystical enlightenment is supposed to take one beyond "the slave-world of literal reference and humdrum prosaic details." It should therefore take us beyond the territory of formal linguistics, beyond "grammar" as traditionally conceived. When it does so, however, and we gain insight into another language's conception of reality, *there is nothing to limit our understanding to matters of "literal reference and humdrum prosaic detail."* Furthermore, *there is nothing to prevent us from making anything we learn our own, by reaccenting it in the tones of our own language.*

Hard-pressed, Whorf addresses this issue a few pages later in the same article, in a discussion of the Coeur d'Alene language:

> If, given a more sophisticated culture, their thinkers erected these now unconscious discriminations into a theory of triadic causality, fitted to scientific observations, they might thereby produce a valuable intellectual tool for science. WE could imitate artifically such a theory, perhaps, but we could NOT apply it, for WE are not habituated to making such distinctions with effortless ease in daily life. Concepts have a basis in daily talk before scientific workers will attempt to use them in the laboratory. Even relativity has such a basis in the western Indo-European languages (and others)—the

> fact that these languages use many space words and patterns for dealing with time. (Whorf 9:266)

Once again, Whorf comes extraordinarily close to affirming the existence of heteroglossia. But he stops short; his use of capital letters alerts us to his nervousness. In this passage he sounds remarkably like Voloshinov, who was so eager to root the poet's authentic word within the bounds of his group, and language, of origin; who wanted to argue that a poet who tries to speak anything else is bound to be inauthentic. And so Western scientists attempting to apply Coeur d'Alene theories of causality must be seen as somehow inauthentic as they do so, because their own society did not develop the theories in question. At best, the poor Western scientist is permitted to "imitate artificially" this theory, which, Whorf assures us, is different from "applying it." Applying it would seem to require Voloshinov's "choral support"; without such support, the effort, like the poet's voice, must fail.

And yet, any new theory, originating within or outside a group of Western scientists, seems "inauthentic" at first. Traditional scientists confronted with a radical new theory must make an effort to understand it, must practice the techniques it requires, if they are to apply it competently. This element—effort, practice, physical and mental rehearsal—is as missing here as it is absent in Whorf's discussion of the mastery of French phonology. Nothing new, not even the language one learns at one's mother's knee, becomes effortless without practice, as any parents who have watched their toddlers struggle with phonology and syntax can testify. It is exactly this sort of effort, this sort of practical activity, that made Whorf an expert in the alien languages he studied. He had, after all, to *study* them. Insight was not always immediate; or, if immediate, it could not be sustained without his making an effort to *learn* the new patterns well enough to retain them for future use. And when one practices that which is new and alien, it has the inevitable tendency to become old and familiar. The distinction between artificial imitation and genuine practice blurs. What is more, Whorf is aware that we are not dependent on alien grammars to supply us with new perspectives. In a final remark, phrased as a hasty afterthought, Whorf allows that metaphorical activity *within* a language (which he elsewhere condemns as a "confusion of thought" [Whorf 4:144]) can supply alternative points of view which are just as challenging to standard opinions as the points of view of outsiders!

Thus, even with a religious-minded audience, we find Whorf choosing to speak in a monological language about dialogical matters. While this language is different from the language of science, and permits him to speak freely on matters which science would censor, it is equally incapable of articulating Whorf's direct authorial word. It is as if an audience of theosophists would be no less offended than an audience of scientists to learn that their concept of a single truth—of "infinite harmony, sympathy and order, of unchanging truths and eternal things"—might be inadequate for, or hostile to, the kind of multilingual consciousness Whorf was advocating. And so he employs equally tortuous prose to avoid accusations of transgression.

With an audience of scientists, by contrast, Whorf doesn't waste time preaching about multilingual consciousness and the overwhelming "flood of aesthetic delight" it makes possible. Rather, in articles like "The Punctual and Segmentative Aspects of Verbs in Hopi," he manipulates style in order to *force* his readers to develop a multilingual consciousness whether they like it or not. Thus these articles are not just texts. For each reader, they simultaneously become events to be reckoned with. As with Dostoevsky according to Bakhtin, "what unfolds in his works is not a multitude of characters and fates in a single objective world, illuminated by a single authorial consciousness; rather a *plurality of consciousnesses, with equal rights and each with its own world,* combine but are not merged in the unity of the event" (1984[1929]:6).

Whorf's texts create *events* for his readers. These texts therefore cannot be understood fully without taking into consideration the nature of the events they trigger in readers every time they are read. One may ask whether Whorf's religious predilections led him to favor the mystical visions of a favored few over the everyday imaginative insights of the many. But if such predilections abide in his explicit statements about Mr. Everyman, they are contradicted by an implicit stylistic structure that makes use of these statements for other purposes. Scientific readers, as Whorf views them, have at least two faces. One is what readers *are*— passive Mr. Everymen—and what they will remain so long as they accept life as complacent monolinguals. The other is what readers may *become* as soon as they reject complacency and risk developing an enlightened multilingual consciousness. Whorf's texts are designed to assist that becoming, to serve as exercises for a sluggish, passive consciousness, to limber that consciousness up and force it into imaginative action almost in spite of itself.

It is instructive to compare Whorf's approach to imaginative insight with that of other linguists attempting to deal with the same phenomenon. Paul Friedrich, for example, is, as we saw earlier, hostile to the "mystical" and "theological" elements he detects in Whorf. And yet, in place of the implicit opposition between science and religion which Whorf's work is supposed to mediate, Friedrich proposes an opposition between science and art. As I noted, Friedrich is sympathetic to Whorf's intentions insofar as these promote awareness of aesthetic patterning in language. What he objects to is taking the further step of concluding that aesthetic patterning is somehow total and inscribed in the grain of the universe.

What is left if one accepts the idea of *partial* patterning which invites the experience of " 'seeing' in one fugitive flash, a whole system of relationships," an experience which "momentarily overwhelms one in a flood of aesthetic delight"? For Friedrich, what is left is art—poetry, in fact: "Poetic language, in sum, is the locus of the most interesting differences between languages and should be the focus of study of such differences" (1986:17). In place of the scientific linguist, he promotes the poet as seer:

> It is the out-and-out poet—whether or not he/she writes it down— who most condenses the teleonomy of language as a quintessential fact of life, as part of an unusually dynamic and fragile point of view—fragile because the medium verges on disintegration or becomes the message. Of course, this is making a special claim for the poet and the poet's language . . . but it also corresponds to a definite reality. (Friedrich 1986:154)

Friedrich emphasizes the aesthetic imagination of individuals, arguing that the poetic creativity of individuals constitutes exactly that aspect of language that is untranslatable, and thus relative not only to a language but to the imagination of a particular person. Friedrich does not entirely neglect language as a group phenomenon. However, he tends to view it monolithically: "the world is uniquely symbolized by a language" (1986:53). Thus, he ignores heteroglossia. He speaks of the language of the group as though it were an individual poetic imagination writ large: "The ways *one poet or tradition* selects, changes, and transposes from another tests, perhaps most sensitively, the coupled hypotheses of linguistic relativism and poetic indeterminacy" (1986:53; emphasis added), and "the metalinguistic and language-using capacities of *any one imagination or culture* are disturbed by the fact that language itself is constantly changing . . ." (1986:143; emphasis added).

Such a manner of speaking about the intersubjective dimensions of language is similar to Whorf's in the way it silently passes over contestation among speakers for control of the terms of debate *within* as well as *across* languages. One may question, however—as Bakhtin questions—whether the only relevant phenomena in the study of language are the individual, on one hand, and "the" language, or culture, or tradition, on the other, even if both are seen as partly chaotic, shot through with radical alterity. Friedrich seems aware that he might be accused of overemphasizing individuality when he concedes that his view corresponds only to "a" definite reality. That there may be other dimensions to reality which are reducible neither to the poetic subjectivity of the individual nor to the determinism of a totalizing linguistic system is not explicitly ruled out, but Friedrich tells us nothing about them.

This same neglect is equally conspicuous in Chatterjee's "solution" to the linguistic relativity problem. Once one abandons the totalizing metaphors of structuralist linguistics, he argues, "as there is no more an encapsulated whole, the relativity-engendering bounds between one language and another disappear, but may crop up between two statements in the same language, between any two statements at all" (1985:54–55). Recognizing that "the dissolution of cross-linguistic relativity in post-structuralist terms results in the appearance of a pervasive *intralinguistic* relativity" (1985:56), he then moves to dissolve the source of the poetic subjectivity Friedrich defends by denying the possibility of an ego possessed of such subjectivity. "Only if one posits an ego, of course, can one speak in terms of a world view or *Weltanschauung* for collections of egos that form speech communities" (1985:58). Thus, he concludes, "if language can be seen as an open-ended series of intersubjective language games, it need have no representation at the individual or communal level. Without such a representation, there is no question of a represented structure on the basis of which one language may be said to be relative to another" (1985:58).

Thus, Chatterjee refuses to recognize polyglossia, heteroglossia, and even the idiolect. It would be fortunate indeed if problems of cross-cultural and cross-linguistic understanding could so easily be defined out of existence. For anyone with significant cross-cultural or cross-linguistic experience, however, Chatterjee's image of the human sociolinguistic world is unrecognizable. His readiness to conceive of speech communities as "collections of egos" betrays an atomistic view of human existence which cannot be sustained without violating his own experience. After all, the English words he writes are not his personal invention, but originated in the mouths and texts of others, with whom he must struggle if he is to make them serve his own intentions. He is thus dependent on others both for the words themselves, and for responses to his use of the words. This is true for every item of culture or language in his life.

Nothing human in his life would be possible for the egoless creature he describes whose identity has no anchor in anything since it does not exist to begin with. Such an image of a human being has a certain nihilistic poststructuralist panache: if self, culture, language, and history are not everything, then they are nothing. But to subscribe to such an image of human nature means to make oneself blind and deaf to broad classes of everyday human experience. Dispensing with polyglossia and heteroglossia, for example, leaves Chatterjee helpless to deal with the concrete, patterned degrees of comprehensibility and incomprehensibility that unite and divide any two people who attempt to communicate with one another. In fact, he is unable to point to any factor which would make most human interaction predictable (as it is), rather than random.

Chatterjee is right to criticize totalizing conceptualizations of language and culture, and to emphasize that individuals can never be totally aware of, or in control of, the various forces at work upon them. But he must not therefore dismiss the very real and active efforts that people make, individually and collectively, in the direction of greater self-consciousness and control, resulting in those social practices and products which we imperfectly call cultures, languages, modes of discourse, grammars, and selves.

And once we begin to pay attention to individuals—be they linguists or poets or decentered subjects in search of coherent selfhood—we may ask again whether the privileged insights of the favored few are indeed so privileged as has been asserted. Perhaps there is not really such a great gulf between the insight attainable by professional seers and the insights of which ordinary alert speakers of a language are capable. Even if we grant that critical faculties become highly refined among such specialists, this need not entail denying them altogether to Mr. Everyman.

The issue at stake is the *status* of that form of consciousness in which one is able to see, in a fugitive flash, "a whole system of relationships never before suspected of forming a unity." The question is the nature, or rarity, of this experience which "momentarily overwhelms one in a flood of aesthetic delight." Whorf explicitly would like to restrict such consciousness to "very few"—and yet he qualifies this immediately by pointing out that he means the ability "to attain such consciousness *as a durable state*" (Whorf 9:254, emphasis added). Such a way of putting things does suggest someone in a permanent trance state, constantly seeing truth face to face, never dropping back into the unreflective consciousness supposedly characteristic of everyday life. Friedrich, too, while not denying a spark of poetic consciousness to everyone—and, indeed, likening the art of the poet to that of ordinary children learning their native tongues (1986:154)—does, as we saw, wish to emphasize the special status of poets, presumably because, in their own individual, partial ways, they are able better than others to maintain their poetic consciousness as a durable state.

But is there such a sharp divide between the unreflective consciousness of Mr. Everyman and the critical self-consciousness of the poet or mystic? Put another way, how difficult is it to make the switch from the unreflective consciousness of everyday practice to that critical self-consciousness which calls everyday practices into question, or views them in a new light? Whorf's rhetorical practices suggest that he believed the switch could be made quite easily for the multilingual, and he deliberately structured his texts in order to create a multilingual event in the consciousness of his readers. But, as we have seen, according to Bakhtin the experience of heteroglossia is equally capable of generating multilingual consciousness.

We have suggested that one of the reasons why Whorf himself avoided analysis of heteroglossia was precisely his need to shake his readers out of the complacent assumption that nonspecialists like themselves already possessed everything they needed for understanding someone else's language. Of course, to the extent that this "understanding" involved nothing more than reducing alien concepts to the standard words and phrases of positivistic English discourse, they *were* wrong, and Whorf *was* right. But a less reductionist and more imaginative approach to heteroglossia *is* possible, even though it is equally unpalatable to positivists. As the recent work of Lakoff and Johnson (1980) has shown, ordinary speakers of a single language can make differential use of its resources to construct different ways of viewing the world through the use of *metaphor*.

Like Whorf and Friedrich, Lakoff and Johnson take into account the "flood of aesthetic delight" that has been associated with the privileged insight of the mystic or poet. For them, however, this is a commonplace experience which occurs every time we grasp the entailments of an apt metaphor:

> The result is a large and coherent network of entailments, which may, on the whole, either fit or not fit our experiences. . . . when the network does fit, the experiences form a coherent whole as instances of the metaphor. *What we experience with such a metaphor is a kind of reverberation down through the network of entailments* that awakens and connects our memories of our past . . . experi-

ences and serves as a possible guide for future ones. (1980:140; emphasis added)

If we begin our analysis from this point of view, then such articles by Whorf as "Languages and Logic" and "The Punctual and Segmentative Aspects of Verbs in Hopi" can be read as extended lessons about, and demonstrations of, the power of metaphorical understanding. And it is a radical demonstration, because it pretends to reach to the very foundations of our way of viewing the world. Here again, Whorf's ambivalence about metaphorical understanding is fascinating. On the one hand, he condemns it as leading to a "confusion of thought" when it occurs interior to one's own language (as when English speaks metaphorically of time as if it were a material commodity) (Whorf 4:144). On the other hand, he highlights it, and works rhetorically to enhance its effect, when trying to promote in his readers insights into someone else's language![2]

Friedrich, interestingly enough, is also ambivalent about the nature of metaphor, but he criticizes attempts to use it as a "master trope" in this foundational way, wishing to restrict it to being merely one of a series of tropes to which a poet, within his own language, may have recourse (1986:3–4).

Whorf's rhetoric suggests that we cannot have "new" thoughts unless they are already present as "old" grammatical forms of a language other than our mother tongue. Only if this were the case would the study of non-SAE languages and propagation of information about their grammatical forms take on the central significance Whorf would like to attribute to them. But it also makes us wonder where—if not via metaphor—language finds the internal resources to elaborate new structures for itself in the presence of new "felt needs," if some other group's grammar is not introduced to provide them.

3 Whorfian Nonverbal Rhetoric
The Drawings

Is cross-linguistic, or cross-cultural, understanding dependent upon words alone? We have seen that those most critical of the "strong version of the Whorfian hypothesis" based their criticism on what they took to be an irrefutable argument: if the grammar of one's native language is monolithic and deterministic, then Whorf should never have been able to learn Hopi, much less translate Hopi grammatical patterns into terms a native speaker of English could understand. The persuasiveness of this argument relies on the assumption that translation and understanding are identical, and can be accomplished only via language. In my analysis of Whorf's verbal style, however, I have suggested that Whorf's ability to convey the meaning of Hopi patterns to his English-speaking readers has almost nothing to do with literal word-for-word or sentence-for-sentence translation (even assuming such a procedure is possible, which is doubtful). Instead, after having prepared his readers to receive it (using the various techniques we have just disclosed), Whorf simply presents them with juxtaposed Native American data and carefully phrased English glosses. He then relies on his readers' presumed capacity for figurative understanding to do the rest. The outcome of this strategy is an event in the mind of the reader: the experience of multilingual consciousness.

If this is truly what Whorf is trying to accomplish, it is then possible to account for one other aspect of his texts that is usually ignored when it is not denigrated: the drawings which appear in the articles "Science and Linguistics," "Linguistics as an Exact Science," and "Languages and Logic." Why did Whorf accompany serious discussion of linguistic matters with these "naive little drawings" as Floyd Lounsbury (in Hoijer 1954:268) called them? Did they not merely show in graphic form matters that could equally well be described verbally—for example, that

Hopi has one word to refer to what English speakers distinguish as airplanes, aviators, and dragonflies (Whorf 6:210; see Figure 1)? Or may they be dismissed as visual aids to a lay audience that professional linguists could do without? After all, the three articles concerned were all published originally for the *Technology Review* at MIT.

Christopher Norris, who equates Whorf's "relativism" with linguistic determinism, bases his criticism of it in part on "the loose but (in practice) indispensable conviction that we know far more than relativist doctrine allows us to know" (1985:216). I believe that the drawings accompanying Whorf's texts can be plausibly interpreted as one means he employs precisely in order to suggest how it is that linguists (or alert, critical observers in general) can know more than relative absolutism allows them to know. The drawings are a significant clue for readers that understanding *cannot* be reduced to verbal translation alone. We *do* know far more than linguistic determinism would allow us to know, because what we understand cannot be reduced to literal rules of grammar, but depends significantly on figurative imagination. And figurative imagination can do its role properly only when the context of speech is made explicit, and related to the words being uttered.

I have argued above that Whorf's texts can be seen to depend for their rhetorical effect upon readers who can become critical of their taken-for-granted concepts. The drawings that accompany articles written for lay readers are a second rhetorical means Whorf employs to encourage these readers to rethink their habitual modes of perception. In fact, he is engaging in what has become a common poststructuralist practice. As Elizabeth Bruss notes, for some contemporary theorists, "graphic display seems to be a way of transcending language. . . . Theoretical discourse resorts to graphics when it grows impatient with or suspicious of language" (1982:123).

Why should writers hope to transcend the limits of language by resorting to pictures? This move seems to be based on the conviction that written words can describe reality only in a roundabout manner, whereas pictures can capture reality directly. In semiotic terms, words are arbitrary symbols, whereas pictures are icons. Charles Sanders Peirce identified three types of sign: the symbol, the index, and the icon. Symbols are related arbitrarily to what they represent; indexes (such as a pointing finger) are related existentially to what they represent (by being copresent and cotemporal with, and close enough to, what they represent for representation to be unproblematic). Icons, however, are related to what they represent by resemblance. The great value of an icon, according to Peirce, "is that by the direct observation of it other truths concerning its object can be discovered than those which suffice to determine its construction" (1932:158). Or, as Wendy Steiner puts it, "This richness in iconic signs—metaphors, analogies, models, diagrams, pictures, and so forth—allows a system to be explored in all its relations and implications, even if these tend to undermine the original thrust of the iconic formulation" (1982:1). Whorf used pictures in his written texts, I submit, precisely *because* they tended to undermine the original thrust of the iconic formulation. He depended on the fact that, again in Steiner's words, "the fit between picture and pictured is so much more extensive than between word and reference that the picture is often confused with the world it pictures" (1982:142)[1]

I believe Whorf included these drawings because he was convinced that the key to cross-linguistic (and cross-cultural) understanding is less a matter of shared grammar than a matter of potentially shareable nonverbal experiences, i.e., of *context*. One way to encourage cross-cultural understanding may involve words: Whorf employed verbal techniques in the content and stylistic structure of the articles we have just studied. But shared nonverbal contextual experiences are equally important for such understanding. By including in his texts drawings which attempt to reproduce for his readers certain potentially shareable nonverbal experiences, Whorf chose the only method available to him in the format of a written essay to introduce this essential contextual element.

If this is so, then we may argue that Whorf's texts—the texts with drawings in particular—support a distinction between translation and understanding similar to the one George Lakoff has recently made: "Accurate *translation* requires close correspondences across conceptual schemes; *understanding* only requires correspondences in well-structured experiences and a common conceptualizing capacity" (1987:312). Understanding of any sophistication, of course, is unlikely to occur without the help of words. But one's understanding may exceed one's ability—especially at the moment when insight is experienced—to plumb the resources of one's native language to find the words which will articulate that understanding in a satisfactory way. Finding the right words to express new insights is rarely a simple matter—for ordinary people, poets, novelists, or ethnographers. The thrill of the multilingual event is the discovery that someone else, in some other language, has found those words and is offering them to you. Indeed the insight you experience accompanies your acceptance of the words offered. And acceptance is possible only because you and the giver are together in a single context meaningful to you both (cf. Bakhtin 1981c[1940]:282).

Whorf includes drawings in order to create a single context that will include *both* his English-speaking readers *and* his heroes, the speakers of Hopi or Shawnee. Sometimes this nonverbal context is fairly straightforward (as with the drawing that illustrates three objects referred to by a single Hopi word, but which require separate words in English; see Figure 1).

Often, however, the context we are intended to share is more complex and ambiguous. Consider, for example, the matrix representing certain "objective" visual features of context which, once we see them with our own eyes, are supposed to illuminate the "contrast between a 'temporal' language (English) and a 'timeless' language (Hopi)" in "Science and Linguistics" (Whorf 6:213; see Figure 2).

Or consider the shared context created by the sketch of a forked outline or a mass of disembodied spots or stripes in "Languages and Logic" (Whorf 8:234; see Figure 3). English speakers and Shawnee speakers, confronting these visual stimuli together, at the same time, should be able to grasp their meaning, and therefore, should be able to

Figure 10. Languages classify items of experience differently. The class corresponding to one word and one thought in language A may be regarded by language B as two or more classes corresponding to two or more words and thoughts.

Figure 1. Whorf's original illustration, and caption, to accompany the article "Science and Linguistics" (Whorf 6:210)

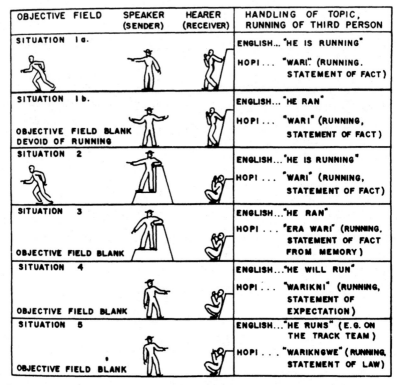

OBJECTIVE FIELD	SPEAKER (SENDER)	HEARER (RECEIVER)	HANDLING OF TOPIC, RUNNING OF THIRD PERSON
SITUATION I a.			ENGLISH... "HE IS RUNNING"
			HOPI ... "WARI" (RUNNING. STATEMENT OF FACT)
SITUATION I b. OBJECTIVE FIELD BLANK DEVOID OF RUNNING			ENGLISH... "HE RAN" HOPI ... "WARI" (RUNNING, STATEMENT OF FACT)
SITUATION 2			ENGLISH... "HE IS RUNNING" HOPI ... "WARI" (RUNNING, STATEMENT OF FACT)
SITUATION 3 OBJECTIVE FIELD BLANK			ENGLISH... "HE RAN" HOPI ... "ERA WARI" (RUNNING. STATEMENT OF FACT FROM MEMORY)
SITUATION 4 OBJECTIVE FIELD BLANK			ENGLISH... "HE WILL RUN" HOPI ... "WARIKNI" (RUNNING, STATEMENT OF EXPECTATION)
SITUATION 5 OBJECTIVE FIELD BLANK			ENGLISH... "HE RUNS" (E.G. ON THE TRACK TEAM) HOPI ... "WARIKNGWE" (RUNNING, STATEMENT OF LAW)

Figure 11.   Contrast between a "temporal" language (English) and a "timeless" language (Hopi).   What are to English differences of time are to Hopi differences in the kind of validity.

Figure 2.   Whorf's original illustration, and caption, to accompany the article "Science and Linguistics" (Whorf 6:213)

grasp the meaning of grammatical forms which depend on them. Without such shared visual experience, however, we would be reduced to relying on words alone to spark insight. And such insight might be long in coming since, as Whorf points out, these "linguistic concepts . . . are not easily definable" (Whorf 8:234).

Nowhere does Whorf explicitly invite reader and hero to meet together in a shared setting whose features they may then compare and contrast, using traditional categories of their native tongues. Yet that such was his implicit aim, and that the drawings are central to achieving that aim, is suggested in an article that appeared in a scholarly publication without accompanying illustrations: "Gestalt Technique of Stem

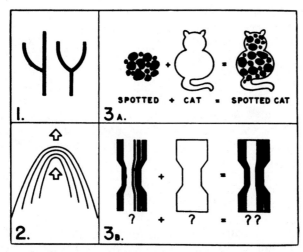

Figure 15. Suggested above are certain linguistic concepts which, as explained in the text, are not easily definable.

Figure 3.   Whorf's original illustration, and caption, to accompany the article "Languages and Logic" (Whorf 8:234)

Composition in Shawnee" (Whorf 5:160–72). In this article, Whorf addresses the problem of making the structure of Shawnee comprehensible to English-speaking readers, and in so doing sets forth a theory of translation in which speaker, listener, and their shared context play central roles.

Shawnee, Whorf tells us, is a polysynthetic language; that is, most Shawnee utterances which we might translate into English in the form of sentences appear in Shawnee as a single complex "word" built up out of several morphemes. The component morphemes, moreover, do not easily correspond to separate words in English; however, they cannot be stuck together in just any order. Whorf's task in this particular article was to explicate the logic behind Shawnee patterning in a manner comprehensible to English speakers. His solution was *to argue that the logic of Shawnee utterances could be grasped if one could grasp the situation the utterance was intended to describe, and to compare the English way of describing that situation with the Shawnee way.* "Our problem is to determine how different languages segregate different essentials out of the same situation" (Whorf 5:162).

By way of illustration, Whorf follows this statement of the problem with an example from Shawnee (the same example that appears, as a set

of paired drawings, in the article "Science and Linguistics," Whorf
6:208; see Figure 4).

> So where we speak of "cleaning (a gun) with the ramrod," Shawnee
> does not isolate any rod or action of cleaning, but directs a hollow
> moving dry spot by movement of tool. . . . This is what makes
> Shawnee so strange and baffling from the standpoint of English, and
> not at all the mere fact that it is polysynthetic. A language can be
> polysynthetic and still say "clean with a ramrod" polysynthetically,
> thereby remaining quite transparent from the standpoint of English.
> (Whorf 5:162)

The difficulty for the linguist comparing the way two languages describe the same situation can be solved if the linguist finds a way "to
analyze or 'segment' the experience *first* in a way independent of any
one language or linguistic stock, a way which will be the same for all
observers" (Whorf 5:162; emphasis added). The scientific linguist must
get beyond, or underneath, all particular, partial views of a situation to
perceive the situation as it truly is, in and of itself. Whorf does not want

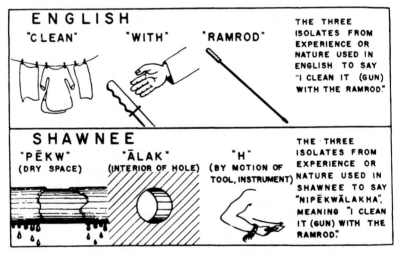

Figure 9. Languages dissect nature differently. The different isolates of meaning
(thoughts) used by English and Shawnee in reporting the same experience, that of
cleaning a gun by running the ramrod through it. The pronouns 'I' and 'it' are not
shown by symbols, as they have the same meaning in each language. In Shawnee
ni- equals 'I'; -a equals 'it.'

Figure 4.   Whorf's original illustration, and caption, to accompany the article "Science
and Linguistics" (Whorf 6:208)

to allow grammatical categories, or any verbal terminology whatsoever, to guide him. He tells us that commonsensical or quasi-scientific terms such as "things, objects, actions, substances, entities, events" must be avoided, since they "are but the creatures of modern Indo-European languages and their subsidiary jargons, and reflect the typical modes of segmenting experience in these tongues" (Whorf 5:162).

On what, then, can all observers agree? Whorf offers a principle from Gestalt psychology: the discovery that "the basal fact of visual perception is the relation of figure and ground" (Whorf 5:163; cf. Holquist 1986:xx). Whorf's concept of "figure" resembles Lakoff's (and Lakoff and Johnson's) concepts of the "experiential gestalt": an embodied set of experiences (including but not limited to visual experiences) that recurs so regularly that the whole set becomes conceptually simpler than the sum of its parts, and on that basis is presumably distinguished from its "ground" (e.g., Lakoff 1987:486–87).

If figure-ground relations were universal and unchanging for all human beings, then close attention to them would provide a way to ground human knowledge apart from language. Surely what we see and touch cannot mislead us the way grammar can mislead us. What if it were possible for speakers of different languages (or the linguist in their stead) to attain, via scientific or mystical discipline, an uncontaminated visual perception of their shared situation? The form of consciousness that made this perception possible would surely be the form of consciousness all people should adopt, since it is broader and deeper than the consciousness made possible by any particular individual language.

Of course, positivist science has long been convinced that it already possesses the requisite form of consciousness. Whorf's critics argue that science long ago eliminated any significant influence of culture and language on its categories. For them the language of science provides a new vocabulary which is faithful to the impersonal, objective "God's-eye" view in a way that other, merely natural human languages are not. Yet speakers of these natural languages can learn the language of science because, as human beings, they too possess the capacity for overcoming error and replacing it with truth. That is what universal rationality is all about. It is also, as we saw earlier, not unlike the message of mystical enlightenment. Religio-philosophical discipline, rather than rigorous empiricism, is seen by the mystical-minded as the pathway to the "God's-eye" view which, while different from scientific objectivity (more compassionate, more humane, perhaps), is no less monological. Making that giant leap from one limited perspective to the unlimited God's-eye view is something which positivists and mystics, each in their own way, have always longed to do. And yet Whorf seems worried that the entire enterprise is doubtful.

The first source of doubt derives from the reliance of both these approaches on meaning as reference, rather than meaning as context. Interestingly, Whorf's exasperation with this reliance is made most powerfully evident in the article he directed to a theosophical audience:

> And while all words are pitiful enough in their mere "letter that killeth," it is certain that scientific terms like "force, average, sex, allergic, biological" are not less pitiful, and in their own way no more certain in reference than "sweet, gorgeous, rapture, enchantment, heart and soul, star dust." You have probably heard of "star dust"— what is it? Is it a multitude of stars, a sparkling powder, the soil of the planet Mars, the Milky Way, a state of daydreaming, poetic fancy, pyrophoric iron, a spiral nebula, a suburb of Pittsburgh, or a popular song? You don't know, and neither does anybody. The word—for it is one LEXATION, not two—has no reference of its own. Some words are like that. As we have seen, reference is the lesser part of meaning, patternment the greater. Science, the quest for truth, is a sort of divine madness like love. And music—is it not in the same category? Music is a quasilanguage based entirely on patternment, without having developed lexation. (Whorf 9:260–61)

In rejecting the reference of individual words as a solution to the problem of meaning, Whorf strives to place such words in context, within patterns of other words. But we have seen how difficult it was for Whorf to decide exactly what kind of pattern was sufficient as a context. He wanted, as we saw, to make patternment coincide with grammar, but this attempt required expanding grammar so greatly that it lost the very precision that recommended it to him in the first place. In the Shawnee article, he goes beyond grammatical context entirely, to the real-world situation which grammars attempt to describe.

So, paradoxically, the first step to cross-linguistic understanding is to avoid words entirely. And yet, in what he tries to craft as a throwaway observation of minor significance, Whorf immediately tells us that words cannot be eliminated, that "cautious use of such terms may be helpful, perhaps unavoidable" (Whorf 5:162). If language can never be abandoned completely, however, we will never be able to attain a perfect, pristine view of the world against which each particular grammar's view can be compared. And this would make translation impossible, if that God's-eye view (and the form of language representing it) were indispensable as a mediating link between one language and another.

Presumably, if we could put our faith in science or religion (and therefore, by extension, in the language of science or in the language of religion), the words we find we must use would not lead us astray the way
everyday language does. But Whorf has his doubts about this too. He
does not disdain science or religion, but neither the language of science
nor the language of religion, as constituted in his day, was able, in his
view, to express an undistorted description of reality. For Whorf, the
language of science as it was constituted in his day was dangerously dependent on the grammatical forms of English and other SAE languages. As
we saw in the foregoing citation, the languages of mysticism and art,
whatever their virtues, were similarly dependent. At the same time, translation clearly was possible; Whorf engaged in it successfully himself.

The one phenomenon that would make cross-linguistic understanding
possible *without* access to the God's-eye view is a phenomenon Whorf
cannot bring himself to name openly: *heteroglossia*. Even within the
boundaries of phonology and grammar recognized by linguistics, each
natural language is internally redundant and unsystematic enough to
allow a variety of different worldviews to find the means for their expression, to allow a variety of different sublanguages to develop and flour-
ish. Friedrich, by contrast, does recognize the redundancies and chaos
internal to language. However, together with traditional philosophers,
critics, and formal linguists, Friedrich continues to view language monolithically, as we have seen. As a result, in Bakhtinian terms, he can
"make no provision for the dialogic nature of language" which is "a
struggle among socio-linguistic points of view, not an intra-language
struggle between individual wills or logical contradictions" (Bakhtin
1981c[1940]:273).

Translation across the sublanguages of heteroglossia is possible because they intersect with each other, overlapping in some ways, opposing one another in other ways. And the places where they intersect
provide the connecting bridges that allow the work of translation to
begin. Thus, no special access to a pure realm of uncontaminated forms
is needed to make translation possible. Each language (or sublanguage)
is loaded with its own resources for building bridges to other languages,
and to their speakers. Yet while heteroglossia is necessary for translation
to take place, it is not fully sufficient for understanding to occur. Understanding requires additional, nonverbal information to which both
speaker and listener have equal access in a shared context. This is true
even for understanding utterances in a sublanguage which all interlocutors share. It is all the more necessary for understanding utterances in
mutually unintelligible languages.

Whorf emphasizes the need for shared context, but cannot avow the role played by heteroglossia. Yet only in the presence of heteroglossia do the multiple possibilities of a single shared context become candidates for verbal articulation. Whorf would like context to clear up the ambiguities and conflicts generated by contesting grammars. The single shared context will show that what appeared to conflict could in fact be made harmonious if related to a nonverbal environment wider and deeper than each grammar individually recognizes. *But what if the shared context is exceedingly complex or ambiguous?* The descriptions provided by two conflicting grammars might help resolve contextual complexity. But contextual ambiguity, far from being resolved harmoniously, might be compounded.

For Whorf not only wishes to paint language as monolithic and constraining; he would like nonverbal situations to be equally monolithic and constraining. Context must speak in a single voice, even if different languages do not. More precisely, he would like to be able to describe a scenario in which the three characters each speak in a single voice: one for the reader (e.g., English), one for the hero (e.g., Hopi), and one for the context (e.g., the voice of Reason? the voice of God? the word of the world?). And yet he cannot bring himself to assert this scenario either, without qualifications. Whorf's struggle produces the tension that characterizes his discussion, in the "Gestalt" article, of the supposed universality of figure-ground perception. In a typical move, Whorf claims that such perception is universal, only to qualify this claim immediately by noting the "fringe of aberrations and individual differences" which may color the essential facts of observation. He cannot deny these aberrations and differences, but he refuses to consider them anything more than "fringe" phenomena, due to "individual" peculiarities. This is the same discomfort we noted in the distinction he made in the earlier text "On the Connection of Ideas" between free and controlled associations.

He is as unwilling to admit openly the existence of heteroglossia as he is unwilling to admit openly that the single situation which two languages describe differently may support more than one valid interpretation. Any such admission to his positivistic readers could only be interpreted by them as a descent into "debilitating relativism." (Indeed, with all the precautions he took, many still interpret his work in this way, as we have seen.) So he struggles manfully to contain his vision within categories acceptable to his audience.

He notes that "special skills or mental effort can rearrange emphases and sometimes change the figure-ground roles of certain items, as when one 'wills' the drawing of a cube seen edgewise to look like a hexagon with three radii" (Whorf 5:163). Such a description of the experience of visual ambiguity is reassuring because it suggests that there is a single "correct" way to view the drawing (i.e., as a cube seen edgewise) which nobody can dispute. And yet he does not speak of other examples of visual ambiguity which cannot be so easily explained away.

Consider, for example, the Necker cube and other visual illusions whose "true" figure-ground roles are completely ambiguous and objectively irresolvable (see Figure 5). One is reminded of Wittgenstein's fascination with the ambiguous drawing that might be a duck or a rabbit, depending on how one forced oneself to see it. One is also reminded of important recent investigation into the nature of visual illusions (Gregory 1983, for example) that emphasizes both the ambiguity of experience and our dependence upon (culturally shaped) patterning for making sufficient sense of it to get on with life.

It is hard to believe that Whorf was unaware of such phenomena if he was acquainted with the visual illusion he describes. And yet he con-

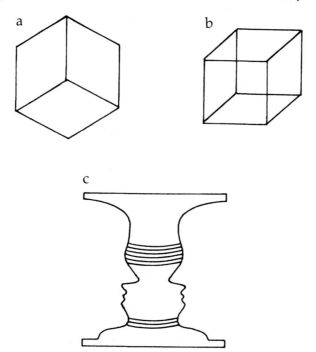

Figure 5.   (a) a hexagon with 3 radii; (b) the Necker cube; (c) the face/vase illusion; (b and c from Schultz and Lavenda 1990:121)

cludes, "The FACTS may differ slightly; the LAWS are the same for all. If the perceptual influences are such as to cause one normal person to see a definite outline, they will cause all other normal persons to see the same outline" (Whorf 5:164). Whorf's use of capital letters for emphasis should make us suspicious. Glaring by its absence is any mention of what will happen when perceptual influences are such as to cause normal persons to see a *variety* of *different* outlines. Under such circumstances, what will determine the particular outline that different normal persons habitually associate with what they perceive? Perhaps a single, universal figure/ground distinction will not appear intuitively obvious. Perhaps "special skills" or "mental effort," far from being an aberration, will be essential if observers are to perceive figure-ground relationships unfamiliar to them but taken for granted by their interlocutors.

And indeed, the example Whorf offers to illustrate the universality of figure-ground perception is overflowing with the very ambiguity he is explicitly trying to eliminate: "For example, all people see the constellation Ursa Major as the outline which we call dipper-shaped, though they may not call it a dipper or have such a utensil in their culture, and though there are, of course, no lines connecting the stars into this or any other outline" (Whorf 5:164). The irony, of course, is that "Ursa Major" is Latin for "Big Bear," the name of a constellation including, but not limited to, the stars that make up the Big Dipper. Moreover, these are not the only two interpretations of the pattern of stars in question. According to Voegelin et al. (1954:33), the Shawnee interpret this pattern as six men hunting and a fox chewing on antlers.

Different cultures elsewhere in the world undoubtedly could offer additional different interpretations. But even the English, Latin, and Shawnee interpretations take effort to reconcile with one another. Reconciliation is not impossible. But it is not due to individual efforts to imitate the "fringe aberrations" or "individual differences" which characterize those descriptions at variance with one's own. This is because, as Whorf had to have been painfully aware, *the differences in question are not individual, but cultural.* Indeed, the "aberrations" are aberrations only if observers are smugly complacent about the adequacy of their own interpretation; and the aberrations are "fringe" only if observers are arrogantly ethnocentric about the correctness of the interpretation they share with other members of their own society.

Perhaps Whorf's lust for scientific precision caused him to overreach himself here. Nevertheless, his claim that cross-cultural/cross-linguistic understanding lies less in language than in the experience language attempts to describe ought not to be overlooked. One can admit that visual experience is complex and sometimes ambiguous without having to conclude that "anything goes." One can admit that heteroglossia exists within every national language, without having to conclude that nothing refracts the expressive will of individual speakers. To admit these things, however, requires rooting language and visual experience within the flow of ongoing practical social activity that characterizes concrete human existence. To do so means to equip human beings with material bodies as well as with consciousness. To do so means to acknowledge the divisions in any society that give rise to alternative worldviews and sublanguages shaped to express such views and debate them. It means to acknowledge oppression and the struggle against oppression by speakers who insist on making their unofficial voices heard.

All of these phenomena are implicit within Whorf's project. Most, however, are masked by Whorf's glossy comic prose. If they had paraded unmasked, how would Whorf have appeared to his readers? How would he have appeared to himself, and to his colleagues, his friends and his family? As a dangerous socialist agitator who belonged in Russia with others of his ilk—like his contemporaries, the members of the Bakhtin circle, for example?

Radical contextualization of language within the ongoing dialogic processes of social life does not rule out cross-linguistic understanding, of course. But it does suggest a very different explanation of how such understanding comes about: namely, with small steps, broadening and deepening the grammar (language, conceptual system) we always begin with by the addition of new insights from the grammars (languages, conceptual systems) we come to learn, or invent, as a result of our practical social experience of the world. Learning is possible, elimination of error is possible—but these gains are not the result of any giant, godlike leap to a single, universal, impersonal truth. Instead, they are ultimately rooted in the concrete process of ongoing dialogue. And the gains will be only as wide-ranging and far-reaching as the dialogue itself. Indeed, despite all the flourishing disclaimers designed to quell the suspicions of his readers (and perhaps his own inner uneasiness), this patient dialogue is what Whorf actually demonstrates in his analysis of stem composition in Shawnee. This article is therefore central if one is to understand what might be called Whorf's theory of translation. How, in fact, does he proceed?

Whorf says that attention to the way figure-ground relations are represented in language has helped him sort out puzzling points of English, Hopi, Aztec, and Maya, and he now proposes to try it on Shawnee. The results of his analysis of the Shawnee data lead him to conclude that, in general, in Shawnee utterances, "figures precedes external field, the more figural precedes the less figural, but the egoic field generally precedes all these" (Whorf 5:166). As an example, he asks us to

> consider the way of saying "among the swamps." Our own manner of lexation is to isolate from the experience an essential that we call "swamp," in the form of a typical English noun. As such a noun, it slides in the grammatical grooves prepared for all nouns, is treated as a typical "thing". . . . There is little difference in linguistic treatment between a swamp and a butterfly, in spite of the enormous difference in the perceptual experience. In Shawnee we have to forget the English type of lexation and fall back on the perceptual situation. The referent of our preposition "among" becomes actually the part of the picture with the most quality of outline—a limited, defined spot in the midst of an indefinite field—which is a field of swampiness. The picture is, as it were, rough sketched by placing first the figural element *laa-* 'midst of area' followed by its ground or setting *tepki* 'swampy terrain." *laa-teepki* . . . '(spot) among the swamps, in the swamp'. . . . (Whorf 5:168)

This patient verbal description has the same intent, if not quite the same immediate expressive power, as Whorf's drawings do. In both cases, the procedure is to create a potentially shareable image (verbally or graphically) and bring two radically different languages into dialogue about what is referentially significant about that image. English and Shawnee interilluminate one another as they both attempt to describe the same thing. Compare the way in which a single set of sketches provides the common context for interpreting the similarities recognized in Shawnee (and the differences recognized in English) in describing actions glossed in English as "I push his head back" and "I drop it in water and it floats," in "Languages and Logic" (Whorf 8:235; see Figure 6).

Whorf speculates about those factors which might explain

> which stem that native regards as most pervasive: i.e., as the occurrent. This may be a question quite apart from that of the method of compounding. I might hazard a guess that it may depend on the degree of analogic pressure behind the various stems in combination. Some stems in the nature of the case would be more productive of combinations than others. The stem with the greatest number of close parallels to the combination in question might be felt by the native as nuclear. (Whorf 5:170)

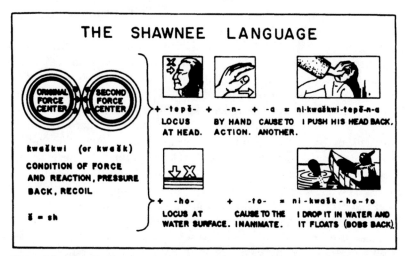

Figure 16. The English sentences 'I push his head back' and 'I drop it in water and it floats' are unlike. But in Shawnee the corresponding statements are closely similar, emphasizing the fact that analysis of nature and classification of events as like or in the same category (logic) are governed by grammar.

Figure 6. Whorf's original illustration, and caption, to accompany the article "Languages and Logic" (Whorf 8:235)

Three points in this rather perplexing passage are noteworthy. First of all, in explaining "which stem the native regards as most pervasive" (i.e., which element in a situation is chosen by a Shawnee speaker as worthy of linguistic representation as "figure," rather than "ground"?), Whorf emphasizes the role of "various stems in combination"—what might be called grammatical or idiomatic constructions—in encouraging Shawnee speakers to notice some things and downplay others. It is worth noting, however, that Whorf does *not* call these stems-in combination *grammatical* constructions. His unwillingness to do so may reflect his own inability to draw a firm line between "grammar" and "discourse," between the formal requirements of "grammar," however unconventionally defined by him, and patterned but unmarked "fashions of speaking" which draw upon the resources offered by grammar, but cannot be reduced to grammatical forms. Put another way, he seems to be struggling here to open up a space for heteroglossia, however primitively conceived.

    In the second place, Whorf tells us that these stems-in-combination exert their force by means of "analogic pressure," a conveniently ambiguous expression, for it leaves unstated whether the analogy involved is of the quasi-mathematical "patternment" kind (related to the obligatory rules of grammar) or the fuzzier figurative kind (dependent upon the more flexible patterns of discourse). Finally, Whorf suggests that these constructions may be related to one another by what we might call family resemblance, such that the "stem with the greatest number of close parallels to the combination in question might be felt by the native as nuclear." This suggests a situation very much like the one Lakoff (1987) describes, in which a prototypical construction can be linked to derived, similar constructions by a "based on"—i.e., analogical—relationship; and in which the prototypical construction itself is prototypical because it is descriptive of certain prototypical situations in terms of which speakers interpret their everyday experiences. The remaining ambiguity here—which Lakoff's treatment also does not escape—is the ambiguity about the universality of figure-ground perception. Both refuse to address squarely the extent to which "well-structured experiences" are universal for all human begins by virtue of their having human bodies, and the extent to which they are but relatively universal to those human beings who make use of shared cultural and linguistic practices (see, for example, Alverson 1987).

Another important figure-ground example to which Whorf makes reference in "Gestalt Technique of Stem Composition in Shawnee" is that of a running boy (Whorf 5:165). What aspects of one's experience of perceiving a running boy need to be noted to give an accurate linguistic representation of this experience? In "Science and Linguistics" Whorf takes this same example and attempts, by means of sketches in a matrix, to represent for his readers six different situations of running and the ways in which English speakers and Hopi speakers differ in their manner of describing these situations (see Figure 2). In some cases, English makes distinctions that Hopi ignores, e.g., distinguishing present progressive from past tense. In Hopi, both situations would be represented by a single verb form, since, according to Whorf, Hopi grammar ignores temporal questions and requires its users to specify instead the validity they attach to particular observations. That is, was the event seen right now with one's own eyes, and thus a statement of fact (verb form 1), or was it an event one is describing on the basis of memory (verb form 2), or is it an event one expects to happen (verb form 3), or is it a statement about an event that recurs with lawlike regularity (verb form 4)? The temporal distinction between a boy who is running now before my eyes and one who was recently running but whom I no longer see is therefore irrelevant when making validity distinctions: the speaker witnessed the running in both cases, and is making a statement of fact that does not depend on whether the "objective field" is empty or contains the runner.

This particular illustration is Whorf's most complex attempt to "capture" in two dimensions on paper the complexity and ambiguity of well-structured situations which—depending on one's language (or one's interest?)—could be validly, if partially, described in more than one way. By combining pictures and text in this way, Whorf is creating what art critics and art historians call *ekphrasis*. Stephen Melville defines ekphrasis as "the presentation of a work executed in another medium within a work of art, typically the presentation of a visual work within a literary text" (1989:91). When words and pictures are combined in this way, typically both deal with the same theme. For example, a written text attempts to describe a painting, or a picture attempts to illustrate a written text. Whorf's illustrated articles would fall into the latter category.[2]

Wendy Steiner explains that in earlier centuries some artists and critics believed that "the temporal limits of painting could be overcome by isolating a moment in the action that revealed all that had led up to it and all that would follow. This is the so-called pregnant moment, and it is obviously associated with historical and iconographic art, since it usually cannot function with full effect unless we already know the story captured in the moment of the painting" (1982:40). When trying to illustrate his linguistic data, Whorf faced the problem faced by painters who want to translate historical or literary texts into iconographic visual images. His solution to this problem, clearest in the running-boy illustration, was to try to capture a series of pregnant moments (see Figure 2). But images alone could not carry all the information Whorf wished to impart, and so he resorted to ekphrasis. As a result, each situation description in Figure 2 attempts to recreate, through the careful juxtaposition of words and images, the active contextual situation which each language reports validly, but differently. Only in this way could the differences in English and Hopi ways of dealing with time be grasped.

Steiner argues that visual images employed as illustrations, together with verbal examples, quotations, illustrations, and allusions, can be viewed as *evidentiary devices* that writers insert into their texts to achieve "intertextuality, that dialogue among the world's written and spoken texts" (1982:113). Evidentiary devices "assure the word-thing relation by making 'things' present in the text" (1982:114). Visual illustrations "are pictures of the thing-world inserted into verbal texts. As pictures, icons, they both signify and contain the characteristics of what they picture. They appear to entrap the thing-world among words, whereas in fact—or in addition—they entrap the pictorial world in the verbal one. By doing so, they and all the other intertextual techniques cited here maintain the crucial dialogic structure necessary to communication, that is, necessary to the maintenance of the relation among message, interlocutors, and signified world" (1982:114). Steiner connects the use of evidentiary devices to Francis Bacon's discussion of the "probational method of argumentation," which "involves a direct gesture to the reader and a recapitulation of the inductive method that gave rise to knowledge in the first place. It is tied to the event of discovery and to the discoverer, for only by retaining this context will the knowledge 'grow' in the mind of the reader" (1982:113). She describes "the linking of image and argument" as "the intersection of word and thing that leads to powerful probational prose. The image in this case has the same function as the quotation, allusion, example, or illustration in bringing about truth-telling" (1982:119). On the basis of our earlier discussion, it seems clear that Bakhtin's artistic prose and Bacon's probational prose have much in common. In fact, Steiner argues that the "triangulation between language system and thing system is the middle way of probational discourse and all dialogic prose" (1982:116).

Steiner's analysis of ekphrasis reinforces the arguments I have offered about the dialogicality of Whorf's texts. Indeed, the line drawings in Figure 2 are explicitly dialogical, in that they include speaker, "hearer" or "receiver," and "objective field" (or context). To be sure, Whorf's matrix does not explicitly attribute the English and Hopi ways of "handling the topic" to either the speaker or the hearer pictured in the corresponding situation. If, however, the verbal material in English were systematically connected to one of the dialogic partners pictured in the corresponding illustration, and the verbal material in Hopi were systematically connected to the other dialogic partner (using cartoonist's balloons, for example), Figure 2 would be transformed into an iconic representation of dialogicality. But such an image might not have been taken seriously even by the MIT engineers in whose journal the article originally appeared, let alone by scientific linguists. By refusing to transform linguistic representations into individual voices, Whorf could maintain the appearance of scientific objectivity.

Visual representation of context allows Whorf to juxtapose not just different verbal accounts, but verbal *and* visual accounts, of the same events. Whorf thus intensifies the multilingual experience for his readers by making it multimodal as well. Peircian verbal symbols are placed alongside image icons which themselves contain indexical icons: note the gestures of the pictured speaker toward the "objective field" and to the "hearer," and the direction of his gaze. Interestingly, Whorf's verbal identification of the rightmost figure as a passive "hearer" or "receiver" is belied by the direction of the speaker's gaze, which indicates indexically that the rightmost figure is also the speaker's actively attentive "addressee." Equally important indexically is the barrier blocking the hearer/addressee's view of the objective field in situations 2 and 3. Finally, symbols, images, and indexes are embedded in a diagrammatic icon, represented by the matrix itself. The result is a *Gesamtkunstwerk,* "a mixture of artistic media epitomized in Wagnerian opera. The *Gesamtkunstwerk* is a gesture toward semiotic repleteness, combining several kinds of sign types and having them comment on each other" (Steiner 1982:144–45). And Whorf could create such a work with impeccable rhetorical justification: as Steiner reminds us, "Rhetoric was seen as the means of presenting knowledge vividly, so as to be experienced in its truth rather than merely referred to" (1982:141).

Grasping the significance of what Whorf is portraying in these illustrations—indeed, Whorf's own ability to decide which features of the situation needed to be portrayed in order to show what was and was not salient for English speakers and Hopi speakers—would seem to depend heavily on the skills and the mental effort he said were responsible for the human ability to reverse figure-ground relationships in visual illusions. The skills and mental effort together constitute our figurative imagination, which makes it possible for us to view the same thing in different ways, or different things in the same way. Indeed, this is the role of metaphor, the Peircian icon that depends on parallelism. Metaphor is the one Peircian sign type that does not appear in Figure 2. But metaphor is not missing from the multilingual/multimodal event that occurs whenever a reader encounters Figure 2 amid the text of "Science and Linguistics." Readers supply the metaphoric links themselves as they exercise their figurative imagination. This capacity for entertaining a multiplicity of views of the world (and of ourselves), without thereby suffering irreparable mental breakdown, is at the root of the versatility, flexibility, adaptability that makes us human beings, rather than automata. The resultant destruction of monologic language does not have to be viewed with dread. It can also be a cause for celebration, for enlightenment, for joyous expansion of human possibilities—and it can keep us honest.

A contrasting attempt to address these issues can be found in the work of Lakoff and Johnson, who are probably the most visible of a new movement in linguistics and philosophy to take seriously both context and the presuppositions of human physical embodiment built into natural languages. However, like their predecessors, they proceed from an atomistic perspective. Speakers, for them, have become talking heads with human bodies. They speak out of a humanly embodied point of view conditioned by context, but each speaker is "expressing" a personal understanding only. Thus any agreement at which different speakers arrive is not socially constructed; it is merely the mechanical outcome of the fact that they possess identical bodies which receive signals from the outside world in identical ways. The cultural shaping of expression plays no explicit role. And, indeed, given atomistic assumptions about human nature, it cannot play a role. This is why Lakoff and Johnson assign no basic role to listeners in their scenario.

Like the traditional linguists and philosophers they criticize, they do not admit that human beings who express a point of view about an object are always, at the same time, addressing a particular listener about it, *evaluating* it for that listener's benefit. For them, listeners are just other isolated talking heads who enter the context in an ad hoc manner—if the speaker's generic expression happens accidentally to strike their ears. Objects, too, remain pure and uncontaminated by socially contextualized perceptions of them. Indeed, "context" for such thinkers is a purely random coming together of socially and historically innocent people and objects.

Such a scenario is built into traditional positivistic science. It makes positivistic "objectivity" possible. It constitutes, in fact, what Bakhtin calls a *chronotope,* that is, a "mode of visualization," a "special artistic conception of space and time" (1984[1929]:31), "the intrinsic connectedness of temporal and spatial relationships that are artistically expressed in literature" (1981a[1937–38]:84). In this positivistic chronotope, speakers and objects are primordially isolated from one another. They are fully equal to their own self-definitions, free of outside "contamination" which might violate that inner identity. This means, of course, that they are unaffected by the passage of time except in ways universal to all objects, e.g., the aging process or, for living objects, the life cycle. Equally ignored are differences in spatial orientation, separate unrepeatable experiences which might become organized over time into traditional points of view. Such factors are "accidents" which cannot affect the "essence" of the objects. Differences, acquired in a particular place or over time, are negligible in the face of similarities, which resist both the passage of time and particularities of place.

Only such a mode of visualization, such a conception of objects (including human beings), could justify the traditional approach of scientific linguistics, which saw social life and cultural tradition and historical fate as equally external to the essence of language, and for that reason superfluous. Indeed, the distinction between human beings and other objects has at different times been considered equally accidental and unimportant, for figures as disparate as La Mettrie and contemporary cognitive scientists. We have been describing, in fact, the chronotope underlying mechanical materialism, the Newtonian chronotope, which, with various modifications, was transferred wholesale from the natural sciences into linguistics and other social sciences.

Lakoff and Johnson do not question the underlying principles of this chronotope. Their innovation consists, in fact, in a minor modification of this venerable scenario. They argue that it is not adequate to think of living organisms, including human beings, as nothing more than complex machines, no different in principle from sophisticated computers. Rather, they stress that human particularity—the specific shape, size, physical and mental properties of human bodies—is *essential,* not accidental, to an understanding of human language. It is a tiny blow against Newtonian absolutism, it chips away at the foundation, but does not do anything to seriously dislodge it or the atomistic (individualistic) assumptions that underlie it. Perhaps Lakoff and Johnson feel the same pressures Whorf felt to speak the language of science to those they criticize, in order to be taken seriously. Attempting to move the argument onto a different plane might only alienate those whom they most ardently desire as listeners, as well as call into question the scientific nature of their own project. Yet using the language of science to speak about matters which science disdains burdens them with a serious handicap.

Bakhtin and his colleagues, by contrast, did not hesitate to shift the grounds of argument. They considered that, from the very outset, atomism in any form was untenable in the human sciences. Language, like the rest of human life of which it was a living part, was social through and through. It is atomistic, impersonal, categories that are secondary: "Just as the body is formed initially in the mother's womb (body), a person's consciousness awakens wrapped in another's consciousness. Only later does one begin to be subsumed by neutral words and categories, that is, one is defined as a person irrespective of *I* and *other*" (Bakhtin 1986[1970–71]:138). As a result, any study of language which ignores this primordially social origin of linguistic consciousness is seriously flawed. "The relationship to others' utterances cannot be separated from the relationship to the object (for it is argued about, agreed upon, views converge within it), nor can it be separated from the relationship to the speaker himself. This is a living tripartite unity" (1986[n.d.]:122). As a result, the study of language must always encompass three sets of relations: (1) among objects, (2) between subject and object, and (3) among subjects. And it must entertain a lively awareness of the way linguistic usage can transform one kind of relationship into another, turning objects into subjects via personification, or turning subjects into objects via reification (1986[1970–71]:138).

Such a scenario explicitly encompasses matters which Whorf habitually refused to make explicit, even when he relied upon them compositionally: the indispensable role of listeners; the relationship of speaker and listener to the diverse, potentially shareable figure-ground relationships that may be discerned in the environment which surrounds both of them; and the metaphorical transformations of figurative imagination which make the perception of new patterns possible. Such a scenario is adequate to account for understanding in situations of polyglossia (Whorf's preoccupation) and in situations of heteroglossia (the domain Whorf neglected). But such a scenario cannot fit into the Newtonian chronotope, which is monologic through and through. In fact, this scenario makes sense only within a totally different chronotope, one which recognizes cultural/linguistic diversity as an irreducible fact of human life. And such a chronotope becomes plausible only when the practical experiences of human life render the monologic view inadequate. "The weakening or destruction of a monologic context occurs only when there is a coming together of two utterances equally and directly oriented toward a referential object. Two discourses equally and directly oriented toward a referential object within the limits of a single context cannot exist side by side without intersecting dialogically, regardless of whether they confirm, mutually supplement, or (conversely) contradict one another, or find themselves in some other dialogic relationship . . ." (Bakhtin 1984[1929]:188–89).

This is, of course, exactly the situation which occurs whenever Whorf applies his "Gestalt technique" in order to find adequate English translations for Shawnee expressions. The monologic context created by English must crumble when an English utterance comes together with a Shawnee utterance, and *both* utterances are directly oriented toward a referential object within the limits of a *single context*. In the same way, the monologic context assumed by the English-speaking reader of Whorf's *Technology Review* articles must crumble when Hopi or Shawnee utterances come together with English utterances (Whorf's carefully crafted glosses), and both sets of utterances are oriented toward referential objects within the limits of a single context. It is the contrastive event, the clash between two or more *diverse* utterances about objects within a *single* context that gives birth to multilingual consciousness. And, in the face of this event, it is impossible to prevent one utterance from casting light on the other; impossible to prevent cross-linguistic/ cross-cultural "contamination"; impossible to ignore the opportunity for new insight—except in bad faith. "Languages are dialogically implicated *in* each other and begin to exist *for* each other (similar to exchanges in a dialogue)" (Bakhtin 1981c[1940]:400). Whorf knows this, and this is why readers who have been lulled into complacency by his seeming alliance with them at the beginning of a text feel betrayed and angry at the conclusion. They must rethink everything or be branded as hypocrites, as bigots—or else as no better than their stereotypical Primitives or Illiterate Peasants: as Mr. Everymen.

And this outcome is not frivolous or easily dismissed, which is why Whorf is still being attacked today, almost fifty years after his death. For the chronotope which must be presupposed for Whorf's writings to make sense in this way (and thus generate controversy) is the chronotope which, according to Bakhtin, must be presupposed if we are to make sense of Dostoevsky's equally controversial writings. For Bakhtin, Dostoevsky's achievements cannot be explained away in traditional stylistic terms, totally separated from the social context in which they took shape. On the contrary, "the objective contradictions of the epoch did determine Dostoevsky's creative work . . . at the level of an objective visualization of contradictions as forces coexisting simultaneously" (1984[1929]:27–28). If Whorf's creative work is similarly rooted in the objective contradictions of his epoch, the lessons to be drawn from it cannot be divorced from those same objective contradictions. Put another way, the stand one takes regarding Whorf has political consequences, as the shrewdest of his critics have always known. This is why, if one deplores the consequences that follow from agreeing with Whorf, it is so important that "Whorfianism" be discredited.

What is the nature of the Dostoevsky chronotope? According to Bakhtin, "The fundamental category in Dostoevsky's mode of artistic visualizing was not evolution, but *coexistence* and *interaction*. He saw and conceived his world primarily in terms of space, not time. Hence his deep affinity for the dramatic form. Dostoevsky strives to organize all available meaningful material, all material of reality, in one time-frame, in the form of a dramatic juxtaposition, and he strives to develop it extensively" (1984[1929]:28). In adopting this scenario, Dostoevsky was breaking with the mode of artistic visualization which had predominated since the Enlightenment, and was most fully developed in the work of Goethe. Goethe saw and conceived his world primarily in terms of time, not space. He saw coexisting diversity and transformed it into an evolving sequence. "In contrast to Goethe, Dostoevsky attempted to perceive the very stages themselves in their *simultaneity,* to *juxtapose* and *counterpose* them dramatically, and not stretch them out in an evolving sequence. For him, to get one's bearings on the world meant to conceive all its contents as simultaneous, and to guess at their interrelationships in the cross-section of a single moment" (1984:28).

The Goethe chronotope is the time-space structure which nineteenth-century unilineal cultural evolutionists assumed. It was also the chronotope assumed by traditional European philology. Anthropologists and linguists who broke with this tradition early in the twentieth century were rightly outraged by the social practices—such as slavery and colonial domination—which unilineal evolutionism could be used to justify. Their growing understanding of the sophistication of non-Western cultures, languages, and their speakers, moreover, was difficult to reconcile with stereotypes about "primitives." All of this was at odds with the mode of understanding presupposed by the Goethe chronotope. But with what might one replace it?

Historically, two different options were taken up, by anthropologists in Europe and in America, respectively. The European option—exemplified by the work of Durkheim, Radcliffe-Brown, and British functionalism—was to return to the Newtonian chronotope: to assume the existence of a universal human rationality and to explain linguistic and cultural differences in terms of deterministic pressures at work within different types of societies. Rather than rejecting unilineal evolutionary aims outright, the functionalists justified their approach as a necessary first step, before social types could be placed scientifically in their proper evolutionary sequence. Each society (or type of society) constituted a Newtonian universe of its own, and its survival depended upon adherence to laws which are absolute, relative to the society in question. Adherence to these laws produced "social solidarity" which kept the society going. Thus, it was not the case that only "primitives" could live certain kinds of lives. Any rational human being required to live in a society of a particular type, however "primitive," would have to abide by the same laws, if solidarity were to be maintained, since the healthy functioning of any part of society depended on the healthy functioning of all other parts. Transgressing these laws would lead to social breakdown and dissolution.

By contrast, the generation of American anthropologists that broke with unilineal evolutionism (including Boas, Sapir, and Whorf) adopted an approach to linguistic and cultural diversity which presupposes the Dostoevsky chronotope. For it is a relativistic chronotope, an Einsteinian chronotope: "It is as if various systems of calculation were united here in the complex unit of an Einsteinian universe (although the juxtaposition of Dostoevsky's world with Einstein's world is, of course, only an artistic comparison and not a scientific analogy)" (Bakhtin 1984[1929]:16). Implicitly or explicitly, post-Boasian American ethnographers aimed to juxtapose, counterpose, consider simultaneously the culture/language of the heroes of the work (the ethnographer's informants) and the culture/ language of their readers (members of the ethnographer's own society, usually the community of fellow ethnographers [see Karp and Kendall 1982:254]). Moreover, such ethnography refrains from presupposing anything in particular about the nature of human "rationality," other than the fact that, whatever it is, all human beings undoubtedly possess it. Put another way, the data of ethnography "are presented not within a single field of vision but within several fields of vision, each full and of equal worth" (Bakhtin 1984[1929]:16). There have, of course, been Tolstoy-like ethnographers who insist on having the final word about their informants' culture, refusing to allow their informants to speak for themselves. But there have also been Dostoevsky-like enthographers who insist on allowing their heroes' voices to be heard, who insist on making their readers listen to those voices.

Although Whorf tries to create a comic mask which will allow him to pass as the former, I believe that Whorf's direct authorial word, almost despite his best efforts, places him among the latter. Many of Bakhtin's observations about Dostoevsky clearly make sense of Whorf as well. For instance, Bakhtin argues that it is incorrect to identify Dostoevsky the novelist with one or another of his characters, as most critics have done, since his direct authorial word is not located in any of them, but is rather to be found in the way he orchestrates *all* of them. This is another way of saying that it is the dialogue among the voices that counts for Dostoevsky, rather than any particular voice. The preceding analysis demonstrates, I believe, that it was the dialogue that counted for Whorf too; that he went to stylistic extremes in order to provoke the dialogue, even when this threatened his own respectable identity.

Almost in spite of himself, Whorf, like Dostoevsky,

> perceived the profound ambiguity, even multiple ambiguity, of every phenomenon. But none of these contradictions or bifurcations ever became dialectical, they were never set in motion along a temporal path or in an evolving sequence: they were, rather, spread out in one plane, as standing alongside or opposite one another, as consonant but not merging or as hopelessly contradictory, as an eternal harmony of unmerged voices or as their unceasing and irrec-

> oncilable quarrel. Dostoevsky's visualizing power was locked in
> place at the moment diversity revealed itself—and remained there,
> organizing and shaping this diversity in the cross-section of a given
> moment. (Bakhtin 1984[1929]:30)

With Whorf, as with Dostoevsky, this visualizing power "made him deaf and dumb to a great many essential things"; at the same time, it "permitted him to see many and varied things where others saw one and the same thing" (1984:30). Bakhtin says that "Dostoevsky offers, in artistic form, something like a sociology of consciousness—to be sure, only on the level of coexistence" (1984:32). This is also what Whorf offers, and this is nothing to sound apologetic about (as Bakhtin does in his sly disclaimer), since the ability of Western thinkers (and many thinkers outside the West) to deal with coexisting others as voices with equal rights, who deserve to be heard, is far from well developed.

In fact, if we believe Wendy Steiner, Whorf and his anthropological colleagues were not the only ones of their generation in the West whose work presumed the Dostoevsky chronotope. Steiner argues that modernist artists are equally concerned to create a multimodal, polyperspectival experience in the consciousness of their addresses. "The search for boundaries and the concomitant need to avoid them, to maintain a dialectic balance between extremes if communication is to be possible, are the drama of twentieth-century art as a whole" (Steiner 1982:174). This is clearest, perhaps, when one considers the work of the painters, and especially the writers, who have been labeled "cubist."

According to Steiner, a list of cubist writers would include Gertrude Stein, William Carlos Williams, Guillaume Apollinaire, and Max Jacob, as well as Ezra Pound, Wallace Stevens, e. e. cummings, André Gide, and Alain Robbe-Grillet (1982:178). Stein, Williams, Apollinaire, Jacob, and Pound were friends with cubist painters, and some of them explicitly acknowledge the influence these painters had on their writing. What sort of influence was it? According to Steiner, cubist painters broke with the artistic canons that had held sway in the West since the Renaissance. They rejected linear perspective and other techniques that facilitated the representation of three-dimensional reality on a two-dimensional surface, emphasizing instead the flatness of the picture plane. Cubist paintings present the objects they depict in ways that disregard the physical laws of appearance. Objects are taken apart and multiple views of them are presented simultaneously; the size of objects depends on their compositional importance rather than on their distance from the putative viewer; the laws of gravity and the directionality of light are ignored. When these

painterly techniques are applied analogically to writing, the results include such literary innovations as experimentation with points of view, the
destruction of causality and motivation, and a heightened emphasis on
punning, contradiction, parody, and wordplay. The result, whether on
canvas or in a literary text, is the simultaneous juxtaposition of a multiplicity of views (Steiner 1982:179–82).

A cubist orientation implies a changed attitude to time as well. Again
breaking with previous understandings, the cubist project transforms temporal sequence into an atemporal "Steinian kaleidoscope" (Steiner
1982:190). "The cubist interaction with the past make a simultaneity of it,
a system whose elements are altered not in substance but in context.
Cubism thus tells us to think of history in a new way, not as a plotted
narrative moving toward a resolution, but as a cubist painting whose
elements maintain their heterogeneity—objects, people; things, signs;
the banal, the dramatic; the contemporaneous, the anachronous—in an
aestheticized structure of interrelations" (1982:191).

The polyphony of modernist art is the central theme of Steiner's book.
And when Steiner describes, for example, the art of Ezra Pound, her
description matches Bakhtin's characterization of double-voiced discourse: "Pound writes a lifelong poem in the *Cantos* juxtaposing elements of every time and civilization. And he translates past art, leaving
it somehow intact in the process" (1982:191). Indeed, Steiner takes the
theoretical inspiration for her approach from early-twentieth-century
Russian linguistics. She relies primarily on the work of Sergej Karcevskij
(1982:101, 103–4, 109, 117, 208–9) and secondarily on Boris Uspenskij
(1982:61–62, 86–87) to justify her defense of dialogicality and polyphonic understanding. But she also cites Bakhtin's *Problems of Dostoevsky's Poetics* (1982:87). In light of the argument set forth in this book, it
is thus all the more ironic that her only mentions of Whorf are in connection with linguistic determinism (1982:27–28).

Keeping this in mind, let us return to Whorf's critics and their dependence on the translatability paradox in order to refute him. The translatability paradox is a paradox only for monological thinkers who persist,
even against their better judgment, in seeing one and the same thing
where others see many and varied things. Only such a mentality could
imagine that cross-cultural, cross-linguistic understanding is a matter of
word-for-word, or even sentence-for-sentence, translation. Only such a
mentality would be threatened by the juxtaposition of two ways of describing a situation with the situation itself, in all its complexity and
ambiguity, in order better to grasp (by grasping the nature of the situation) how each language chooses to describe it. Only such a mentality

would begin by denying the possibility of multilingual consciousness, or at best, try to pass off the language of science as multilingual consciousness by fiat, since all other languages, by force, can be assimilated into it. Only such a mentality could interpret the absence of a systematic monological point of view in Whorf's works as a flaw, rather than as the entire *point* of his project. Only such a mentality could be alarmed to discover that what it took to be all the truth was only partial truth. Only a monological mentality would perceive no difference between partial truth and a lie.

The multilingual or heteroglot mentality is not similarly dismayed. Such a mentality has no difficulty admitting that it is only by grasping the nature of the situation in its complexity and ambiguity that understanding is possible. It is not threatened to learn that understanding has more to do with human imaginative capacities than with language per se. On the contrary, understanding the situation in this complex cognitive sense makes it possible to understand, in turn, the logics employed by different languages as they offer their own particular, and partial, definitions of the situation. Therefore, understanding is not reducible to a single logic any more than it is reducible to a single language. If each grammar embodies a "logic" of its own, that logic is partial. Or, in the view of psychologist James Wertsch, the speaker of each language takes up a different *referential perspective* with regard to the nonlinguistic context of speech (1985:168). Wertsch has been deeply influenced by the writings of Russian psychologist Lev Vygotsky, who was a contemporary of Bakhtin, and Wertsch has recently tried to incorporate Bakhtin's insights into his own work. This has led him to conclude that referential perspectives are always at the same time *ideological perspectives:* "Just as one must use some referential perspective when speaking of objects and events, one must also use some ideological perspective" (1985:229). This means that each language of heteroglossia or polyglossia "carries with itself a great deal of sociohistorically specific ideological baggage" (1985:229).

Whorf argues that understanding the situation makes it possible for us to grasp the validity of each partial form of linguistic logic—of each referential perspective—even as we recognize its partiality. If this is indeed the basis of cross-linguistic understanding, then it rules out as utterly misconceived those attempts at word-for-word or sentence-for-sentence translation so beloved of analytic philosophers. One has to grasp the *situation* before one can make sense of words and sentences, or know which words and sentences in one language can be used to gloss which words and sentences in another language. Thus, the attempt by philosophers such as Putnam or Davidson to equate sentences with propositions and proceed on a sentence-by-sentence (or proposition-by-proposition) basis to translate from Language *A* to Language *B* is absurd, because it presumes that one language can be mapped onto another, *apart from situations,* by disembodied, decontextualized minds. The artificiality of such a translation scenario must lead one to agree with Stephen Tyler, who remarks that one

> gets the distinct impression that those who argue that translatability signifies the underlying unity of language or reason have never struggled with translation or attempted to see the world from the point of view of another language. They have a naive notion that translation is only a process of code-matching, when in fact far more than simple decoding is involved. Every language presumes the context of its appropriate world, and it is this context that the translator must somewhow evoke without at the same time succumbing so completely to it that the translation becomes unintelligible. (1978:70)

Or, as Talal Asad has put it, "the anthropologist's translation is not merely a matter of matching sentences in the abstract, but of *learning to live another form of life* and the speak another kind of language" (1986:149).

While this emphasis on context would seem, if pushed far enough, to argue for the necessity of studying foreign languages in context before translation could be attempted, Whorf shies away from making such an assertion outright. This is, by now, a familiar omission. Whorf spent no extended time in the field; we know that his favored research situation was picking the informant's brain in a laboratory-like setting, but not engaging the informant himself in verbal or practical activities that usually come under the heading of "participant observation." He was willing to relate a language to other activities of its speakers, but only insofar as these activities were traditional matters *internal* to their *own* society (as he does, for instance, in his discussion of the importance to the Hopi of "repetition," in "The Relation of Habitual Thought and Behavior to Language" (Whorf 4:134–59)). Nowhere in his texts does he openly allow speakers of different languages to debate one another about social, political, religious, or ethical matters affecting them jointly. The only context in which dialogue is allowed is the context of reference to material objects and events.

It is surely the case that Whorf's primary occupation as an insurance executive made extended periods of participant observation impossible for him, but this only deepens the mystery. Why should someone who seemed so clearly to understand the centrality of context *refuse* to engage wholeheartedly in participant observation? Why didn't he become a full-time linguistic anthropologist, give up his insurance job, and do his research the way it should have been done? A partial answer undoubtedly concerns his prototype of science as a laboratory science, and his need to equate informants with apparatus to make linguistics respectably scientific. But that might equally well be seen as an excuse to mask his squeamishness when faced with a direct and prolonged confrontation with Otherness.

A preoccupation with reference to material objects, of course, is a traditional means, in science and philosophy, to eliminate from consideration those factors which are believed to "contaminate" the data. Paradoxically, however, Whorf's willingness to go along with this preoccupation in his own analyses of human language (and the cultures of the human beings who speak them) sets him up for another attack by his critics. Part of the rationale for concentrating on reference to the exclusion of all else is rooted in the faith that the identity of material objects is free of the ambiguities that cloud political or ethical matters, for example. By restricting their analysis of language to matters of reference, and assuming one can translate sentence-by-sentence, these critics imply that there can be only one legitimate (i.e., unambiguous) way in which any given sentence in language *A* can be translated into language *B*. That is, since sentences must be thought of as propositions, they must therefore be translated as literal statements whose material, referential truth value (or lack of it) can be clearly established. On these grounds, Whorf is faulted either (1) for translating metaphorical expressions too "literally" when such translation leads a Western observer to questions their truth value (e.g., Lenneberg 1953:465–66; Brown, 1958:231ff.), or (2) for masking the "deep," literal sameness or difference of expressions from different languages (which would presumably reveal their common truth value, or lack of it) by attaching too great an importance to their "superficial," figurative or formal similarities or differences (e.g., Longacre 1956:306).

It seems that Whorf cannot win. On the one hand, if he wishes to be faithful to the peculiarities of a particular tongue (for example, in his discussion of cleaning rifles with ramrods in English and Shawnee), he will be accused of making a translation so literal-minded as to be "ludicrous," to use Lenneberg's term. To avoid such an outcome, Lenneberg would urge the translator clearly to distinguish between literal and metaphorical statements in both the source and the target languages, and be so kind as not to mistake a mere metaphor for a serious literal statement whose truth value the natives respect. Like Putnam and Davison, Lenneberg urges the translator to exercise a "principle of charity" which assumes that speakers of the foreign tongue would not be so irrational as to take literally a statement which could only be metaphorical in the English of scientific linguists. Longacre, on the other hand, appears *unwilling* to extend a principle of charity to the speakers of other languages, and he criticizes Whorf for according the same truth value to sentences which only appear superficially equivalent to one another. Thus, everything informants say must in principle be taken as literal statements of belief, and we Western scientists must feel free to criticize such statements from the standpoint of our superior scientific knowledge.

The appropriate form translation should take now becomes highly problematic and politically charged. The key decision is not so much which sentences in one language should be matched with which sentences in another, as how we wish to portray the speakers of the language being translated. Do we want them to appear as rational, as "human," as we do? If so, we will want our translation to highlight the similarities between their speech and ours, and to downplay those aspects which, in Whorf's words, make their speech "so strange and baffling from the standpoint of English" (Whorf 5:162). If, on the other hand, we are convinced that the speakers of the language being translated are indeed "primitives" utterly unlike ourselves, we will want our translation of their language to reflect this fact, and we will not allow the loophole of figurative language to save their false beliefs from being exposed (cf. Brown 1958:231–33).

So, paradoxically, an idiomatic translation highlights rationality. With this sometimes goes a corollary assumption that "their" idioms must be easily translatable into "our" idioms; otherwise we are impugning their rationality. This view can be found in Au (1983:182–83), who asserts that

> Hockett was right that we should make sure the translations are idiomatic before we draw conclusions from the findings of cross-cultural research on language and thought. Many French teachers have told their English-speaking students that "Comment allez-vous?" which is literally "How go you?" actually means "How are you?" . . . I wonder if some day an Apache speaker will tell us that Whorf's English translation, "as water, or springs; whiteness moves downward" actually means "It is a dripping spring"; and if a Shawnee speaker will one day tell us that "direct a hollow moving dry

spot by movement of tool" actually means "cleaning a gun with a ramrod."

Yet, as we have seen, Whorf demonstrates in his discussion of the gun-cleaning example that idiomatic translation, by itself, is *insensitive* "toward the brute materiality, the typicality . . . in how the world is seen and felt, ways that are organically part and parcel with the language that expresses them" (Bakhtin 1981c[1940]:367). Only a monolingual, monological consciousness could fail to detect, or to take seriously, such material differences. And when Whorf contrasts the Shawnee and English ways of describing cleaning a gun, he is speaking from the perspective of a multilingual consciousness, which brings into sharp focus the material differences between different languages. It is the multilingual consciousness which can encompass two (or more) materially different ways of describing a shared situation. Only the multilingual consciousness grasps fully that a speaker's understanding of language cannot proceed without awareness (1) of the interlocutor's point of view/language and (2) of the shared situation whose features both are trying to describe.

This is eloquently illustrated by the "dripping spring" example referred to by Au. Whorf's discusses this example in his article "Languages and Logic" as follows:

> We might isolate something in nature by saying "It is a dripping spring." Apache erects the statement on a verb *ga:* "be white (including clear, uncolored, and so on)." With a prefix *no-* the meaning of downward motion enters: "whiteness moves downward." Then *to,* meaning both "water" and "spring" is prefixed. The result corresponds to our "dripping spring," but synthetically it is "as water, or springs, whiteness moves downward." How utterly unlike our way of thinking! (Whorf 8:241)

Whorf's vague reference to "something in nature" makes it unclear whether the "spring" he refers to is the season of the year or a source of fresh water, though his definition of *to* suggests the latter. Whorf appears to interpret the Apache expression *ga,* "whiteness," in its "clear, uncolored" sense, suggesting that the whiteness moving downward is the water. However, this interpretation is at odds with the one offered by Hoijer (1953:559). Hoijer writes:

> A final, and revealing, illustration may be added from the language of the Chiricahua Apache, the place name *tonoogah,* for which the English equivalent (not the translation) is "Dripping Springs." Dripping Springs, a noun phrase, names a spot in New Mexico where the

water from a spring flows over a rocky bluff and drips into a small pool below; the English name, it is evident, is descriptive of one part of this scene, the movement of the water. The Apache term is, in contrast, a verbal phrase and accentuates quite a different aspect of the scene. The element *to*, which means "water," precedes the verb *noogah*, which means, roughly, "whiteness extends downward." *tonoogah*, as a whole, then, may be translated "water-whiteness extends downward," a reference to the fact that a broad streak of white limestone deposit, laid down by the running water, extends downward on the rock.

If we compare these two analyses, we could argue perhaps that, although "dripping spring" is a noun phrase, the participle "dripping" is, after all, a verbal, and does convey the idea of water in (slow) motion. Likewise, if the Apache expression is actually referring to the streak of white limestone, this is very nounlike, and has nothing to do with the moving water which deposited it upon the rock. This being said, and despite the differing interpretations of the Apache phrase, the basic insight defended by both Whorf and Hoijer stands. Speakers of English and Apache use their respective languages to describe the *same physical scene* in *materially different ways:* English emphasizes the slowly moving water, Apache emphasizes the limestone streak left by the water on the rock. Furthermore, both descriptions are logically relatable to the potentially shareable experience of Anglos and Apaches going together to Dripping Springs, New Mexico, observing the phenomenon in question simultaneously, and juxtaposing for one another their respective language's typical way of describing the scene.

Once this is done, it is possible to argue that both versions are valid, if partial, descriptions of the scene, each being relative to the standard referential perspective of Anglos and Apaches, respectively. By relating the two descriptions to the phenomenon itself, moreover, both Anglos and Apaches should be able to relate the perspective taken in one language to the perspective taken in the other. With a little effort, Anglos might even come up with an equivalent of the Apache expression— "Limestone Streak," for example. No doubt Apache speakers could construct an equivalent to "Dripping Springs" as well. But none of this eminently plausible activity would be possible without English speakers and Apache speakers (or the English and Apache voices within an individual multilingual consciousness) addressing one another about these referential matters *within the bounds of a single, specific context.*

The task for the translator seems paradoxical: how do you highlight the humanity—the "rationality"—of those who speak the language you are translating without obscuring the very real differences in the way they use their language to talk about the world? If we believe Bakhtin, however, this task is paradoxical only for a monological consciousness. Only a consciousness that can report another's words without drowning them out in its own voice can accomplish translation with anything like success. The form of consciousness in question is, of course, multilingual consciousness, prose consciousness: " 'retelling in one's own words' . . . poses on a small scale the task implicit in all prose stylistics: retelling a text in one's own words is to a certain extent a double-voiced narration of another's words, for indeed 'one's own words' must not completely dilute the quality that makes another's words unique; a retelling in one's own words should have a mixed character, able when necessary to reproduce the style and expression of the transmitted text" (Bakhtin 1981c[1940]:341).

Whorf's attempt to translate from Shawnee or Hopi or Nootka is an attempt to retell in English words without diluting the material uniqueness of the Amerindian words he is translating. This is why neither word-for-word nor sentence-for-sentence translation is adequate by itself. Either procedure may suffice for limited purposes—purposes of "explanation," in Bakhtinian terms, where only one consciousness, one subject is present. *Both* procedures, however, are needed for comprehension, which requires "two consciousnesses and two subjects. . . . Understanding is always dialogic to some degree" (1986[n.d.]:111). Bakhtin argues that "the prose writer as a novelist does not strip away the intentions of others from the heteroglot language of his works, he does not violate those socio-ideological cultural horizons (big and little worlds) that open up behind heteroglot languages—rather, he welcomes them into his work" (Bakhtin 1981c[1940]:299). So, too, Whorf—the scientific linguist as seer—does not want to violate the socio-ideological cultural horizons that open up behind polyglot languages. He, too, wants to welcome them into his work. According to Bakhtin, moreover, such an orientation is not misplaced "even in the narrowly scientific disciplines," for "any gifted, creative exposition defining alien world views . . . is always a free stylistic variation on another's discourse; it expounds another's thought in the style of that thought even while applying it to new material, to another way of posing the problem: it conducts experiments and gets solutions in the language of another's discourse" (1981c:347).

To conduct such an experiment successfully, however, requires enormous attention to artistic composition. The Whorfian text, like the novelistic hybrid, "is *an artistically organized system for bringing different languages in contact with one another,* a system having as its goal the illumination of one language by means of another, the carving out of a living image of another language" (Bakhtin 1981c:361). And the successful Whorfian text—that is to say, the controversial Whorfian text, several of which we have examined—is like the successful novel. In both cases readers are drawn into "the process of coming to know one's own language as it is perceived in someone else's system . . . an ideological translation of another's language, and an overcoming of its otherness—an otherness that is only contingent, external, illusory" (1981c:365). It is this experiment, this process, that produces the multilingual event; the same experiment, the same process, produces the polyphonic novel: "the artistic will of polyphony is a will to combine many wills, a will to the event" (Bakhtin 1984[1929]:21).

"The event" is crucial for Bakhtin and for Whorf. Its centrality to Bakhtin's perspective has been noted by his translators, who have emphasized the importance of his Russian neologism *sobytie.* Emerson, for example, expounds at some length on this term in a footnote on the second page of her translation of *Problems of Dostoevsky's Poetics* (1984:6):

> *Sobytie* (event) and its adjective *sobytiinyi* (full of event potential) are crucial terms in Bakhtin. At their root lies the Russian word for "existence" or "being" (*bytie*), and—although the etymology here can be disputed—*so-bytie* can be read both in its ordinary meaning of "event," and in a more literal rendering as "co-existing, co-being, shared existence or being *with* another." An event can occur only among interacting consciousnesses: there can be no isolated or solipsistic events.

According to Bakhtin, Dostoevsky was the literary master of multilingual, multicultural "co-being." "What unfolds in his works is not a multitude of characters and fates in a single objective world, illuminated by a single authorial consciousness; rather a *plurality of consciousnesses, with equal rights and each with its own world,* combine but are not merged in the unity of the event" (1984[1929]:6). In his own way, Whorf was equally a master of multilingual, multicultural co-being. His texts endeavor to show that the languages of polyglossia, no less than the languages of heteroglossia, "do not *exclude* each other, but rather intersect with each other in many different ways" (1981c[1940]:291). This realization, as Bakhtin goes on to note, might lead one to conclude (as Chatterjee concluded) "that the very word 'language' loses all meaning in this process—for apparently there is no single plane on which all these 'languages' might be juxtaposed to one another" (1981c:291). This conclusion can, in fact, seem inescapable when the various languages in question are the languages of heteroglossia: it is possible to assume, along with Mr. Everyman, that each of us speaks as we individually choose to speak, encountering neither inner nor outer constraint.

But Bakhtin explicitly rejects this conclusion: "In actual fact, however, there does exist a common plane that methodologically justifies our juxtaposing them: all languages of heteroglossia . . . are specific points of view on the world"—points of view that grow out, and point back toward, diverse, *shared* ways of life; diverse, *shared* practical activities. "As such, they encounter one another and coexist in the consciousness of real people—first and foremost in the creative consciousness of people who write novels" (1981c:291).

Whorf appears to agree with Bakhtin. By choosing, moreover, to concentrate on the languages of *poly*glossia, he has considerably heightened the dramatic impact of his text. His "will to the event" is demonstrated by three techniques, as we have seen. First, he gives "literal-minded" word-for-word translations of alien expressions, to shock his readers into recognizing the material linguistic differences separating the alien language from their own (as in the gun-cleaning or dripping-spring examples). Second, he offers "figurative" or idiomatic English glosses to emphasize the way in which these alien expressions intersect with familiar English expressions. Finally, on occasion he provides drawings designed to represent the potentially shareable experience, the single context, from which the differences and similarities can both be validly drawn. Together, these techniques gives us a feel for the unique perspective of a particular language, even as they demonstrate the ways in which relating "their perspective" and "our perspective" to shareable human experience can create the possibility of each party grasping something of the perspective of the other.

Bakhtin's work, particularly his analysis of Dostoevsky, was focused primarily on heteroglossia, although we have seen that polyglossia was not something he ignored, especially in his studies of Greek and Latin texts. The remarks he did make, however, would seem to endorse Whorf's project. In a late text, he asks, "Can languages and dialects (territorial, social jargons), language (functional) styles (say, familiar daily speech and scientific language and so forth) . . . speak with one another and so forth? Only if a nonlinguistic approach is taken toward them, that is, if they are transformed into a 'world view' (or some language or speech sense of the world), into a 'viewpoint,' into 'social voices,' and so forth" (1986[n.d.]:119). This is what Whorf undertook to accomplish with SAE and Amerindian languages. The approach of scientific linguistics, according to him, would make this transformation from "language" to "world view" possible, via concentration upon grammar. To do so meant, however, that the only worldviews he could recognize would be those articulated by languages of polyglossia, since the phonological and grammatical rules which separate such languages are maximally different.

But what happens when such maximally different languages are juxtaposed? The sorts of things taken for granted by speakers of dialects of a single language, or of specialized jargons within a single dialect, no longer exist: no shared history, no shared traditions, no shared way of life at all. And yet, Bakhtin tells us, "Two utterances, separated from one another both in time and in space, knowing nothing of one another, when they are compared semantically, reveal dialogic relationships if there is any kind of semantic convergence between them (if only a partially shared theme, point of view, and so forth)" (1986[n.d.]:124). The only matters on which semantic convergence might rest become physical characteristics of the interlocutors' human bodies (as Lakoff and Johnson stress) *and shared physical features of their shared, single context.* The Other, and a context in which the Other and the speaker may meet, and whose features they can discuss, is indispensable. And so Whorf included drawings, or attempted to paint word pictures, to illustrate the indispensable context which his readers and his heroes were to share.

Such a translation strategy, of course, far from providing readers with an exhaustive, unambiguous rendering of one language in terms of another, in actuality only creates the possibility for embarking upon cross-linguistic understanding. It circles around the problems of translation, offering possible paths to insight and examples of insights achieved, but guaranteeing nothing (although Whorf is optimistic). Readers, in fact, must accomplish the translation, the understanding, on their own. This is bound to be unsatisfactory for readers who are relying on Whorf to explain the meaning of Shawnee words or Hopi sentences in the monological language of science. They are bound to accuse him of duplicity, or of failing to demonstrate what he claimed he would demonstrate. But Whorf is not interested in such monological explanation, even though he writes in a parodic version of the monological language of science. Like Dostoevsky, Whorf takes on a different artistic task: "A plurality of voices, after all, is not meant to be eliminated in his works but in fact is meant to triumph" (Bakhtin 1984[1929]:204).

 If this is Whorf's goal, then there is a central role to be played by nonidiomatic translation. We may agree, on some level, with Lenneberg when he objects that "it makes no sense to equate the global meaning of an utterance with the sequence of abstracted, general meanings of the morphemes that occur in that utterance" (1953:465). Yet such an action is necessary in order to jostle and stimulate the reader's awareness of the material uniqueness of any particular language's habitual way of describing the world. Of course, translation and comprehension must involve more than this alone, as we have seen. Still, nonidiomatic translation achieves its aim if it forces readers to recognize that there is, indeed, something profoundly *alien* (from the point of view of English) about the way Shawnee goes about describing the way a rifle is cleaned, however commonplace and idiomatic that description may be in Shawnee. This of course highlights the troubling but inescapable fact we encounter in all translation, linguistic or cultural: one person's (language's, culture's) idiom is another's unjustified false belief; one person's (language's, culture's) metaphor is another's literal description of reality. And neither figurative nor literal statements come with labels attached that allow translators unerringly to avoid mistaking one for the other as they go about their work. Once again, the matter can be resolved— insofar as is humanly possible—only by reintegrating contradictory statements made by speakers of different languages back into the *single* concrete social context they are *both* intended to describe.

Whorf, like Dostoevsky, "placed the idea on the borderline of dialogically intersecting consciousness. He brought together ideas and world views, which in real life were absolutely estranged and deaf to one another, and forced them to quarrel" (Bakhtin 1984[1929]:91). Whorf's art, like that of the prose novelist, "presumes a deliberate feeling for the historical and social concreteness of living discourse, as well as its relativity, a feeling for its participation in historical becoming and in social struggle; it deals with discourse still warm from that struggle and hostility, as yet unresolved and still fraught with hostile intentions and accents" (Bakhtin 1981c[1940]:331). Whorf dared to face this aspect of human discourse and expose it. And yet the very activity seems to have frightened him to death. Seeing this revolutionary view of language through to its conclusion meant calling into question much more than the rules of English grammar (cf. Bakhtin 1981c:367). It meant calling into question much more than the religious and scientific doctrines he had been taught. It required a thoroughgoing reassessment of his society's relations with the speakers of the languages he studied; it required a thoroughgoing reassessment of the role of his social class within that society. Whorf appears to have known this, and to have feared it. He tried to hide behind a focus on grammar and reference, and he restricted his informants to these topics as well. He tried to hide behind a comic persona, or, more accurately, an elusive parody of a serious scientific persona. But to hide completely would defeat his project, so he risked exposure, tearing himself apart in the process.

This unsettling mixture of terror and glee is perhaps most evident in Whorf's article "A Linguistic Consideration of Thinking in Primitive Communities." He describes the following situation:

> Let us suppose that an ethnologist discovers that the Hopi speak about clouds in their rain prayers, etc., as though clouds were alive. He would like to know whether this is some metaphor or special religious or ceremonial figure of speech, or whether it is the ordinary and usual way of thinking about clouds. Here is the sort of problem to which language might be able to give a very meaningful answer, and we immediately turn to it to see if it has a gender system that distinguishes living from nonliving things, and, if so, how it classes a cloud. We find that Hopi has no gender at all. (Whorf 3:79)

Since, however, Whorf extends the notion of grammar to include not just the formally marked elements in language but also the patterned but unmarked usages (which he calls cryptotypes), he finds that Hopi does distinguish a cryptotypic animate class of nouns, and the Hopi word for "cloud" is always pluralized in the animate way. Having discovered this, Whorf concludes: "And so the question whether the animation of clouds is a figure or formality of speech or whether it stems from some more deep and subtly pervasive undercurrent of thought is answered, or at the least given a flood of new meaning."

But what sort of conclusion is this? What is this "flood of new meaning"? Apparently it is occasioned by Whorf's introduction of the concept of cryptotype. Yet Whorf's concept of a cryptotype is fascinating in its ambiguity. It refers to a "covert linguistic class," that is, a patterned linguistic usage which nonetheless is not formally marked in the grammar (Whorf 3:70). Whorf would like to be able to argue that grammar forces people to think in terms of its formal categories. Thus, if cryptotypes are part of grammar, and if, cryptotypically, clouds are animate, then Hopi grammar forces Hopi speakers not just to talk about but also to think about clouds as if they were animate. But the flaw in this argument consists precisely in the fact that *cryptotypes are not formally marked,* so that there is nothing about them (apart from *unmarked* patterns of usage) to force Hopi speakers to think about them in one way rather than another.

Perhaps Whorf means to refer to these unformalized patterns as fashions of speaking, or discourse practices, which draw upon but are not reducible to the formally marked patterns of a language. If this is the case, then it is possible that speaking of clouds as if they were alive is but a figurative discourse practice of which Hopi are fully aware, and the practice becomes comprehensible once one understands the Hopi worldview and the place of clouds within it. Hopi "rationality" is saved. *And yet how can we be sure that this usage does not reflect a Hopi attempt, via discourse practices, to force their language to represent a literal belief of theirs which remains uncaptured by formal grammar but which they find justified and true and are determined to assert?*

Perhaps it is this disquieting possibility that Whorf is referring to when he asks whether the animation of clouds in Hopi "stems from some more deep and subtly pervasive undercurrent of thought." In any case, despite his assertion to the contrary (which he immediately and characteristically qualifies so extensively that one may question whether anything is left of it), *Whorf offers no answer.* Nor does he provide any "flood of new meaning," unless—perverse thought!—the "new meaning" consists precisely in this unsettling discovery that the line between the literal and the figurative can never be drawn unambiguously, at least when one is working cross-linguistically. And if heteroglossia is equally real—i.e., if fashions of speaking exist *within* each separate language—perhaps the distinction can never be made *at all.* What remains, then, is unfinalizable dialogue.

Unfinalizable dialogue, of course, need not be a free-for-all. Although never resolved into a single point of view valid for everyone, it can nevertheless be asymptotic in effect: each partner to the dialogue (including, importantly, the context) acts as a control on the others, correcting for bias, filling in blind spots. Such a view of dialogue is optimistic. Certainly, the burden of achieving total lucidity about ourselves would lessen considerably if we could rely on others to see what we do not see, and point it out to us, and keep us honest; and if we could be relied upon to perform the same service for them. But to the monological consciousness, such a devolution of power is immensely threatening. It threatened the traditional scientist in Whorf, even the traditional mystic. What is admirable about Whorf is that he had the courage to face the threat, regardless of the consequences.

Conclusion

It seems fairly clear that one part of Whorf wanted to persuade his readers that, ultimately, his brand of scientific linguistics had the potential to make fully and unambiguously clear the dimensions of reality which individual languages could describe only partially and therefore, ambiguously. Nevertheless, he admitted that no linguist had yet come close to amassing the kind of metalinguistic knowledge that would make this possible. In the late twentieth century, Whorf's faith may seem naive at best, and irritating at worst, since, as Friedrich reminds us, the state of our world gives us little reason for optimism. Yet to read Whorf today can still prove invigorating for the delight he takes in discovering and sharing with his readers new ways of talking about experience, quite apart from what these discoveries might tell us about the grammar of the universe. To read him can also prove fascinating as one explores the tortuous way in which he fashioned a discourse that, far from being reducible to some finite set of rules of English grammar, stretched, bent, and otherwise exploited those rules in order to cultivate ambiguity about complex matters. To note his rhetorical strategies is to admire his shrewdness and his intellectual honesty at the same time; his desire to seem to offer simple and radical new insights, and yet his scrupulous unwillingness to allow his text to commit him to anything simplistic.

Bakhtin similarly cultivated ambiguity about complex matters. He never attacked the censors of his own day directly. But in attacking the censors of previous epochs (such as the medieval church), or of different genres (such as poets), he delivered a barrage against "epistemological monomania" (to use Holquist's expression), whose metaphorical aptness the censors of his own day found it impossible to ignore. The result for him was arrest and internal exile. The result for Whorf has been, largely, the hostility of two generations or more of philosophical and social scientific critics. That two thinkers with similar ideas about language, working in societies so different from each other, should have been equally notorious is fascinating. But it is due to the fact, I believe, that each used insights gained from his understanding of language to attack the sensitive underbelly of the particular social world in which he lived.

Both recognized the two linguistic processes which Bakhtin called *canonization* and *reaccentuation*. Each chose to highlight only one of these processes. Whorf tried to alert his readers to the power of canonization: the social endorsement of certain grammatical rules and generic speech forms which are taken as a standard to which everyone's speech must conform if it is not to sound alien. Only marginally would he acknowledge that speakers have the creative imagination and flexibility to manipulate canonical usage to their own ends. Bakhtin, while having much to say about canonization, nevertheless inspired his readers most by what he had to say about reaccentuation: for instance, "In each epoch, in each social circle . . . there are always authoritative utterances that set the tone. . . . the unique speech experience of each individual . . . can be characterized to some degree as the process of *assimilation*—more or less creative—of others' words. . . . These words of others carry with them their own expression, their own evaluative tone, which we assimilate, rework, and re-accentuate" (1986[1952–53]:88–89).

Bakhtin's elaboration of the ways in which reaccentuation can occur is a useful supplement for Whorf's insistence on the power of canonical forms. He highlighted the various ways in which authoritative utterances could be undermined even as they were repeated—with a parodic-ironic intonation, of course. The reward for coming to understand the nature of the chains that bind us, for Bakhtin, is very much like that which Fishman claims as the reward of a Whorfian perspective: "The better our command of genres, the more freely we employ them, the more fully and clearly we reveal our own individuality in them (where this is possible and necessary), the more flexibly and precisely we reflect the unrepeatable situation of communication—in a word, the more perfectly we implement our free speech plan" (Bakhtin 1986[1952–53]:80). Freedom of speech, for Bakhtin as for Whorf, is not something we are born with, but something we have to work at, to achieve. At the same time, it is something potentially accessible to anyone, and a goal worth pursuing vigorously for everyone. "Only in the form of a confessional self-utterance . . . could the final word about a person be given, a word truly adequate to him" (Bakhtin 1984[1929]:55–56).

And this is a message of particular relevance for ethnographers and anthropological linguists who have not always been sufficiently aware of what is needed if they are more perfectly to implement their own free speech plan. Bakhtin's advice to literary critics about novels is equally good advice for ethnographers about ethnographies (and the cultures they are supposed to illuminate): "What is present in the novel is . . . a system of *images* of languages, and the real task of stylistic analysis consists in uncovering all the available orchestrating languages in the composition of the novel, grasping the precise degree of distancing that separates each language from its most immediate semantic instantiation in the work as a whole, and the varying angles of refraction of intentions within it, understanding their dialogic relationships and—finally—if there *is* direct authorial discourse, determining the heteroglot background outside the work that dialogizes it" (1981c[1940]:416). Bakhtin explicitly warns analysts against the temptation to explain away apparent contradictions: "Especially dangerous is any vulgarizing that oversimplifies re-accentuation (which is cruder in all respects than that of the author and his time) and that turns a two-voiced image into one that is flat, single-voiced" (1981c:420).

To resist in this way the temptation to epistemological monomania should make the critic, and the ethnographer, more sensitive to the ground of diversity and dialogue out of which social and linguistic change arises. Linguistic and cultural freedom is discerned in the way people reaccent and mix the generic forms they inherit from the past or borrow from contemporaries. We never begin with a clean slate, but this does not mean that we cannot attain, with effort, a significant degree of expressive liberty. Of course, a similar effort must be exercised if outsiders—literary critics or ethnographers—are to come to understand the forms of expression they encounter in texts or in social relations. Bakhtin saw "*depth* of understanding as one of the highest criteria for cognition in the human sciences. The word, if it is not an acknowledged falsehood, is bottomless" (1986[n.d.]:127). At the end of his life he could claim, "Meaning cannot (and does not wish to) change physical, material, and other phenomena; it cannot act as a material force. And it does not need to do this: it itself is stronger than any force, it changes the total contextual meaning of an event and reality without changing its actual (existential) composition one iota; everything remains as it was but it acquires a completely different contextual meaning (the semantic transformation of existence). Each word of a text is transformed in a new context" (1986[1974]:165).

What is the lesson for linguists and ethnographers? If meaning as reference will never be sufficient to unlock the meaning of context, is there hope for a "scientific" study of the relationship between human thought, language, and culture? Are we condemned to mapping mish onto mash? Bakhtin thinks not. If science is a matter of precise measurement, clearly the forms of measurement adequate for the material world, and reference within it, will be too crude in the human sciences. But this does not mean that precision is impossible. Rather, it must take a different form. "In the human sciences precision is surmounting the otherness of the other without transforming him into purely one's own" (1986[1974]:169). This is the kind of precision Whorf seems to have aimed at, in his own way. His preoccupation with "patternment" (Whorf 7:231), and his desire to get an adequate reading of the precise forms patternment took in different grammars, seem to presuppose Bakhtin's axiom. Whorf aimed to make alien grammars comprehensible to his English-speaking readers, which meant that the otherness of these grammars needed to be surmounted. Yet, at the same time, he refused to efface the materiality of those alien grammars entirely, he refused to assimilate them to English patterns, to make them purely his, or his readers', own. As we have seen, Whorf was clearest on this point in his discussion of Shawnee grammar. But it is exactly this point that Whorf's critics cannot accept.

For Bakhtin, of course, Dostoevsky was the figure who was better able than anyone else to surmount the otherness of the other without transforming him into purely one's own. "Dostoevsky was capable of *representing someone else's idea,* preserving its full capacity to signify as an idea, while at the same time also preserving a distance, neither confirming the idea nor merging it with his own expressed ideology" (1984[1929]:85). And Bakhtin's reading of Dostoevsky offers an example from which ethnographers might learn; indeed, it describes what always occurs in the best ethnography: "only a dialogic and participatory orientation takes another person's discourse seriously. . . . Only through such an inner dialogic orientation can my discourse find itself in intimate contact with someone else's discourse, and yet at the same time not fuse with it, not swallow it up, not dissolve in itself the other's power to mean" (1984[1929]:64). Rationalist philosophers and formal linguists want precisely to dissolve the other's power to mean with the corrosive acid of their own categories. Of course, repression of difference by force does give the appearance of unanimity. But it remains willfully blind and deaf to a great many things. Opening one's eyes and ears to diversity takes courage. Conveying an understanding of that diversity to a potentially hostile audience takes courage plus artistry. As Bakhtin observed, with typical understatement, "To preserve distance in the presence of an intense semantic bond is no simple matter" (1984:64).

The ideal ethnographer or anthropological linguist, then, would be very like the ideal novelist whom Bakhtin found in Dostoevsky: "a higher type of disinterested artist who takes nothing from the world" (1984[1961]:286). In one of the few pessimistic utterances to be found in his works, Bakhtin continues, "Such consistent antihedonism is no longer anywhere to be found" (1984:286) And yet Whorf, Bakhtin's contemporary, came very close. In his texts, be strove with extraordinary dedication and artistry to take as little from the world as possible, and to restore what he did take away as best he could. The price he paid cognitively to achieve this seems to have been enormous. And if his voice, as Bakhtin tells us, cannot be separated from his worldview and fate and entire individuality, the struggle which appears in his texts cannot have failed to affect his life beyond them.

Why is Whorf so threatening to rationalist philosophers and formal linguists? If his project is legitimate and if its lessons are unforgettable, it gives the lie to their project. Their pursuit of a single, objective, impersonal truth valid in all times and all places for all people turns out to be misguided. The hope of being able to assimilate the whole of truth within the harmonious categories of a single consciousness is similarly doomed. The image of the rational man of Western philosophy and science, the rugged individualist who masters the universe on his own, is shown to have feet of clay. Indeed, the self-image of Western man since the Enlightenment is called seriously in question, as are vast areas of knowledge and practice which depend on the plausibility of that self-image (see Taylor 1985a:4–5; cf. Bakhtin 1984[1929]:82). Bakhtin understood this, and he believed that Dostoevsky understood it. "Capitalism created the conditions for a special type of inescapably solitary consciousness. Dostoevsky exposes all the falsity of this consciousness, as it moves in its vicious circle. . . . man in class society . . . has been driven into forced solitude, which the unsubmissive strive to transform into *proud solitude* (to do without recognition, without others)" (1984[1961]:288). Rationalist philosophers and positivist scientists, each in their own way, claim mastery from a position of proud solitude. Dostoevsky is scandalous because he confronts "all decadent and idealistic (individualistic) culture, the culture of essential and inescapable solitude. He asserts the impossibility of solitude, the illusory nature of solitude" (1984:287).

So, too, Bakhtin and Whorf, in their own ways, assert the impossibility of solitude. Bakhtin was able, in his discussions of heteroglossia, to show again and again how any individual voice depends on the voices and words of others even to come into being. He could demonstrate that struggles to get past the censor could succeed, paradoxically, only by manipulating other people's words for one's own ends. Whorf, as we said, had to convince his readers that the censor even existed. The linguistic ideology of his society drew upon the same individualism, the same proud solitude, of the philosophers and scientists which Bakhtin and Dostoevsky decried.

Both Whorf and Bakhtin resist the attempt by their critics to reduce sociolinguistic points of view to mere struggle between individual wills or logical contradictions. But their critics, who seem convinced that to resist this reduction is to endorse nihilism, protest equally vigorously. And, of course, Whorf is not their only target. Other figures, like Robin Horton in anthropology, for example, are equally scandalous when they attempt to set up a dialogue among different points of view on a common theme, as Horton does in his essay accompanying Meyer Fortes' *Oedipus and Job in West African Religion* (1983). Horton refuses to make it easy for his readers by reducing four indigenous West African theories of personhood to the Freudian model originally suggested by Fortes. On the contrary, he explicitly urges his readers to consider Freud's voice as only one other voice (albeit an important one) in the dialogue (Horton 1983:79). In his own way, Horton refuses to allow "the transformation of a dialogue of styles into a simple coexistence of various versions of one and the same style" (Bakhtin 1986[1970–71]:135).

Clearly, critics are afraid that to allow dialogue would be to allow Truth to degenerate into mere Opinion—and as our freshman students always tell us, "everyone is entitled to their own opinion." But this fear is based on the assumption that voices in dialogue must always disagree; that the only alternative to this cacophonous disagreement is unanimity, imitation, identity, fusion of perspective. Some of Bakhtin's supporters, indeed, value his work precisely because it, like deconstruction, promises to tear things down in an orgy of joyful relativity. Emerson, for example, writes that "in place of the comfortable patterns of synthesis and *Aufhebung,* Bakhtin posits a dualistic universe of *permanent* dialogue. Life in language is in fact dependent upon the preservation of a gap. Two speakers must not, and never do, completely understand each other; they must remain only partially satisfied with each other's replies, because the continuation of dialogue is in large part dependent on neither party knowing exactly what the other means" (1984:xxxii). But this makes dialogue sound unnatural, contrived, the result of deliberate preservation of a gap in perspective which would otherwise naturally close.

Emerson reads Bakhtin as suggesting that we need to create gaps deliberately, like a coquette playing hard to get, since otherwise dialogue would collapse, fusion of perspective would ensue. Of course, if the only alternative to disagreement is fusion with another, the preference for lively disagreement to stagnant imitation is understandable.

And yet this emphasis misses an important element in Bakhtin's message: his suggestion that unanimity and cacophony are *not* the only alternatives. The third alternative, as we mentioned earlier, is a voluntary assent to a unified truth which includes the partial truths of each point of view, but is greater than any one of them taken by itself. *Dialogic agreement* of this sort is thus not ruled out. It is dialogic agreement that makes the heteroglot elements in a culture hang together despite the absence of rigorous policing of boundaries or routing out of contradiction. It is dialogic agreement, in ideology and in practice, that makes culture, in Bakhtin's expression, an "open unity." A culture hangs together, but not by force alone. If force were all, to speak of *a* culture would be false and misleading.

But to speak thus is not false, because it is possible for individuals speaking from different perspectives to acknowledge the validity of one another's points of view without being forced to deny their own. It is not always easy, of course. But an insight into human affairs to which a group of variously situated observers could freely assent, even though it surpassed in scope their own personal visions, would be no less objective, no less true than an insight into the nature of physical bodies which could be freely ratified by a range of differently situated observers. This dialogic objectivity, if we may call it that, was something Bakhtin recognized in Dostoevsky's novels (1984[1929]:51).

The difference between traditional, "rational" objectivity and dialogic objectivity might be phrased as the difference between a focus on how we know and a focus on how we learn (cf. Smith 1988:11). Indeed, according to Bakhtin's description, Dostoevsky's artistic procedure resembles the learning process, and the outcome of that process can include dialogic agreement as well as disagreement: "His entire material unfolds before him as a series of human orientations. His path leads not from idea to idea, but from orientation to orientation. To think, for him, means to question and to listen, to try out orientations, to combine some and expose others. . . . Even *agreement* retains its *dialogic* character. . . . it never leads to a *merging* of voices and truths in a single *impersonal* truth, as occurs in the monologic world" (1984[1929]:95).

Agreement in this sense "cannot be a monologic act, but rather presumes the attachment of the hero's voice to the chorus" (1984[1929]:249).

This is the sort of dialogic agreement Whorf appears to seek: he employs all the artistry he can muster to encourage his readers to assent voluntarily, to attach their voices freely, to the chorus. But Whorf realizes, as Bakhtin believes Dostoevsky realized, that "for this to happen . . . it is necessary to subdue and muffle the fictive voices that interrupt and mock a person's genuine voice" (Bakhtin 1984[1929]:249). The agonizing paradox Whorf faced was the necessity of distorting the genuine voices of his heroes and his readers, in order to impress the latter that the former possessed a genuine voice that had been subdued and muffled and mocked by their stereotypes, but that deserved to be heard.

What is the outcome of dialogic agreement? It would seem to be the same outcome that follows any intensive learning experience. Rather than merely asserting previous suppositions without questioning them, learners broaden and deepen their understanding of those suppositions, rejecting some, confirming some, and adding new ones. The result is a change in perspective. This scenario has been insightfully described by W. C. Smith:

> The question is not whether you agree with what I say, and certainly not with the imperfect way that I am saying it; rather, whether you see some of the things that I see and am trying to point to and am offering a vocabulary to talk about and whether you see other things of this ilk that I have not seen, and can point them out to me. And finally, of course, the question is whether those things that various ones of us have seen are indeed there. The purpose is that we may all live enriched. . . . (1988:11)

As with all learning, the lesson may be upsetting. We discover that some of the things we took most for granted are *not* there. Bakhtin observes: "As a result of Enlightenment criticism, the world, as it were, became qualitatively poorer in the most immediate way; there turned out to be much less that was actually real in it than was previously thought." Nevertheless, the loss made important new gains possible: "this abstract negative criticism of Enlightenment thinkers . . . helped reality to gather itself together and condense into the visible whole of the new world. New aspects and infinite prospects were revealed in this condensing reality" (1986[1936–38]:44–45).

The world no longer looks the way it did before, but it is still a familiar world. Dialogic agreement is the means by which change is incorporated into human understanding. Both Whorf and Bakhtin believed such change was healthy and necessary. In particular, the outcome of linguistic change, being dialogic, would not require speakers of one language to renounce it entirely in favor of someone else's. As Bakhtin put it, "the growth of literature is not merely development and change within the fixed boundaries of any given definition; the boundaries themselves are constantly changing" (1981d[1941]:33). Interanimation of languages destroys boundaries, but, like carnival, also makes way for a rebirth of new and different ones: "Languages quarreled with each other, but this quarrel—like any quarrel among great and significant cultural and historical forces—could not pass on to a further phase by means of abstract and rational dialogue, nor by a purely dramatic dialogue, but only by means of complexly dialogized hybrids. The great novels of the Renaissance were such hybrids, although stylistically they were monoglot" (1981b[1940]:82).[1]

The controversial Whorfian texts we have examined, of course, are also complexly dialogized hybrids, which stylistically are monoglot (usually in the language of positivist science, sometimes in the language of mysticism). Whorf is trying to persuade his readers to allow themselves to develop a hybrid consciousness, a multilingual consciousness, in order that they may learn, that they may see more than they have been able to see until now. And he is not asking them to renounce everything they have known up until now, except in parody. He respects science and religion and does not want to destroy either. But the unity he envisions is, as Bakhtin put it when speaking of Dostoevsky, "unity not as an innate one-and-only, but as a dialogic *concordance* of unmerged twos or multiples" (1984[1961]:289).

Dialogic agreement is a form of consensus to which people voluntarily assent. As such it should not be unfamiliar to anthropologists who have studied the political practices of many non-Western societies. It is a form of consensus that recognizes the autonomy of individuals who may not be coerced, but may only be persuaded, to cooperate with one another. And it relies on the ordinary willingness of autonomous individuals to decide freely to cooperate with one another in order to further the welfare of the group (cf. Schultz and Lavenda 1990:370–73). It is probably the most ancient of political practices, at least as ancient as coercion. But it has flourished in the modern world primarily in societies of "primitives," where the spread of Western civilization has not stamped it out entirely. Primitive or not, however, it is "democratic" in the most basic sense of the term: "Active agreement/disagreement (if not dogmatically predetermined) stimulates and deepens understanding, makes the other's word more resilient and true to itself, and precludes mutual dissolution and confusion. The clear demarcation of two consciousnesses, their counterposition and their interrelations" (Bakhtin 1986[1970–71]:142).

Such an understanding of freedom is deeply threatening, however, to those—like Whorf's science-minded readers especially—who believe that freedom lies in allegiance to a single point of view. Yet Bakhtin points out (as Western historians of science such as Kuhn and Feyerabend have pointed out) that "there has not been a single scientific age when only one trend existed (but there has almost always been one dominant trend). This is not a question of mere eclecticism: the merging of all trends into one and only one would be fatal to science (if science were mortal). The more demarcation the better, but benevolent demarcation. Without border disputes. Cooperation. The existence of border zones (new trends and disciplines usually originate in them)" (Bakhtin 1986[1970–71]:136–37). This sounds like a retelling in Bakhtin's words of Whorf's position.

What would science be like if it embraced a search for dialogical truth rather than monological truth? Neither Bakhtin nor Whorf believes that it would cease to exist, cease to be "scientific." Whorf in particular is urging us to recognized that the scientific undertaking would be even truer to itself, objective and self-correcting in a more radical way. His tone is optimistic. Bakhtin seems equally optimistic, most of the time. But what if the only stable thing in the world is change? What if the final word, for all time, is that there is no final word as long as we are alive? A pessimistic shadow falls across his image of dialogism when he describes what he finds in Dostoevsky as a "lofty and tragic game" (1984[1929]:91); and when he remarks, in at least three places, that the religious solution Dostoevsky claimed to have found in life—Christ as the Final Word—did not transfer into his art (1984[1929]:97, 249,252). Of course, this entire study has documented the intense struggle Whorf endured as he tried to proclaim a vision of harmony in the face of disturbing signs that it might be illusory. There is for all these men (Dostoevsky included) the uncomfortable suggestion that to "remain with the mistake, but with Christ" is simply not good enough any longer, not for someone who also knows about Allah and Buddha and Brahma and Hopi clan spirits, and who cannot avoid taking them seriously.

And so we must face the price that must be paid for joyful relativity. Some commentators on Bakhtin seem under the impression that the joyful relativity he espouses comes with no strings attached. A good example is Emerson, who characterizes dialogism this way:

> But this "violence" among languages—although deadly serious—is ultimately a *happy* war. Here Bakhtin resembles his beloved Rabelais: when Friar John lops off heads in the monastery vineyard, we see all the bloody parts but no one seems hurt. (1984:xxxvii–xxxviii)

Such an understanding betrays, it seems to me, an insufficient appreciation of what is entailed by taking dialogism seriously, an insufficient appreciation of what is deadly serious about joyful relativity. Emerson may be able to view the violence in the monastery garden as a happy war that does no serious damage, perhaps because she believes that wars of words do not draw real blood, no matter how seriously writers take them. This belief may seem plausible to academic litterateurs living today in the United States. Such a faith is much more difficult to sustain, however, if context is widened to include the rest of the world, and the rest of the century. Challenging established dogma elsewhere has often carried penalties far stiffer than heated criticism in the pages of an academic journal. To fail to see this is to cheapen Bakhtin's commitment to dialogism, to reduce carnival (as he refused to reduce it) to "empty frivolity" or "vulgar bohemian individualism" (Bakhtin 1984[1929]:610). It is a failure to come fully to terms with the fact that the laughter that makes relativity joyful is *ambivalent* laughter, laughter with an edge. Rabelais and Bakhtin lived through dangerous times and managed to survive when many of their friends and colleagues perished for challenging established dogma. To ignore this is to reduce Bakhtin's position to that of other postmodern consciousnesses whose laughter is without ambivalence. It is either to class him with those who, like small boys, cannot see beyond their naive pleasure in destruction to the need to replace what they have destroyed with something else; or it is to place him among the nihilists.

Bakhtin, however, was neither naive nor nihilistic. That he could continue to proclaim allegiance to joyful relativity in spite of the great suffering and deprivation he endured throughout his life testifies to this. Unlike Western academics whose scandalous writings will do no more than provoke scandalized responses from other equally well-heeled, physically and politically unthreatened readers, Bakhtin and his colleagues put their careers and their lives on the line. His most famous collaborators were purged, and he lived for years in exile, plagued by illness that eventually cost him a leg, improverished and unknown. To continue to have faith in humanity's ability to redeem itself from unspeakable violence and injustice is truly remarkable and testifies to a spiritual generosity and lack of bitterness that are exemplary. The moral question is how one uses one's surplus of vision. From all accounts, Bakhtin tried to imitate "Dostoevsky's use of this surplus. Not for materialization and finalization" but for "love . . . confession, forgiveness . . . an active . . . understanding, a willingness to listen . . . never . . . as an ambush, as a chance to sneak up and attack from behind. This is an open and honest surplus" (Bakhtin

1984[1961]:299; cf. Smith 1988:15). To pay attention just to Bakhtin's texts, and refuse to place them in this context, is to distort their significance. It is, in fact, to violate the very canons for understanding which Bakhtin himself endorses.

This story of his texts, and his life, in fact seem to suggest that joyful relativity is possible *only* for someone who is prepared to risk everything for it. It requires an ability to face without fear the fact of inevitable human finitude and partial grasp of the truth. If we consider Dostoevsky together with Bakhtin, we see that both of them were people who knew much suffering and who nevertheless were unwilling to endorse simplistic (i.e., monological) solutions that promised an end to suffering. It is almost as if relativity can be joyful only for those who simultaneously love life and do not fear death. Some may not fear it because, like children, it seems unreal to them; others, because they have stared it in the face and yet defy its power to destroy anything that truly matters.

Bakhtin addresses this in notes written for a revision of *Problems of Dostoevsky's Poetics* (1984[1961]:298):

> The problem of catastrophe. Catastrophe is not finalization. It is the culmination, in collision and struggle, of points of view (of equally privileged consciousnesses, each with its own word). Catastrophe does not give these points of view resolution, but on the contrary reveals their incapability of resolution under earthly conditions; catastrophe sweeps them away without having resolved them.

Elsewhere he remarks, "To kill is not to refute" (1984[1961]:284). Truth, even the partial truth of an individual consciousness, will not turn into a falsehood just because that individual's voice is silenced. Only a faith in the ongoing, living hope for regeneration of the human species—a faith which does have something in common with Rabelais—could sustain such a commitment. He writes that carnival "absolutizes nothing, but rather proclaims the joyful relativity of everything. . . . it is not naked, absolute negation and destruction (absolute negation, like absolute affirmation, is unknown to carnival)." Rather, what one finds in carnival is "the image of constructive death." Such a notion can be dismissed as merely one more variation on the Christian view of redemption. And yet if what Bakhtin says about Dostoevsky's understanding of Christ is true, that he is on the same plane as other human beings, whose consciousnesses are equally privileged, the variation is significant. It is not Christ become man, but men seeking to become Christ that matters. And the image of Christ has nothing to do with hierarchy and power and the supernatural and life after death as conventionally understood. If each human being must become a Christ, then each must be willing to face death, martyrdom, in defense of the truth each of us sees with our own surplus of vision. The only eternal life we can hope for is the life of our species, the chance that in the fullness of time, perhaps long after we as individuals are gone, the truth that we saw will be rediscovered and proclaimed, "have its homecoming festival" (Bakhtin 1986:170).

The most we can hope for is, of course, that dialogic agreement will be achieved. Failing that, however, courage may be fortified by what Bakhtin sees as "the catharsis that finalizes Dostoevsky's novels": "*nothing conclusive has yet taken place in the world, the ultimate word of the world and about the world has not yet been spoken, the world is open and free, everything is still in the future and will always lie in the future.*" As he then goes on to remind us, "this is, after all, the *purifying* sense of ambivalent laughter" (1984[1929]:166).

Of course, a commitment to dialogism requires that we rethink what it is to be human. Bakhtin is betting that our chief attribute is not what we have in common with other objects—being subject to determinism from without and within—but what sets us apart: critical self-consciousness. And not just *some* of us, but *all* of us. To understand what is essential about human nature is to venture (as he says Dostoevsky ventured) "not into the depths of the unconscious; rather into the depths of the heights of consciousness. . . . Consciousness is much more terrifying than any unconscious complexes" (1984[1961]:288).

This is also to understand, I believe, what is essential about Whorf. The voices that speak to us from the pages of his writings point back to a consciousness that suffered. It almost seems that the torture Whorf underwent was worse than the outright persecution, imprisonment, and exile suffered by Bakhtin or Dostoevsky. For if he was imprisoned, it was in a comfortable, complacent world of capitalist success. And he liked his prison, knew how to make it work, fit in with consummate skill. At the same time, he was cursed with a surplus of vision that, if pursued fully, could only call into question all the standard justifications for the comfortable existence he enjoyed with other members of his class. Had he been a "baggy monster" like Bakhtin (to use Michael Holquist's expression), he might have been able to deal with relativity in a more relaxed manner, he might have become a more conventional eccentric. But he was instead so great a lover of order that he was irresistibly attracted to *different orders* wherever he found them—with the result that he could not avoid undermining any lingering hope he harbored for finding the key to any conventional kind of single cosmic order. He was a Moses-like figure: knowing of the promised land, even seeing it, but incapable of actually, physically entering into it, except in his imagination. As a result, his *œuvre* as an utterance is a particularly poignant example of the "contradiction-ridden, tension-filled unity of two embattled tendencies in the life of language" (Bakhtin 1981c[1940]:272).

Critical self-consciousness and its chief product, a fully developed surplus of vision, not just for a few, but for all—this is the kind of "more" which Whorf kept trying to urge his readers to see. And this is exactly what is missed when Stephen Murray, for example, summarizes (and endorses) Peter Rollins' assessment of Whorf's project as "reconciling new science (notably quantum physics) with old doctrine (divine creation and the 'Genesis paradigm' and Vedic notions of time and space)" (1982b:156). To begin with, there is something odd to an anthropologist—and, one hopes, by now to the reader—about this willingness to lump Judeo-Christian and Hindu doctrines together as though all "old doctrine," whatever its source, is basically the same. More fundamentally, in view of the preceding discussion, it should be clear that "reconciling" science and the Christian tradition (or one of its variants), or "reconciling" science and the Hindu tradition (or one of its variants) is an inadequate way of speaking about Whorf's project. "Reconciliation" is redolent of the monological consciousness: it suggests fusion, merging, effacement of difference. Whorf's tragedy, if one may use such a term, was that he spoke the language of reconciliation, merging, effacement while realizing (and forcing his readers to realize) that such effacement was fundamentally wrong. He pursued the path of enlightenment radically, to discover at the end that his reward was both less and more than he had been promised, both by traditional science and by traditional religion.

I believe that Whorf's intellectual journey continues to appall some readers today precisely because it led him beyond science, beyond Christianity, indeed beyond the Western tradition, in the pursuit of truth. It is this strain in Whorf, I believe, which resonates so profoundly in the postmodern world. Such a radical undertaking makes those whose defense of critical self-consciousness is inseparable from a defense of the Western philosophic tradition appear guilty of bad faith (cf. Bakhtin 1984[1929]:32). Whorf is telling us not only that Western thought and its most precious product, Western science, must be subjected to critical examination; he is also making the shocking assertion that the best way to remain true to the principles and goals of Western science is to enter into serious dialogue with a form of Eastern mysticism.

It is precisely this suggestion in Whorf's writing that makes it, and the "relativism" associated with it, the prized spoils in a contestation of discourse within the human sciences today. To domesticate "relativism," to reduce it to either subjectivism or determinism, is to turn it into a concept which is easily disarmed by the Western philosophic tradition. To argue against such domestication is to defend relativism as a perspective which reduces human sociocultural practices neither to the sum of purely arbitrary individual preferences nor to the predictable outcome of implacable, inscrutable forces of biology or history. It is therefore to defend a perspective which eludes the grasp of "normal" philosophy, which is no doubt why "normal" philosophers so fear it.

Such a perspective on the human condition, articulated so well by the Bakhtin circle during the years Whorf wrote, is one of the most valuable legacies of American anthropology. It is, of course, a perspective that is difficult to grasp in our culture, as Whorf himself was painfully aware. It is however, a perspective that has become subtler and better articulated over time. One of the purposes of this study, indeed, is to suggest how a dialogue with Bakhtin can enrich our previous understanding of "the Whorfian hypothesis." This ongoing enrichment and development of relativity can be usefully compared with the ongoing enrichment and development of the theory of evolution by natural selection first set forth by Darwin. The truths revealed by a multilingual consciousness can no more be eliminated by showing "where Whorf went wrong" than the truths of modern evolutionary theory can be eliminated by discrediting Darwin.

Whorf's texts are, I believe, eminently "writable" texts, to borrow the expression of Roland Barthes. They have proved themselves to be so by the enormous amount of commentary they have generated in the past fifty years. And this has not necessarily been wasted effort. It may well be, as Eagleton suggests (1983:138), that writable texts are "plural and diffuse, an inexhaustible galaxy of signifiers . . . through which the critic may cut his own errant path." Nevertheless, as Edmund Leach remarks somewhere about Claude Lévi-Strauss, "he gives me ideas even when I don't understand him." Perhaps all "writable" texts do this; their elusive qualities suggest all sorts of fresh possibilities to alert and attentive readers. It may thus be to our advantage to resist attempts to circumscribe the Whorfian canon or to systematize Whorf's ideas. We may be better served (and do greater justice to Whorf) by opening ourselves up to those insights which may arise from a direct confrontation with paradox.

Notes

References

Index

Notes

Introduction

1. Unlike most writers who associate Whorf with linguistic determinism, Arnheim has clearly read Whorf closely. When he links Whorf with the other "linguistic determinists" he mentions, he cites chapter and verse to support this move.

Arnheim begins by asserting that "all of them [Herder, Humboldt, Cassirer, Sapir, and Whorf] eloquently describe the visual world as shapeless" (1972:140). In Whorf's case, he supports this accusation by citing a passage from "Science and Linguistics": " 'the world is presented in a kaleidoscopic flux of impressions which has to be organized by our minds—and this means largely by the linguistic systems in our minds.' The world of sight appears as a colorful nightmare, truly the invention of men of words" (1972:140; see my discussion of this passage, pp. 000 above). Arnheim continues: "Language is assumed to be the mold into which the amorphous raw material of vision is cast. . . . [Whorf says that] 'segmentation of nature is an aspect of grammar. We cut up and organize the spread and flow of events as we do, largely because, through our mother tongue, we are parties to an agreement to do so, not because nature is segmented in exactly that way for all to see' " (1972:140; the citation is from "Languages and Logic"; see my discussion of this passage, p. 82ff above). Arnheim's final citation of Whorf is somewhat conciliatory: "Occasionally, the adherents of this introverted approach to the psychology of cognition acknowledge that there are facts not easily reconciled with their view. Thus Whorf commends Gestalt psychology for 'the discovery that visual perception is basically the same for all normal persons past infancy and conforms to definite laws, a large number of which are fairly well known.' In fact, the main antidote to the prevalent introverted slant has come from Gestalt psychology" (1972:143; the passage is from "Gestalt Technique of Stem Composition in Shawnee"; see my discussion of this article p. 102ff above). And yet Arnheim makes no attempt to suggest why a "linguistic determinist" should be so open to the main antidote to linguistic determinism!

Either Arnheim has unwittingly gotten caught in one of Whorf's loopholes, or he is making use of that loophole for rhetorical purposes of his own. Notice that Arnheim repeatedly claims that it is the *visual* world that the linguistic determinists say cannot be known without language. However, in none of the passages he cites from Whorf's texts does Whorf make this claim. Whorf speaks of grammar segmenting "the world" or "nature," or "the spread and flow of events." And while the world and nature and the spread and flow of events have undeniable visual aspects, their content is not exhausted by those visual aspects. Arnheim's trick is to reduce the broader and deeper experiential world of which Whorf speaks to the visual world, and then to criticize linguists who argue that visual experience is dependent upon language. A better target than Whorf would be Nelson Goodman, who borrows from linguistics to make exactly this sort of reduction, for which he has been repeatedly criticized.

Indeed, those who criticize Goodman frequently attribute his views to Whorf. Douglas Arrell, as we saw, does this. So does Wendy Steiner, who writes: "A less troublesome way of handling the peculiar semantic thrust of art grows out of the Whorf-Sapir theory of language. According to it, the world is directly reflected in language and the particular language one speaks determines the world one lives in" (1982:27). Steiner then provides a critique of the work of E. H. Gombrich, Nelson Goodman, and Sol Worth, all of whom she sees supporting "the Whorfian argument" or "the relativist approach" (1982:28ff.).

As we shall see later, in a discussion of the line drawings Whorf included in three of his articles, Whorf's attitude toward the visual world cannot be equated with Goodman's attitude. I will be arguing that Whorf's use of pictures in his texts results from much the same motivation which Steiner detects behind cubist art.

I am grateful to Bela Petheo, who brought Arnheim's article to my attention.

2. After the manuscript of this book was completed, Michael Silverstein drew my attention to John Lucy's 1987 doctoral dissertation, "Grammatical Categories and Cognitive Processes: An Historical, Theoretical, and Empirical Reevaluation of the Linguistic Relativity Hypothesis." Lucy describes his study as an attempt to "work through exactly what Whorf did say and, implicitly, to correct many of the misunderstandings" (1987:8).

Lucy delimits the Whorfian canon in a way which places highest value on the Sapir festschrift paper, "The Relation of Habitual Thought and Behavior to Language," yet he does not dismiss the articles written for the *Technology Review* and the *Theosophist* (1987:43). As Lucy "works through" the texts, he often uncovers ambiguity rather than consistency on Whorf's part. For example, as he attempts to wrest from Whorf a coherent definition of the Whorfian concept of cryptotypes or covert categories, he points out that "Whorf's use of these alternate terms can be confusing. . . . In a later writing . . . Whorf moved toward using phenotype and cryptotype more exclusively for meaning as opposed to marking, but in a way that was inconsistent with his earlier uses" (1987:31). Lucy is aware of intralanguage variety, as embodied in different modes of thought (1987:250, 293) or genres of speech (1987:341–42). He stresses the importance of including a "referential anchor" in the world beyond language if cross-linguistic comparison is to succeed (1987:294ff., 451). He creates such an anchor inductively, by comparing nominal number systems in several unrelated languages in order to make explicit the range and patterns of distinctions such systems might formalize (e.g., table 14, 1987:363). Moreover, his testing procedure involves the use of pictures as stimuli designed to elicit the desired kinds of linguistic and nonlinguistic responses from subjects (1987:455ff.), and he notes twice that Whorf resorted to a similar technique in his "popular" articles (1987:39 footnote 13, 162).

Lucy's dissertation gives the impression of being open, in principle, to a less traditional understanding of Whorf. Nevertheless, in practice, he carries out his test of the "linguistic relativity hypothesis" in a thoroughly traditional manner. His virtual silence on all but the traditionally respectable items in the Whorfian canon might be interpreted as a kind of professional discretion, not unlike that shown by John Carroll, who tried to avoid awkward questions about Whorf's "mysticism" (but see 1987:51, footnote 21). He describes his own research as an effort to correct the theoretical and methodological shortcomings of Whorf and his successors in anthropology and linguistics (1987:284ff.). In some respects, his decision to confine grammar to morphosyntactic relations, in the traditional manner of formal linguistics, is crucial. Thus, he does not explore the ambiguity surrounding Whorf's characterization of "grammar" (see my discussion, e.g., p. 41 above). Having delimited the grammatical focus in this way, he tests for relativity effects by focusing on formal-functional analogues of nominal number marking in two unrelated languages, English and Yucatec. "The goal of the cognitive assessment is to identify patterns of habitual thought in the two languages that could plausibly stem from corresponding differences in the morphosyntactic treatment of nominal number. Habitual thought will be inferred from patterns of attention, memory, and classification exhibited by samples of individuals from both groups. . . . experimentally controlled tasks will provide the crucial evidence for language effects in this study" (1987:301). He administers projective tests to individual subjects in traditional laboratory-like settings, and obtains results that "were consistently in line with expectations based on the general linguistic analysis" (1987:448).

As a result, the outcome of Lucy's analysis of Whorf and linguistic relativity is somewhat anticlimactic. Although he claims to be able to demonstrate relativity effects in a narrow grammatical domain under controlled testing conditions, he admits that this falls short of Whorf's aim to analyze relativity "at the level of general cultural worldview" (1987:390). Indeed Lucy's results have more in common with other recent research in cognitive psychology that demonstrates the way in which linguistic patterns facilitate such mental processes as recall (1987:391). His awareness of linguistic varieties and speech genres does not translate into an awareness of the way these linguistic patterns might serve as the "fashions of speaking" that Whorf wanted to study. This seems to be due to the fact that he views languages monolithically (see his discussions of "functional relativity," 1987:125ff., 250). From a dialogical perspective, his induction-based framework for analyzing nominal number represents a major achievement, based as it is on the recognition that partial knowledge of the structure of reality is all we can ever hope to attain. Yet he insists repeatedly on the necessity of developing a descriptive metalanguage that will "produce an explicit, neutral characterization of reality" for the purposes of linguistic comparison (1987:295). And, indeed, the perspective he takes on language, in keeping with his traditional understanding of grammar, is not dialogical at all (see, e.g., 1987:279, 297).

1 Bakhtin and Whorf

1. The notion of individual human agency has had its ups and downs in the history of twentieth-century social scientific theorizing. Early in the century, attempts were made to undermine popular notions of autonomous individual self-determination and transparent individual self-consciousness by such figures as Saussure, Durkheim, and their followers in a number of social scientific disciplines. Boas, Sapir, and Whorf were part of this movement. In American sociology, the work of Talcott Parsons, with its reduction of individually motivated action to socially conditioned action, became the cornerstone of what Anthony Giddens calls the "orthodox consensus" in the academic sociology of the 1950s and 1960s. It its own way, however, the reduction of human individuals to passive automata which Parsonian orthodoxy seemed to require was as problematic as the individualism it was designed to combat. In the 1970s and 1980s, social thinkers like Pierre Bourdieu (1972), Marshall Sahlins (1976, 1981), and Giddens himself (1976, 1979, 1981) began seriously to rethink the role of human agency in social life. Giddens, in particular, has developed a sophisticated account of individual human agents as acting subjects who help constitute themselves as individuals in the context of ongoing, culturally and historically shaped social life which they themselves (re)produce. For a recent summary of the influence of this work on anthropological theorizing about human agency, see Karp (1986).

2. Levic Jessel (1978) argues that Whorf did not pursue his insights on linguistic relativity to their logical conclusion which, in Jessel's opinion, is that linguistic diversity is only one feature of the sociocultural diversity of irreducible "ethnic speech communities." He writes that "Whorf's 'world view' was actually the outlook of an ethnic community" (1978:83). As a result, the "world view of the native speaker, then, could have been interpreted basically as the typical mental attitude of a specific people—a behavior embodying an historically evolved cultural background *within* a relatively segregated and historically developed segment of the world. That step Whorf did not take" (1978:83–84). Jessel attributes Whorf's reluctance to take this step to the "ideological and intellectual climate of the times" which would have led his readers to conclude "that he was leaning too far in the path of ethnicity—an approach that could smack of a reactionary nationalism!" (1978:83).

Jessel's motive is apparently to claim an empirical basis for demands for national homelands made by "emergent peoples" (1978:99) and/or "oppressed peoples" (1978:102). He seems to believe that such demands cannot be made legitimate unless they can be shown to be rooted "in the primeval, and even animal, past"; in "the whole societal, cultural and traditional experience of living within relatively isolated immemorial conditions of one sort of another" (1978:100). He then offers a naive sociobiological explanation for the irreducibility of ethnicity (1978:103ff.).

J. A. Laponce (1985) attempts to deny the viability of multilingual consciousness for similar reasons. He argues that "languages are territorial. By concentrating 'their' speakers in physical space, languages increase their chances of surviving, prospering, and assimilating the competitiors that enter their midst" (1985:3). He claims that "Sapir and Whorf . . . hypothesized that the bilingual cannot translate thought, hence attitudes, from one language into another without introducing a bias imposed by the language in which he or she thinks, speaks, or writes" (1985:4). His aim is to go "beyond the Whorf/Sapir hypothesis and pose the questions: are bilinguals different from unilinguals, neurophysically as well as psychologically, and, if so, are there political consequences" (1985:4). Like Jessel, he seeks neurophysiological evidence to explain what he takes to be the obvious fact of language territoriality. Even though he finds no such evidence, however, this does not prevent him from concluding that "the costs of learning, storing, maintaining, and using two languages contribute to the tendency of language groups to form cohesive territorial units' (1985:9).

Interestingly, Laponce refers to research suggesting that one benefit of bilingualism is the way it "facilitates the dissociation of the signified from the signifier" (1985:7). This is, of course, a point made explicitly by Bakhtin and implicitly by Whorf. Moreover, Bakhtin's discussions of heteroglossia would predict a similar phenomenon even within a national language. But Laponce avoids developing the consequences of this argument in the radical direction which Bakhtin took. Instead, he merely observes, "It would violate common sense to expect that we learn other languages for the sake of detaching the word from the idea, the thing, the person, or the animal it stands for" (1985:7). Whorf, of course, can plausibly be interpreted as urging his readers to learn other languages (or to listen to a linguist who has learned them) *precisely* in order to learn how to detach words from the things they stand for. Bakhtin, in contrast, stresses that learning other languages is not something we have any choice about. Since every language is shot through with sublanguages we must master if we are to engage in dialogue with other people, the real issue for Bakhtin is not whether we choose to learn a second language, but rather how we go about choosing one of these diverse languages we already know as the vehicle of our thought.

The arguments of both Jessel and Laponce are vulnerable to the same objections we have presented in our critique of relative absolutism in Whorf and Voloshinov. Jessel's very dissatisfaction with Whorf on this issue supports our contention that Whorf was not a linguistic determinist. Indeed, Jessel's arguments illustrate exactly the kinds of simplistic and untenable claims one would have to make in order to defend linguistic determinism—claims Whorf and Voloshinov were, for good reasons, unwilling to make. Furthermore, the eagerness both Jessel and Laponce display to find biological explanations for cultural practice is fascinating. Both seem to want to discover an unshakeable foundation from which to defend the linguistic or cultural right to exist of minority groups. And both seem to think that the answer must lie in biology. Laponce puts it baldly: "The biological explanation is more likely than the social to offer us the constants, the universal effects that can be used to measure the strength of the cultural factors that either reinforce or contradict them" (1985:3). And he is not deterred when the requisite biological factors cannot be found. An anthropologist can only wish that these writers (who both appear to be political scientists) had studied some linguistics or some bio-anthropology, or read something by Stephen Jay Gould, before venturing into the unknown. As it is, one is hard put to distinguish their arguments from the reactionary nationalism it is presumably designed to combat.

3. Michael Silverstein reminds us that Whorf relied "on the fundamental analytic bases of phonology (phonemics) as the predecent for all of 'scientific' linguistics, in contrast to the seemingly a priori semantics of the philosophers he criticizes. In this he duplicates Leonard Bloomfield who, all the while endorsing the programs of both behaviorism (influenced by Albert Paul Weiss) and physicalism, criticizes the Vienna Circle authors" (1979:237–38). However, as he goes on to show, Whorf and Bloomfield did not see eye to eye on everything: Bloomfield saw linguistics as "Science rescuing language from students of culture" whereas Whorf saw "Cultural Science rescuing students of science . . . from language in the Technology Review" (1979:238). This may help explain why the scientists who found greatest fault with Whorf were not the MIT engineers (if we are to believe Carroll 1956:20) but the linguists following a purer Bloomfieldian program. Silverstein makes a plausible distinction between the "addressees" (the engineers) and the "implicit audience (e.g., Bloomfield himself . . .)" of the *Technology Review* pieces (1979:238). This distinction provides Whorf with yet another loophole: he can criticize his professional linguist colleagues while appearing to be criticizing nonlinguists. This conjecture is supported by the fact that the stylistic techniques he uses in the *Technology Review* articles turn up in articles addressed to professional linguists as well (e.g., "The Punctual and Segmentative Aspects of verbs in Hopi").

2 The Politics of Style

1. This might be termed the translatability paradox facing analytical philosophers. Take any sentence they regard as a proposition with self-evident truth value—for example: "Snow is white." The unique and self-contained meaning of this (or any other) proposition is shattered as soon as one utters it in an ironic tone of voice. This inescapable loophole dogs the best efforts of the formal philosophy of language. For every solemn attempt to erect a single meaning,

there will always be gadflies, like Dostoevsky, or Bakhtin, or Whorf, to reaccent it. As Bakhtin wrote about Dostoevsky (1984[1929]:30): "Where others saw a single thought, he was able to find and feel out two thoughts, a bifurcation; where others saw a single quality, he discovered it in the presence of a second and contradictory quality. Everything that seemed simple became, in his world, complex and multi-structured."

2. Moreover, he is careful, in his comparison of Hopi and English treatments of time and space, to claim *only* that Hopi does not conceptualize time metaphorically in terms of space: "The absence of *such metaphor* from Hopi speech is striking. Use of space terms when there is no space involved is NOT THERE—as if on it had been laid the taboo teetotal!" (Whorf 4:146; italics added). Nevertheless, his rhetorical intent to persuade us that Hopi lacks metaphor entirely is quite plain, and in fact allowed George Lakoff to conclude that "Whorf claimed that Hopi had no metaphors, which he took as being another sign of its superiority" (1987:325)

3 Whorfian Nonverbal Rhetoric

1. The status of the icon has been subject to intense debate in artistic circles. Leading the attack against the possibility of iconicity as understood by Peirce has been Nelson Goodman, who is also the figure whom defenders of iconicity usually have most clearly in their sights. Goodman (1968) argues that pictures resemble what they picture not by virtue of similarity, but by convention. The marks the painter makes on the canvas, like the sounds of language, are only arbitrarily related to what they represent. If we lack knowledge of the conventional meaning assigned to these painterly marks by the painter and other members of his community, we are unable to decipher the painted image. Evidence to support this thesis includes ethnographic reports of non-Western people who were unable to decipher photographs and other two-dimensional drawings the first time they encountered them. Only after they learned the conventions associated with "reading" these images did they interpret them the way Westerners do.

The ethnographic evidence Goodman cites exists. But interpreting the responses of non-Western people to their first encounter with photographs and drawings is a far more complex undertaking than Goodman and his followers seem to allow (for a summary, see the discussion in Schultz and Lavenda (1990) chapt. 5). Research on visual perception carried out since Goodman published his classic account in 1968 further complicates the issue. For instance, Karen Neander (1987) reports on research showing that apes and small children typically respond to two-dimensional depictions as if they were the three-dimensional objects depicted. "Apes have been observed responding to ape-pictures as they normally would to apes," and "children can, under certain favourable circumstances recognize *what* a picture is *of* before they can tell (or can fully understand) *that* it is a picture" (1987:218–19).

Neander cites the work of psychologist Ralph Norman Haber, who argues that the ethnographic data can be reconciled with the data on the responses of apes and children if they are related to different rates of development in flatness perception and depth perception. "Adults who are unfamiliar with picturing rule out any depth interpretation, because for them the picture is clearly perceived as flat. Children, less able to perceive that the picture is a flat object in its own right (perhaps because of the immaturity of stereopsis) perceive the picture as though it is a window opening into space. If Haber is correct, learning to perceive pictures involves the normal maturation of depth processing, plus the quickly acquired knack of assimilating apparently conflicting perceptual information into the understanding that what is seen is a flat surface which represents a three-dimensional scene" (1987:219). Neander also cites the work of David Marr (1982), and, although she did not, she might have cited the work of J. J. Gibson (1979). Both men, each in his own way, provide evidence to show that "a surprisingly large amount of information about the surfaces and distances of objects turns out to be computable *without* the use of higher level knowledge about what the objects are, or what the objects are likely to be" (Neander 1987:222).

However, the barrier to Goodman's acceptance of iconic resemblance is less empirical than logical. Goodman's position on pictorial representation is based on a linguistic analogy. His linguistic model is that provided by formal linguistics, which bases itself on symbolic logic. As David Blinder points out, "The first argument [against iconic resemblance] turns on the logic of resemblance relations. Pictorial representation cannot be explained by resemblance, the formalist argument alleges, since resemblance is a symmetric relation while representation is not" (1986:19–20). That is, the formalist argument insists on interpreting "resemblance" as "identity." For A to *resemble* B entails that A be an identical copy of B. A picture which *represents* B, however, is not an identical copy of B. Thus, since pictures are not identical copies of what they represent, they cannot resemble what they represent. Blinder points out, however, that "the formalist argument overlooks the root meaning of 'resemblance' in mimetic theory," which is to simulate, to imitate, to mimic. "The point is that there is a relation of *ontological dependence* implicit in the notion of mimetic resemblance that holds between the pictorial image and the original model. . . . The dependence of image on model (real or imagined) is missed entirely if we construe mimetic resemblance as a formal, symmetric relation" (Blinder 1986:20).

The other argument against iconic resemblance is based on the supposed "ontological difference" between pictures and what they depict. This argument is illustrated by Goodman's famous claim that a picture of Marlboro Castle looks more like another picture than it looks like the castle, even though it represents the castle and not another picture. As Blinder reminds us, however, "properly construed, the mimetic claim is that the resemblance relation holds between the *look* of realistic pictures and the things they depict, not between two-dimensional images and three-dimensional reality" (1986:20). And as Douglas Arrell emphasizes, "Surely it depends on the context whether we notice the properties of the painting which make it similar to the Castle or similar to another picture. This seemingly willful ignoring of the relativity of resemblance is found also in Goodman's main arguments against the notion that resemblance is necessary for representation. . . . Goodman argues from the fact that there are properties of pictures that are not shared by their subjects to the conclusion that pictures need not resemble their subjects. . . . This argument assumes that similarity depends on the sharing of properties. But according to the relativized view of resemblance, similarity depends only on the *noticing* of shared properties" (1987:43). Goodman, vilified by many as the arch-relativist, is in fact not relativist enough. He neglects to note that "claims about visual resemblance are always relative to context" (Neander 1987:214).

Another figure who is sometime lumped together with Goodman as a "relativist" is Ernst Gombrich, primarily on the basis of his famous work *Art and Illusion* (1960). In this work, Gombrich shows in great detail the extent to which artistic "realism" is dependent on the artist's mastery of acquired techniques and conventions. Neander notes that Gombrich's argument has often been interpreted as evidence that representation is not the same as resemblance. "However, we should not fail to notice that throughout the book, Gombrich is explaining what it is to 'render a *likeness*' within a style and medium" (1987:222). Rendering a likeness depends on knowledge and technique, but "there is nothing in any of this to suggest that resemblances between picture and pictured are unimportant. . . . Showing that the artist has to render a likeness does not detract from the fact that it is a likeness that must be rendered" (1987:222).

On the basis of the evidence, I must agree with Neander's conclusion: "There is much experimental and phenomenological data supporting the claim that meaningful sight requires interpretation, but it is compatible with the further highly plausible claim that innate visual processing provides information about the surfaces of objects which constrains possible interpretations. The information may be ambiguous, while still severely constraining" (1987:222). Neander avoids the hyperbolic posturing both of Goodman and of the extremists among his critics (Gibson, for example) who understand perception narrowly and treat linguistic or cultural influences on perception as negligible. For these reasons, and with these qualifications, I endorse, and will continue to use, the concept of "icon" in this book.

2. The term *ekphrasis* is used by specialists in the arts to refer to a range of works that, in one way or another, combine words and pictures.

For literary critics such as Michael Davidson, ekphrasis is "the use of literature to imitate a work of plastic art," and he quotes Murray Krieger, who elaborates: " 'The object of imitation, as spatial work, becomes the metaphor for the temporal work which seeks to capture it in that temporality. The spatial work freezes the temporal work, even as the latter seeks to free it from space. *Ekphrasis* concerns me here, then, to the extent that I see it introduced in order to use a plastic object as a symbol of the frozen, stilled world of plastic relationships which must be superimposed upon literature's turning world to "still" it' " (M. Davidson 1983:70). When used in this way, the "spatial work" is ordinarily a painting and the "temporal work" is a poem; poetry of this kind is called ekphrastic poetry (see also Wendy Steiner's discussion [1982:40–41]). Davidson distinguishes ekphrastic poetry from what he calls a "painterly poem" such as Frank O'Hara's "On Seeing Larry Rivers' *Washington Crossing the Delaware* at the Museum of Modern Art." For Davidson, a poem like O'Hara's "attacks a static ekphrasis" and "refuses to constitute the painting in an act of linguistic recovery," instead mediating the historical event "by a series of perspectives, the multiplicity of which undermines the event's autonomy and objectivity" (1983:72).

Davidson does not appear to consider the two long paragraphs of description of Rivers' painting which he provides in his text to be ekphrasis (the painting itself is not reproduced). However, ekphrasis can be used to refer to a "verbal recreation of a painting" (Carrier 1987:20). Art historians favor this usage, referring to the descriptions of paintings contained in such books as Giorgio Vasari's *Lives of the Artists* (1550, rev. ed. 1568) as ekphrasis. And Vasari's model derived from a literary genre of antiquity, ekphrasis as "the set-piece description of a work of art" (Grigg 1984:400). Understood in this way, "an ekphrasis tells the story represented, only incidentally describing pictorial composition" (Carrier 1987:21). Carrier compares ekphrasis (which he sees as brief, general, superficial, incapable of generating debate) with "interpretations" of paintings which, according to him, are like philosophical arguments, providing systematic analyses of style and revealing deeper meanings. In addition, Carrier claims that ekphrasis is biased, whereas interpretations are objective: "for Vasari, to identify the sacred scene is already to tell us what attitude we are to take. . . . Berenson and Fry [i.e., practitioners of "interpretation"] claimed to respond with indifference to the content of Renaissance art" (1987:24). Carrier does not appear to intend any irony.

Wendy Steiner describes the origin of ekphrasis within the *ut pictura poesis* ["as is painting, so is poetry"] tradition of Western art. Early attempts to make paintings depicting events from literary sources such as the Bible led painters to develop pictorial devices capable of representing significant human action in a "static" visual medium. One such device was the "pregnant moment": that is, "isolating a moment in the action that revealed all that had led up to it and all that would follow" (1982:40). This attempt by painters to translate literary material into visual images then gave rise to the attempt by poets to translate visual material into literary texts "by stopping time, or more precisely, by referring to an action through a still moment that implies it. The technical term for this is *ekphrasis*, the concentration of action in a single moment of energy" (1982:40–41).

Viewed broadly, I think it is clear that the tension between pictures and words which are somehow connected within a single work is common both to the literary and painterly understanding of ekphrasis. Therefore, following Melville, I will use the term ekphrasis in a generic, descriptive sense: "the presentation of a work executed in another medium within a work of art" (Melville 1989:91). Such a definition would embrace ekphrastic poetry, "painterly poems," textual passages (such as Davidson's) which aim to offer adequate verbal descriptions of visual works, and illustrated texts such as Whorf's.

Conclusion

1. One of the more interesting loopholes Bakhtin leaves himself concerns the nature of cultural/linguistic hybrids. In an early text (1981c[1940]:360) he distinguishes *intentional semantic hybrids* from *historical, organic hybrids:* "In an intentional novelistic hybrid . . . the important activity is not only (in fact not so much) the mixing of linguistic forms—the markers of two languages and styles—as it is the collision between differing points of view on the world that are embedded in these forms. Therefore an intentional artistic hybrid is a *semantic* hybrid; not semantic and logical in the abstract (as in rhetoric), but rather a *semantics that is concrete and social.*

"It is of course true that even in historical, organic hybrids it is not only two languages but also two socio-linguistic (thus organic) world views that are mixed with each other; but in such situations, the mixture remains mute and opaque, never making use of conscious contrasts and oppositions. It must be pointed out, however, that while it is true the mixture of linguistic world views in organic hybrids remains mute and opaque, such unconscious hybrids have been at the same time profoundly productive historically: they are pregnant with potential for new world views, with 'internal forms' for perceiving the world in words.

"Intentional semantic hybrids are inevitably internally dialogic (as distinct from organic hybrids). Two points of view are not mixed, but set against each other dialogically."

The contrast between intentional and historical, between novelistic and organic, is not unlike the contrast between the literary (bilingual) consciousness and the consciousness of the illiterate peasant. In regard to the first members of each of these opposing pairs—intentional, novelistic, literary (bilingual) consciousness—the suggestion is that choice, and struggle, are involved. In regard to the second members of these pairs—historical, organic, illiterate peasant—the suggestion is that choice, and struggle, are absent. The rhetorical force of the passage quoted above would seem to be that mixing of languages or cultures that occurs over time is evolutionary, rather than revolutionary; that the people who do the mixing are unaware of it; or, if aware, are nevertheless passive, inarticulate, unable to affect the course of change. Indeed, the passage quoted in the text which credits the great novels of this period with passing the cultural/linguistic quarrels of the Renaissance "on to a further phase" has a Leninist flavor: it is the great novelists who point out what the masses are too brutish to see, and in their works carry out the dialogical hybridizing revolution that makes historical, organic hybrids possible!

Yet we have seen that the rhetorical effort he makes to portray the illiterate peasant as Mr. Everyman is, in fact, undercut by loopholes which recognize that peasants are less dull-witted and passive than their stereotype allows. And in the passage above, similar loopholes exist. Particularly in light of his remarks about dialogic agreement—e.g., "unity not as an innate one-and-only, but as a dialogic *concordance* of unmerged twos and multiples" (1984[1961]:289)—one must ask what the difference is between dialogic agreement and historical, organic hybrids. In both cases, languages and cultures mix without merging, but also without impasse. If dialogic agreement includes agreement without fusion, what is the outcome except the multicultural mixing of an organic, historical hybrid? If intentional semantic hybrids are inevitably internally dialogic (as distinct from organic hybrids), this can be interpreted as meaning that organic hybrids are *not internally* dialogic. But it can also be interpreted as meaning that organic hybrids are *not inevitably* dialogic, although they *may* be!

Many years later, this same ambivalence about dialogic agreement reappears (1986[1970]:7). Bakhtin states that "a dialogic encounter of two cultures does not result in merging or mixing. Each retains its own unity and *open* totality, but they are mutually enriched." Such a statement, however, would seem to rule out the very kind of historical, organic hybrid of which he spoke in the earlier citation. It would seem to suggest that boundaries around cultures are so stable that such a thing as a hybrid culture could never come about. And yet, a few paragraphs earlier in the same article, he says, "Even the culture of an epoch . . . cannot be enclosed within itself as something ready made, completely finalized, and irrevocably departed, deceased. . . . the unity of a particular culture is an *open* unity." But if the culture is an open unity, it must needs be open to the possibility of eventually mixing with another culture or cultures to create something totally new and greater than the sum of all of the cultures that gave birth to it. It is this kind of openness without effacement that permits W. C. Smith to argue, plausibly, "that the West is bicultural, having received one major stream of its inheritance from Greece and Rome, one from Palestine" (1988:11–12).

Openness is not openness without the risk of change and growth. Bakhtin may have wrestled with his prose in these passages because he was conscious that many of his readers would not take kindly to an open declaration that no historical events (not even the October Revolution) were without this risk. But his entire oeuvre, and his life, suggest that the risk is the point. In 1924, before the purges, he seems to be speaking in his own voice when he writes, "Every cultural act lives essentially on the boundaries: in this is its seriousness and its significance; abstracted from boundaries, it loses its soil, it becomes empty, arrogant, it degenerates and dies" (1984[1961]:301, footnote). Without the risk of change (and sometimes the risk of death), the seriousness and significance of all human acts disappear.

References

Writings by Benjamin Whorf

All are referred to in the text by number and page in Carroll 1956 (e.g., Whorf 1:36). Date of original composition or publication is indicated.

1. On the Connection of Ideas. 1927. Pp. 35–39.
2. The Punctual and Segmentative Aspects of Verbs in Hopi. 1936. Pp. 51–56.
3. A Linguistic Consideration of Thinking in Primitive Communities. Circa 1936. Pp. 65–86.
4. The Relation of Habitual Thought and Behavior to Language. 1939. Pp. 134–59.
5. Gestalt Technique of Stem Composition in Shawnee. 1939. Pp. 160–72.
6. Science and Linguistics. 1940. Pp. 207–19.
7. Linguistics as an Exact Science. 1940. Pp. 220–32.
8. Languages and Logic. 1941. Pp. 233–45.
9. Language, Mind, and Reality. 1941. Pp. 246–70.

General references

Alford, D. K. H. 1981. Is Whorf's Relativity Einstein's Relativity? Berkeley Linguistic Society, *Proceedings* 7:13–26.

Alford, D. K. H. 1978. The Demise of the Whorf Hypothesis. Berkeley Linguistic Society, *Proceedings* 4:485–99.

Alverson, Hoyt. 1987. Metaphor and the Language of Experience: The Baby and the Bathwater in George Lakoff's "Women, Fire, and Dangerous Things." Invited paper delivered at the session "Metaphor Theory in Anthropology." Annual meeting of the American Anthropological Association, Chicago.

Arnheim, Rudolf. 1972. The Myth of the Bleating Lamb. *Toward a Psychology of Art,* pp 136–50. Berkeley and Los Angeles: University of California Press.

Arrell, Douglas. 1987. "What Goodman Should Have Said about Representation." *Journal of Aesthetics and Art Criticism* 46:41–49.

Asad, Talal. 1986. The Concept of Cultural Translation in British Social Anthropology. In James Clifford and George E. Marcus, eds., *Writing Culture*, pp. 141–64. Berkeley: University of California Press.

Au, T. K. F. 1983. Chinese and English Counterfactuals—The Sapir-Whorf Hypothesis Revisited. *Cognition* 15(1–3):155–87.

Bakhtin, M. M. 1981a(1937–38). Forms of Time and of the Chronotope in the Novel. In M. Holoquist, ed., *The Dialogical Imagination*, pp. 84–258. Austin: University of Texas Press.

Bakhtin, M. M. 1981b(1940). From the Prehistory of Novelistic Discourse. In M. Holquist, ed., *The Dialogic Imagination*, pp. 41–83. Austin: University of Texas Press.

Bakhtin, M. M. 1981c(1940). Discourse in the Novel. In M. Holquist, ed., *The Dialogic Imagination*, pp. 259–422). Austin: University of Texas Press.

Bakhtin, M. M. 1981d(1941). Epic and Novel. In M. Holquist, ed., *The Dialogic Imagination*, pp. 3–40. Austin: University of Texas Press.

Bakhtin, M. M. 1984(1929, 1961). *Problems of Dostoevsky's Poetics*. Ed. and trans. Caryl Emerson. Minneapolis: University of Minnesota Press (Theory and History of Literature, 8).

Bakhtin, M. M. 1986. *Speech Genres and Other Late Essays*. Trans. Vern W. McGee, Ed. C. Emerson and M. Holquist. Austin: University of Texas Press.

Bernstein, Richard. 1983. *Beyond Objectivism and Relativism*. Philadelphia: University of Pennsylvania Press.

Black, Max. 1962(1959). Linguistic Relativity. In Max Black, *Models and Metaphors*, pp. 244–58. Ithaca, NY: Cornell University Press.

Blinder, David. 1986. In Defense of Pictorial Mimesis. *Journal of Aesthetics and Art Criticism* 45(1):19–27.

Booth, Wayne. 1984. Introduction to M. M. Bakhtin, *Problems of Dostoevsky's Poetics*, ed. and trans. Caryl Emerson, pp. xiii–xxvii. Minneapolis: University of Minnesota Press (Theory and History of Literature, 8).

Bourdieu, Pierre. 1972. *Outline of a Theory of Practice*. Cambridge: Cambridge University Press.

Brown, Roger. 1958. *Words and Things*. Glencoe: Free Press.

Bruss, Elizabeth. 1982. *Beautiful Theories: The Spectacle of Discourse in Contemporary Criticism*. Baltimore: Johns Hopkins University Press.

Bucci, Wilma. 1985. Dual Coding—a Cognitive Model of Psychoanalytic Research. *Journal of the American Psychoanalytic Association* 33(3):571–607.

Carrier, David. 1987. Ekphrasis and Interpretation: Two Modes of Art History Writing. *British Journal of Aesthetics* 27:20–31.

Carroll, John B., ed. 1956. *Language, Thought, and Reality: Selected Writings of Benjamin Lee Whorf*. Cambridge: MIT Press.

Chatterjee, Ranjit. 1985. Reading Whorf through Wittgenstein—A Solution to the Linguistic Relativity Problem. *Lingua* 67(1):37–63.

Clark, Katerina, and Michael Holquist. 1984. *Mikhail Bakhtin*. Cambridge: Belknap/Harvard.

Crawford, T. D. 1982. Plato's Reasoning and the Sapir-Whorf Hypothesis. *Metaphilosophy* 13(3–4):217–27.

Davidson, Donald. 1984. *Inquiries into Truth and Interpretation.* Oxford: Clarendon.

Davidson, Michael. 1983. Ekphrasis and the Postmodern Painterly Poem. *Journal of Aesthetics and Art Criticism* 42:69–79.

Dillon, G. L. 1982. Whorfian Stylistics. *Journal of Literary Semantics* 11(2):73–89.

Eagleton, Terry. 1983. *Literary Theory.* Minneapolis: University of Minnesota Press.

Emerson, Caryl. 1984. Editor's preface to M. M. Bakhtin, *Problems of Dostoevsky's Poetics,* pp. xxix–xliii. Minneapolis: University of Minnesota Press.

Fernandez, James. 1986. *Persuasions and Performances: The Play of Tropes in Culture.* Bloomington: Indiana University Press.

Fernandez, James. 1982. *Bwiti: An Ethnography of the Religious Imagination in Africa.* Princeton: Princeton University Press.

Feuer, Lewis S. 1953. Sociological Aspects of the Relation between Language and Philosophy. *Philosophy of Science* 20(2):85–100.

Fishman, Joshua. 1980. The Whorfian Hypothesis—Varieties of Valuation, Confirmation and Disconfirmation. 1. *International Journal of the Sociology of Language* 26:25–40.

Friedrich, Paul. 1986. *The Language Parallax: Linguistic Relativism and Poetic Indeterminacy.* Austin: University of Texas Press.

Gibson, J. J. 1979. *The Ecological Approach to Visual Perception.* Boston: Houghton-Mifflin.

Giddens, Anthony. 1976. *New Rules of Sociological Method: A Positive Critique of Interpretative Sociologies.* London: Hutchinson.

Giddens, Anthony. 1979. *Central Problems in Social Theory: Action, Structure and Contradiction in Social Anthropology.* Berkeley: University of California Press.

Giddens, Anthony. 1981. *A Contemporary Critique of Historical Materialism.* Vol. 1. *Power, Property, and the State.* Berkeley: University of California Press.

Gipper, Helmut. 1977. Is There a Linguistic Relativity Principle? In Rik Pinxton, ed., *Universalism versus Relativism in Language and Thought.* pp. 217–28. The Hague: Mouton.

Gombrich, Ernst. 1960. *Art and Illusion.* New York: Phaidon Press.

Goodman, Nelson. 1968. *The Languages of Art.* Indianapolis: Indiana University Press.

Gregory, Richard 1983. Visual Perception and Illusions: Dialogue with Richard Gregory. In Jonathan Miller, *States of Mind,* pp. 42–64. New York: Pantheon Books.

Grigg, Robert. 1984. Relativism and Pictorial Realism. *Journal of Aesthetics and Art Criticism* 42:397–408.

Handler, R. 1985. On Dialog and Destructive Analysis—Problems in Narrating Nationalisms and Ethnicity. *Journal of Anthropological Research* 41(2):171–82.

Hoijer, Harry, ed., 1954. *Language in Culture.* Chicago: University of Chicago Press.

Hoijer, Harry. 1953. The Relation of Language to Culture. In A. L. Kroeber, ed., *Anthropology Today,* pp. 554–73. Chicago: University of Chicago Press.

Holquist, Michael. 1986. Introduction to Mikhail Bakhtin, *Speech Genres and Other Late Essays,* trans. Vern W. McGee, ed., Caryl Emerson and Michael Holquist, pp. ix–xxiii. Austin: University of Texas Press.

Holquist, Michael. 1981. Introduction to Mikhail Bakhtin, *The Dialogic Imagination,* ed. and trans. C. Emerson and M. Holquist, pp. xv–xxxiv. Austin: University of Texas Press.

Horton, Robin. 1983. Social Psychologies: African and Western. In Meyer Fortes, *Oedipus and Job in West African Religion.* pp. 41–82. Cambridge: Cambridge University Press.

Jessel, L. 1978. Whorf: The Differentiation of Language. *International Journal of the Sociology of Language* 18:83–110.

Karp, Ivan. 1986. Agency and Social Theory: A Review of Anthony Giddens. *American Ethnologist* 13:131–37.

Karp, Ivan, and Martha B. Kendall. 1982. Reflexivity in Field Work. In P. Second, ed., *Explanation in Social Science,* pp. 249–73. Los Angeles: Sage.

Lakoff, George. 1987. *Women, Fire and Dangerous Things.* Chicago: University of Chicago Press.

Lakoff, George, and Mark Johnson. 1980. *Metaphors We Live By.* Chicago: University of Chicago Press.

Laponce, J. A. 1985. The Multilingual Mind and Multilingual Societies—In Search of Neuropsychological Explanations of the Spatial Behavior of Ethnolinguistic Groups. *Politics and the Life Sciences* 4(1):3–9.

Lenneberg, Eric. 1953. Cognition in Ethnolinguistics. *Language* 29:463–71.

Longacre, Robert A. 1956. Review of *Language and Reality,* by Wilbur M. Urban, and *Four Articles on Metalinguistics,* by Benjamin Lee Whorf. *Language* 32:298–308.

Lucy, John Arthur. 1987. Grammatical Categories and Cognitive Processes: An Historical, Theoretical, and Empirical Reevaluation of the Linguistic Relativity Hypothesis. Dissertation, University of Chicago.

Marcus, George E., and James Clifford. 1986. *Writing Culture.* Berkeley: University of California Press.

Marcus, George E., and Michael M. J. Fischer, eds. 1986. *Anthropology as Cultural Critique.* Chicago: University of Chicago Press.

Marr, David. 1982. *Vision.* San Francisco: Freeman.

Melville, Stephen. 1989. Review of *Salome and the Dance of Writing,* by Françoise Meltzer, and *Pictures of Romance: Form against Context in Painting and Literature,* by Wendy Steiner. *Journal of Aesthetics and Art Criticism* 47:91.

Miller, G. A. 1978. Review of *Language, Thought and Reality,* by Benjamin Lee Whorf. *Human Nature* 1(6):92–96.

Murray, Stephen O. 1982a. *Group formation in Social Science.* Edmonton, Alberta: Linguistic Research, Inc.

Murray, Stephen O. 1982b. Review of *Benjamin Lee Whorf—Lost Generation Theories of Mind, Language, and Religion,* by P. C. Rollins. *Historiographia Linguistica* 9(1–12):156–61.

Neander, Karen. 1987. Pictorial Representation: A Matter of Resemblance. *British Journal of Aesthetics* 27:213–26.

Norris, Christopher. 1985. *The Contest of Faculties.* London and New York: Methuen.

Norris, Christopher. 1983. *The Deconstructive Turn: Essays in the Rhetoric of Philosophy.* London and New York: Methuen.

Peirce, Charles Sanders. 1932. *Collected Papers.* Vol. 2 Cambridge: Harvard University Press.

Penn, Julia M. 1972. *Linguistic Relativity versus Innate Ideas: The Origins of the Sapir-Whorf Hypothesis in German Thought.* The Hague/Paris: Mouton (Janua linguarum, series minor, 120).

Putnam, Hilary. 1983. *Realism and Reason.* Cambridge: Cambridge University Press.

Putnam, Hillary. 1981. *Reason, Truth and History.* Cambridge and New York: Cambridge University Press.

Rabinow, Paul. 1977. *Reflections on Fieldwork in Morocco.* Berklely: University of California Press.

Rollins, P. C. 1980. *Benjamin Lee Whorf—Lost Generation Theories of Mind, Language, and Religion.* Ann Arbor: University Microfilms International for Popular Culture Association.

Sahlins, Marshall. 1976. *Culture and Practical Reason.* Chicago: University of Chicago Press.

Sahlins, Marshall. 1981. *Historical Metaphors and Mythical Realities: Structure in the Early History of Sandwich Island Kingdoms.* Ann Arbor: University of Michigan Press.

Schultz, Emily, and Robert Lavenda. 1990. *Cultural Anthropology: A Perspective on the Human Condition.* 2d ed. St. Paul: West Publishing Company.

Sherzer, Joel. 1987. A Discourse-Centered Approach to Language and Culture. *American Anthropologist* 89(2):295–309.

Silverstein, Michael. 1979. Language Structure and Linguistic Ideology. In Paul Clyne, William Hanks, and Carol Horbauer, eds., *The Elements: A Parasession on Linguistic Units and Levels,* pp. 193–247. Chicago: Chicago Linguistic Society.

Smith, W. C. 1988. Transcendence. *Harvard Divinity Bulletin* 18(3):10–15.

Steiner, Wendy. 1982. *The Colors of Rhetoric. Problems in the Relation between Modern Literature and Painting.* Chicago and London: University of Chicago Press.

Taylor, Charles. 1985a. Introduction to *Human Agency and Language* (*Philosophical Papers, 1*), pp. 1–12. Cambridge: Cambridge University Press.

Taylor, Charles. 1985b(1979). Atomism. In *Philosophy and the Human Sciences* (*Philosophical Papers, 2*), pp. 187–210. Cambridge: Cambridge University Press.

Tyler, Stephen A. 1978. *The Said and the Unsaid.* New York: Academic Press.

Vasari, Giorgio. 1963. *The Lives.* Trans. A. B. Hinds. London.

Voegelin, C. F., John F. Yegerlehner, and Florence M. Robinett. 1954. Shawnee Laws: Perceptual Statements for the Language and for the Content. In Harry Hoijer, ed., *Language in Culture,* pp. 32–46. Chicago: University of Chicago Press.

Voloshinov, V. N. 1987(1926). Discourse in Life and Discourse in Art (Concerning Sociological Poetics). In Titunik I. and Bruss N., eds., *Freudianism,* pp. 93–116. Bloomington: Indiana University Press.

Waterman, John T. 1957. Benjamin Lee Whorf and Linguistic Field Theory. *Southwestern Journal of Anthropology* 13(3):201–11.

Wertsch, James V. 1985. *Vygotsky and the Social Formation of Mind.* Cambridge: Harvard University Press.

Index

Absolutism, 43
Alford, Danny, 14, 16–18
Arnheim, Rudolf, 12, 157–58
Artistic (or novelistic) prose, 6, 26, 50, 52, 116
Atomism: in America, 23; in Chatterjee, 94; in Lakoff and Johnson, 118; rejected by Bakhtin circle, 119
Authentic word, 25, 33, 44–45, 49

Background phenomena of language, 41, 53, 65–68
Bakhtin, Mikhail, 5–6; and catastrophe, 150; and cohabitation of languages, 86; compared with Whorf, 20; and explanation, 132; the image of constructive death, 150; and precision in the human sciences, 142; and social languages, 52; and "the event," 133; and understanding, 132
"Based on" relationships, 114
Big Bear, 110
Boas, Franz, 4, 122

Canonization, 8, 140
Carnivalesque literary tradition, 50, 52, 57
Censorship, 25, 43, 46, 144; in America, 22, 24; for Bakhtin, 35; and Hopi, 78; in Whorf, 90
Chronotope, 118, 120; in Dostoevsky, 121–22, 124; in Goethe, 122; in Newton, 119–20, 122; in positivism, 118
Clown, 60

Comic style, 57–58, 60; in Whorf, 19, 59, 62, 82, 111
Context, 107–8, 111, 120, 127, 131, 135, 136; in Bakhtin, 29, 49; in Lakoff and Johnson, 118; in Voloshinov, 30–31; in Whorf, 99, 106, 108
Controlled associations, 35, 76, 108
Critical self-consciousness, 55, 151–52
Cryptotypes, 42, 137, 158
Cubist art, 124–25, 158
Cultural relativism, 4

Darwin, Charles, 153
Deconstruction, 5, 144
Determinism, 41, 43, 153
Dialectic of fieldwork, 53
Dialogic agreement, 145, 147, 151, 168; and learning, 145–46
Dialogical relationships, 21
Dialogic analysis of stem-composition in Shawnee, 111–12
Dialogism in anthropological fieldwork, 53
Dialogized hybrids, 147
Dialogizing background, 22, 141
Dialogue, 50, 52; in Whorf, 43
Direct authorial word, 47, 58, 61–62, 88, 92, 123, 141
Discourse, 42, 49; for Bakhtin, 21, 52–53; in Whorf, 113
Dostoevsky: and catharsis, 151; and Christ as the Final Word, 148, 150; and co-being, 133; and the unity of the event, 92

175